There are only a few works that aim for a comprehensive mapping of what games as a culture are, and how their complex social and cultural realities should be studied, as a whole. Daniel Muriel and Garry Crawford have done so, analyzing both games, players, associated practices, and the broad range of socio-cultural developments that contribute to the ongoing ludification of society. Ambitious, lucid, and well-informed, this book is an excellent guide to the field, and will no doubt inspire future work.

Frans Mäyrä, *Professor of Information Studies and Interactive Media, University of Tampere*

This book provides an insightful and accessible contribution to our understanding of video games as culture. However, its most impressive achievement is that it cogently shows how the study of video games can be used to explore broader social and cultural processes, including identity, agency, community, and consumption in contemporary digital societies. Muriel and Crawford have written a book that transcends its topic, and deserves to be read widely.

Aphra Kerr, *Senior Lecturer in Sociology, Maynooth University*

VIDEO GAMES AS CULTURE

Video games are becoming culturally dominant. But what does their popularity say about our contemporary society? This book explores video game culture, but in doing so, utilizes video games as a lens through which to understand contemporary social life.

Video games are becoming an increasingly central part of our cultural lives, impacting on various aspects of everyday life such as our consumption, communities, and identity formation. Drawing on new and original empirical data – including interviews with gamers, as well as key representatives from the video game industry, media, education, and cultural sector – *Video Games as Culture* not only considers contemporary video game culture, but also explores how video games provide important insights into the modern nature of digital and participatory culture, patterns of consumption and identity formation, late modernity, and contemporary political rationalities.

This book will appeal to undergraduate and postgraduate students, as well as postdoctoral researchers, interested in fields such Video Games, Sociology, and Media and Cultural Studies. It will also be useful for those interested in the wider role of culture, technology, and consumption in the transformation of society, identities, and communities.

Daniel Muriel is a Postdoctoral Research Fellow and Lecturer at the Leisure Studies Institute, University of Deusto, Bilbao, Spain.

Garry Crawford is a Professor of Sociology at the University of Salford, Manchester, UK.

ROUTLEDGE ADVANCES IN SOCIOLOGY

For a full list of titles in this series, please visit www.routledge.com/series/SE0511

236 "Helicopter Parenting" and "Boomerang Children"
How Parents Support and Relate to Their Student and Co-Resident Graduate Children
Anne West and Jane Lewis

237 New Directions in Elite Studies
Edited by Johan Heilbron, Felix Bühlmann, Johs. Hjellbrekke, Olav Korsnes, Mike Savage

238 Reflections on Knowledge, Learning and Social Movements
History's Schools
Edited by Aziz Choudry and Salim Vally

239 Social Generativity
A relational paradigm for social change
Edited by Mauro Magatti

240 The Live Art of Sociology
Cath Lambert

241 Video Games as Culture
Considering the Role and Importance of Video Games in Contemporary Society
Daniel Muriel and Garry Crawford

242 The Sociology of Central Asian Youth
Choice, Constraint, Risk
Mohd. Aslam Bhat

243 Indigenous Knowledge Production
Navigating Humanity within a Western World
Marcus Woolombi Waters

VIDEO GAMES AS CULTURE

Considering the Role and Importance of Video Games in Contemporary Society

Daniel Muriel and Garry Crawford

Routledge
Taylor & Francis Group
LONDON AND NEW YORK

First published 2018
by Routledge
2 Park Square, Milton Park, Abingdon, Oxon OX14 4RN

and by Routledge
711 Third Avenue, New York, NY 10017

Routledge is an imprint of the Taylor & Francis Group, an informa business

© 2018 Daniel Muriel and Garry Crawford

The right of Daniel Muriel and Garry Crawford to be identified as authors of this work has been asserted by them in accordance with sections 77 and 78 of the Copyright, Designs and Patents Act 1988.

All rights reserved. No part of this book may be reprinted or reproduced or utilized in any form or by any electronic, mechanical, or other means, now known or hereafter invented, including photocopying and recording, or in any information storage or retrieval system, without permission in writing from the publishers.

Trademark notice: Product or corporate names may be trademarks or registered trademarks, and are used only for identification and explanation without intent to infringe.

British Library Cataloguing-in-Publication Data
A catalogue record for this book is available from the British Library.

Library of Congress Cataloging-in-Publication Data
Names: Muriel, Daniel, author. | Crawford, Garry, author.
Title: Video games as culture: considering the role and importance of video games in contemporary society/Daniel Muriel and Garry Crawford.
Description: Abingdon, Oxon; New York, NY: Routledge, 2018 | Series: Routledge advances in sociology; 241 | Includes bibliographical references and index.
Identifiers: LCCN 2017049860 | ISBN 9781138655102 (hbk) | ISBN 9781138655119 (pbk) | ISBN 9781315622743 (ebk)
Subjects: LCSH: Video games–Social aspects. | Video gamers–Psychology. | Popular culture.
Classification: LCC GV1469.34.S52 M87 2018 | DDC 794.8–dc23
LC record available at https://lccn.loc.gov/2017049860

ISBN: 978-1-138-65510-2 (hbk)
ISBN: 978-1-138-65511-9 (pbk)
ISBN: 978-1-315-62274-3 (ebk)

Typeset in Bembo
by Deanta Global Publishing Services, Chennai, India

Printed in the United Kingdom
by Henry Ling Limited

For Nuria and Nicolás – D.M.
For Victoria, Joseph, and Grace – G.C.

CONTENTS

List of illustrations   x
Preface and acknowledgements   xi

1   Introduction: contemporary culture through the lens of video games   1

2   The emergence and consolidation of video games as culture   16

3   Video games and agency within neoliberalism and participatory culture   60

4   Video games as experience   84

5   Video games beyond escapism: empathy and identification   115

6   Video gamers and (post-)identity   143

7   Conclusion: this is not a video game, or is it?   180

Glossary   185
Index   189

ILLUSTRATIONS

Figures

2.1	The rise of the walking simulators: screenshot from *Firewatch*	40
4.1	A 'Very long phase' in *Gone Home*	87
4.2	Changing a diaper in *Heavy Rain*	97
4.3	A *Bloodborne* wiki	106
4.4	Screenshot from *Bloodborne*	106
5.1	Screenshot from *Papers, Please*	121
5.2	Different face representations in *Papers, Please*, *This War of Mine*, and *Gone Home*	125
5.3	Licking other guy's guns in *The Tearoom*	128

Table

1.1	List of interviews	7

PREFACE AND ACKNOWLEDGEMENTS

This book is the outcome of over three years' research. It has been a long and sometimes difficult journey, yet a very gratifying one. Although, as long-term gamers and scholars we were already well-aware of the growing importance of video games in today's world, this process has helped us to more fully realize and explore just how significant video games are for understanding contemporary society. Video games are undoubtedly an important part of our cultural landscape, and as with other media forms, such as films, music, television, or books, are increasingly becoming embedded in our everyday lives and impacting on other areas of social life. But video games are more than just another media product. Video games, we suggest, are also informing and driving the very culture that determines our lifestyles, meanings, and relationships. That is why this book is about not just video game *culture*, but rather also, and more than this, video games *as* culture.

It is almost an impossible task to thank everyone and everything (we must acknowledge, at least generically, the importance of our fellow non-humans) that made this book possible. We will try our best, though.

As rewarding as doing research is, this usually needs some form of material support, and mostly typically, money. Therefore, we need to thank the Basque Government and its Postdoctoral Programme for their funding support and for making the research and the meeting of these authors possible. In relation to this institutional support, we also wish to thank the University of Salford – in particular the Directorate of Society in the School of Health and Society, and the University of the Basque Country – and the Department of Sociology 2, in particular the research centre 'Social Change, Precarity, and Identity in Contemporary Society'. In Salford, we would particularly like to thank Muzammil Quraishi, Gaynor Bagnall, Victoria Gosling, Ben Light, Christopher Birkbeck, Anthony Ellis, Steve Myers, and Carlos Frade. In the Basque Country, we would particularly like to thank Joseba García Martín, Ivana Ruíz Estramil, Ander Mendiguren, Iñaki Robles,

Carlos García Grados, and Benjamín Tejerina. In both places, their help, conversations, and views – including shared thoughts, coffees, and meals – were always inspiring and refreshing (and this goes beyond the book and the topics it covers). We think that Ying-Ying Law, from Salford, deserves a special mention; we both were lucky enough (alongside Victoria Gosling) to have her as a PhD candidate, and from whom we learnt probably more than she would concede or imagine. Also, we are particularly fond of the many fruitful discussions with Iñaki Martínez de Albeniz and Diego Carbajo (Basque Country), full of video games, brownies, candies, donkeys, mediations, and *agencements*.

Besides funding, institutional and material support, social research would not be possible without those who kindly agree to participate in it. Their generosity to help us better understand the vicissitudes of video game culture from such a diverse and range of points of views was astounding. The research participants offered rich, varied, and insightful knowledge; we hope to have done it, and them, justice. For obvious methodological and ethical reasons, we cannot thank them personally by name, but we would like to acknowledge their fundamental contribution to our research and this book. We owe you a lot. What we can do is to personally thank Karla Zimonja, Pawel Miechowski, and Víctor Somoza, not only for participating in the research, but for being so kind (and brave) by letting us use their 'real' names in the book to facilitate the connection of their discourse with their work. We really appreciate your kindness and openness.

If research needs funding and participants, a book needs a publishing house. In this sense, we would like to express our gratitude to Routledge for placing their trust in our work. Specifically, we would like to thank Emily Briggs – Editor for Sociology, who showed her interest in our research from the outset and whose help was fundamental in bringing our work to Routledge; and Elena Chiu – Editorial Assistant for Sociology, who has accompanied us during a big part of this endeavour and has always offered her help. Both Emily and Elena have always been very kind and supportive, so we hope they are as proud of this book as we are.

We are also grateful to those video game publishers and developers that were open to our questions and gave us permission to use their video games' images (whether their games are directly cited in the book or not). Our thanks to Sony PlayStation (Cameron Wood, Ignacio Rodrigo), Square Enix (Ian Dickinson), Bethesda (Alistair Hatch), Fulbright (Karla Zimonja), 11 bit studios (Pawel Miechowski), Lucas Pope, Campo Santo (Erin Yvette), Robert Yang, EA Maxis (Nicole Rauschnot), Nordic Games (Reinhard Pollice), Frictional Games, Funcom (Tor Egil Andersen), Red Thread Games, Bloober Team (Rafał Basaj), Failbetter Games (Hannah Flynn), IMGN.PRO (Jakub Ryłko), Tale of Tales (Michael Samyn), Giant Sparrow (Ian Dallas, Janelle Grai), and Everything Unlimited (Davey Wreden).

Furthermore, any research or book in progress needs to be debated and scrutinized by the public eye in order to test its limits and detect any shortcomings. In this sense, we have expounded our findings in different academic spaces, including seminars, conferences, courses, and symposia. Events where early drafts of our work were presented at include: The British Sociological Association

Annual Conference in Glasgow (Scotland), the joint DiGRA-FDG conference in Dundee (Scotland), the Directorate of Social Sciences Research Seminar Series at the University of Salford, both the Research Seminar Masters and the Research Seminar for Undergraduates at the University of the Basque Country, the Cabueñes International Youth Conference in Gijón (Spain), the Sociology of the Ordinary Meeting in Madrid (Spain), the Workshop Identity and Video Games at Carlos III University in Madrid (Spain), and the 2nd Forum on Social Change in Santander (Spain). We would like to thank the organizers and delegates at each of the events, at which we came across a multitude of enthusiastic scholars and individuals interested in our research, who exceed our capacity to mention them here. Nevertheless, we would like to thank them all, and in particular (even at risk of forgetting many names) Carlos Gurpegui, Chuso Montero, Antonio Planells, Daniel Escandell, Justyna Janik, Alexander Muscat, Daniel Vella, Óliver Pérez-Latorre, César Díaz, Jorge González, Ruth García, Josué Monchán, Claire Dormann, Iris Rodríguez Alcaide, Adam Duell, Karl Spracklen, Elena Casado, Amparo Lasén, Antonio García, Rubén Blanco, Pablo Santoro, Luca Carrubba, and Miguel Sicart.

We also wish to thank Alberto Murcia, for his intelligent remarks and great sense of humor (the invasion of the body snatcher is here!); Jon López Dicastillo, for the opportunity to debate these issues in a political arena; Héctor Puente, for his incessant energy and passion for video games and his ability to open the academic world to other areas of society (and this includes the *Enjuegarte* collective and other friends, a peculiar group of young individuals with a multitude of interesting things to say: Costan Sequeiros, Mélida López, Marta F. Ruíz, Sheila Moreno, Erika García); Steve Conway, for his tremendous ability to read between the lines of our work and his more than useful comments on some of our drafts; Borja R. Surís, who is no academic, but whose wisdom and friendship we had the pleasure to share along a pint (or two!) and a good game of chess; Paul Joyce, a sociologist working outside of academia, who was always willing to listen to our ramblings and offer ideas; and finally, Richard Montgomery and Daniel Hancock for their insights into, and discussions on, esports and cosplay (respectively).

There were other forums and media where our work was tested and open to a wider audience in the form of non-academic writings. We would like to thank Guillermo G. M. – a real curator of video games and advocate of video games as culture – and the opportunity he gave us to share some of our ideas in one of the most stimulating online spaces for video games understood as culture (*Deus Ex Machina*, where we also came across interesting and nice people like Nacho Bartolomé, Fran G. Matas, Carmen Suárez, Marçal Mora, Ricardo Lázaro, Jenn Scarlett, Fu Olmos, Ricardo Suárez); Alberto Venegas and his journal *Presura*, one of the most prolific individuals we know and who always has something of relevance to say; Víctor Martínez from *AnaitGames*, whose openness to new approaches to video games and their culture and capacity to analyze video games in unexpected (always brilliantly) ways seems to be infinite (like his beard!); and Raúl García from *Zehngames*, Antonio Santo from *FSGamer*, Javier Alemán and Juanma from *Nivel*

Oculto, Koldo Gutiérrez from *Cactus*, and John Tones from *Canino* for making their online spaces available to some of our diatribes.

But this book (and everything else, to be honest) would not be here without the support and love of those who are around us. The ones who support us (and this includes putting up with us), no matter what, and fill our lives with love, comfort, and happiness. We owe them more than it can be expressed here. During this journey, some new members have joined our families, while others have sadly left us (I would like, this is Daniel speaking, to specially thank my mum, who could not see the end of this journey and many other – and more important – things: *un beso muy grande, ama*). So, this 'big thank you' is for our families and friends, and in particular, for our wonderful partners Nuria Fernández and Victoria Gosling, and our beautiful and full of life (and often tiring) children Nico, Grace, and Joseph.

1
INTRODUCTION

Contemporary culture through the lens of video games

Introduction

In the new preface for the 2010 edition of the first volume of the book *The Information Age*, Manuel Castells (2010: xvii) states that we 'live in confusing times, as is often the case in periods of historical transition between different forms of society'. It is difficult not to agree with this statement, but that is probably because we always live in confusing times: we are perpetually between different forms of society. Almost two decades into the twenty-first century and the diagnosis has not changed; social reality is the outcome of complex and major transformations that affect how we experience, think, and act within contemporary society.

The main task of sociologists is to understand the social reality that surrounds them. The social sciences in general, and sociology in particular, are concerned with a particularly sensitive area of study because they affect a portion of reality – the social – that heavily influences how we are as individuals and groups, societies and communities, citizens and human beings. Sociology dangerously participates in the construction of regimes of knowledge – or even of *truth* – that determine the social life and its structure. In this sense, Bourdieu, Chamboredon, and Passeron (1991: 69) suggest that 'the frontier between common knowledge and science is more blurred than elsewhere'. This *proximity* between the sociologist and their object of study brings about several risks, and not least a conflation between the knowledge generated by the academic and that produced by other social actors.

However, precisely because society and sociology are so intertwined, there is room for using this proximity as an epistemological vantage point; that is, it is a position, or lens, we can use to try to better understand contemporary social reality. As Georg Simmel (2004: 53) proposed more than a century ago, society can be found even in the most, apparently, insignificant interactions: the work of research thus lies in the possibility of 'finding in each of life's details the totality of its meaning' (Simmel, 2004: 53). We do not claim that in this book we will be able to grasp the totality of contemporary social life, but we can certainly shed new light on important aspects of contemporary society through the study of video game[1] culture.

Of course, the (very valid) argument could be made that one cannot discuss a single and coherent video game 'culture'. The argument has often rightly been made that we cannot homogenize video games, their players, and their culture. It is, of course, obvious to anyone with even a passing knowledge of video games that playing a game such as *World of Warcraft* (Blizzard Entertainment, 2004) on a personal computer is very different to playing *Call of Duty* (Activision, Infinity Ward, 2003–to date) on a games console, which is vastly different to playing *Candy Crush Saga* (King, 2012) on a mobile phone. Similarly, how video games are played and experienced in the UK is very different to how this happens and is socially located in, for example, India (see Chhina, 2016). This is, of course, something we recognize and acknowledge, and seek to elaborate in this book. Video game culture is diverse, complex, and constantly evolving. Hence, we recognize that it is problematic to talk about a singular video game culture. All cultures are complex and never static, and inevitably video game culture is the same. Nonetheless, just as we can at a certain level discuss the contemporary nature of 'British culture' or 'Spanish culture', we can articulate an area of study, even if this is at the level of the imagination, that is video game culture. As Simmel (1964) argues, it is obvious that in the same way that we can talk about the behaviour of the Greeks and the Persians in the Battle of Marathon without knowing the behaviour of each and every individual involved, it is possible to separate – if only analytically – form (video game culture in general) and content (the concrete cases: the different types of video games, styles of play, gamers, platforms, social contexts, and so forth).

The fundamental premise of this book is that there is a growing and consolidating video game culture (understood as the institutionalization of video game practices, experiences, and meanings), which permeates our societies, and provides a significant lens from which we can analyze wider social issues in contemporary society. Video games are therefore understood as an expression of life and culture in late modernity. Hence, this book provides an important perspective for understanding video games as experience, culture, and sociotechnical assemblage, but it also provides a consideration of how video games and their culture can help us understand aspects of social life such as work, education, culture, agency, power, experience, empathy, and identity in today's world. In particular, the book introduces complex notions that affect contemporary society through video game culture, making these ideas more tangible and accessible.

This book, then, makes an original and novel contribution to knowledge, particularly in the fields of sociology, media and cultural studies, and game studies. In this sense, the book employs insights from a range of social actors implicated and influential in various areas of video game culture. While most research in this field tends to focus on a particular aspect of gaming, or a particular type of social actor such as certain kinds of video gamers, developers, or other professionals of the industry, this research considers the roles and attitudes of those in various positions ranging from casual to avid gamers, to games designers, journalists, and also those often missing from research in this field, such as games academics, and those involved in the wider cultural interpretation of games, such as museum directors. This text also integrates a number of key concepts and ideas frequently employed in game studies, but rarely is their meaning, value, or use fully elaborated. Thus, the book pushes game studies into a number of scarcely explored areas, and sets out new theoretical and methodological frameworks for the analysis of video games, gamers, and video game culture.

Why video games?

So why and how do video games and their culture allow us to understand wider social issues? Primarily, the decision to study video games in order to understand contemporary society and the transformations that define it is based on four key assumptions:

1. Video games are an undoubtedly contemporary reality;
2. Video games embody some of the most important aspects of contemporary society;
3. Video games are established cultural products;
4. There is a growing and consolidating video game culture.

First, video games are, undoubtedly, a contemporary reality. If the aim of this book is to shed light on key aspects of contemporaneity from a sociological and cultural and media studies point of view, the universe of video games is then an excellent field to help us illustrate those aspects. The phenomenon of video games has only been relevant, at least socially speaking, since the 1980s (Kirkpatrick, 2015). From then onwards, video games have grown exponentially, especially in the last decade or so, with the so-called 'casual revolution' (Juul, 2010), and the expansion of video gaming to mobile devices and online social networking sites, such as, most notably, Facebook. Video games are postmodern, and as such, contain promises of a coming new reality:

> Digital games emerged in an era when discourses of the post-industrial and the post-modern dominated and when existing public regulation of the media and communications institutions was being dismantled. […] It is perhaps unsurprising that they should at the same time hold out the promise of new spaces for sociality, virtuality and identity construction while also embodying fears about the increasing levels of violence, individualisation and consumption in society.
>
> *(Kerr, 2006: 2)*

This then directs us to our second reason, which is to suggest that video games are a key vantage point from which to approach the ongoing crucial transformations of society. In this sense, video games embody some of the most important aspects of wider society such as a pervasive digital culture, the hegemony of neoliberal political rationalities, the emergence of participatory culture, and the rise of new modes of meaning construction, to name but a few. We face a world that has been completely inundated by digital technology (Castells, 2010), which affects our social lives in multiple and significant ways (Gere, 2008), and mediates how we interact with our environment. Video games, digital by definition, are bound to be one of the most important cultural products of this digital age (Kirby, 2009); which turns them into one of the best entry points to understand digital culture. Similarly, video games reflect and reproduce the hegemonic political rationalities of contemporary society, those of neoliberalism, in which individuals are governed through their freedom to choose, and responsibility is bestowed upon the individual (Rose, 1999). The central role attributed to the video game player as the demiurge of what happens in the act of playing video games, reinforces this position. However, video game culture also involves more collaborative and participatory rationalities and cultures: it is a 'participatory culture' (Jenkins, 2006), which can be defined as the culture that enables ordinary consumers to actively participate in the construction and modification of media content. Video game culture is full of participatory potential, such as the production or use of wikis, tutorials, walkthroughs, fan fiction, cosplay, modding, and much more (Newman, 2008). Finally, video games also exemplify how identities are formed today; the 'gamer' category and the communities that are built around video games are clear examples of fluid, multiple, and fragmented identities (Bauman, 2004; Giddens 1991), to the point that they anticipate post-identity scenarios (Agamben, 1993).

Third, video games appear as one of the most relevant cultural products and objects of our time. If, as Kirby (2009) suggests, digimodernism is the hegemonic cultural logic of contemporary society and both the video game and the video gamer are its principal object and subject, then studying video game culture provides us with the key tools with which to understand our contemporary cultural landscape. The video game industry is a thriving culture industry that is becoming hegemonic in the field. Revenues of video game companies are higher each year (Chatfield, 2011; ESA, 2016) and do not seem to have reached their peak. Statistics tell us that video games are played by increasing numbers of people, regardless of their demographics (ESA, 2017; Ukie, 2017). In a similar way, video game exhibitions and museums (Antonelli, 2013), along with conferences, festivals, tournaments, and all sorts of events on video games (Taylor, 2012; Law, 2016) have proliferated in the last few years. Also, not only have the number of specialized websites on video games vastly increased in number, but also the traditional media has started to regularly include sections dedicated to video games. Additionally, a multitude of jobs, courses, and degrees focusing on the development, design, and study of video games have emerged in the sectors of education and work (Kerr, 2017). In relation to the academic world, the emergence of the discipline of games studies (Aarseth, 2001; Wolf and Perron, 2015), along with a growing interest in studying video games from a wide range of disciplines (social sciences, humanities, arts, natural and technical sciences) corroborate the relevance of video games in our contemporary society.

Finally, it can be argued that there is a growing and consolidating video game culture (Mäyrä, 2008; Crawford, 2012) understood as the institutionalization of video game practices, experiences, and meanings in contemporary society, which permeates almost every corner of the social fabric. This means that many aspects of our society can be increasingly understood in terms of video games, that is, we are in a growing process of the videoludification of society (Raessens, 2010; Walz and Deterding, 2014; Zimmerman, 2014; Mäyrä, 2017). Not only do video games reflect wider social issues, but they also shape those social matters and drive their transformation. This can be seen in how certain areas of social reality are being gamified, that is, the use of game elements – particularly from video games – applied to other fields such as, education, labour, therapy, business, warfare, academia, and social relationships. Social reality is turned into a (video) game, and, in doing so, video game culture significantly affects society as a whole. Therefore, though there might be social actors that ignore video games as culture, the culture of video games is affecting them. It is affecting all of us, regardless.

For all these reasons, this book advocates and explores the value of video games as a focus and tool for understanding wider social and cultural changes and processes. It is therefore an exploration of *video game culture*, *video games in culture*, and *video games as culture*.

Methods

From a methodological point of view, the research on which this book is based builds on an actor–network theory approach, in accordance with the works of Latour (2007) or Law (2004), focusing especially on the innovative aspects of a digital ethnography (Hine, 2000), and how it intertwines with more traditional methods (Thornham, 2011). This approach seeks to focus not only on social agents or actors and their discourses, but also on their ways of doing and proceeding. For example, this is why the interviews included questions about the interviewees' regular activities, aims, and feelings, along with more theoretical interrogations about their views on certain issues related to video game culture.

Hence, this book draws on data gathered from ethnographic research on video game culture, conducted between January 2014 and June 2017. This employed a mixture of research tools including the use of formal semi-structured interviews, observations, informal interviews, a focused engagement with video game culture online and offline, and the use of play as a method of research. All the data gathered is used to illustrate, and give voice and weight, to the arguments and ideas we set out in the book.

In order to gather a wide range of opinions of various social actors, the research involved semi-structured interviews with 28 participants in Germany, Sweden, Luxembourg, and the United States, but primarily, in the UK and Spain – some face-to-face, but most commonly via Skype. The interviewees were categorized, by the researchers, to broadly include individuals from a range of video game-related roles or groups. This includes, (but is not limited to) video gamers, developers (such as designers, programmers, and artists), academics, journalists, website contributors and bloggers, and those in the arts and culture sector. It is important to note that these categories are only an analytical tool, and were simply used to gather a broad range of actors implicated within video game culture. These categories are not necessarily mutually exclusive or even clearly bounded. Therefore, significantly, where most empirical studies of video game culture focus on only a particular type or role of actor, such as video game players, developers, or journalists, this book explores the nature of this culture and its networks from multiple perspectives.

The aim of this varied pool of participants is to grasp – on a small but detailed scale as we are using an in-depth qualitative and ethnographic approach – the diversity of actors that are part of video game culture. Our purpose is not to establish differences between video game industry professionals and video gamers, or between individuals from different nationalities or backgrounds (which are taken into account, nonetheless), but to study video game culture as a whole and its impact on society. All participants cited in the research have been given pseudonyms except three interviewees who appear with their real names, with their explicit consent, in order to be able to refer to their works with more freedom. This is the case for: Pawel Miechowski, senior writer at 11 bit studios, developers of *This War of Mine* (2014); Karla Zimonja, co-founder of Fullbright, developers of *Gone Home* (2013), and Víctor Somoza, director of the documentary on video games *Memorias: más allá del juego*, which translates into English as *Memories: Beyond the Game*.[2]

With regard to 'video gamers', the interviewees were purposefully sampled according to their (self-defined) various levels of involvement within video game culture and their own identification as (or not) a 'gamer'. For example, some of them were highly involved in aspects of video game culture and self-identified as gamers, while others were less active and did not necessarily label themselves as gamers. The interviewees who were members of the video game industry were chosen again to provide a range of participants according to their role within the industry (such as, managers, programmers, designers, artists, and marketing), type of company (size, if they are developers and/or publishers), and the kind of video games they worked with (AAA, indie, free-to-play games). The interviewees categorized as belonging to 'the media' were again purposefully selected in relation to their primary type of medium (primarily print or online), and the role they play in that particular media form. Finally, we interviewed individuals working in the 'arts and culture' sector relating to video games, such as directors of video game museums.

Additionally, gender and age were also taken into consideration to try and again get a diverse range of participants, which provided us with a sample age range of 24–54 and a gender divide of 7 women and 21 men (among video gamers the divide was fifty-fifty). Interviews were recorded, transcribed, and analyzed thematically. Also, notes were taken from more informal conversations and communications with the interviewees and fed into the research; for example, information about their work and experiences. See Table 1.1, which sets out the list of interviewees and some basic information. In the book, in each chapter, the pseudonyms of the interviewees and some basic information is provided the first time they are mentioned, then after that, we only refer to them using their pseudonym.

In part, this research is also autoethnographic. Both of the authors identify as gamers, and both have been playing video games since early childhood. Hence, the research elicits and draws on the authors' own gaming knowledge and experiences; however, the decision was made to engage more deeply with video game culture, and play games much more regularly and analytically, during the research period. Over the entire period of the project, detailed research diaries were kept, documenting this (auto)ethnographic process, including thoughts, observations, play sessions, and informal conversations.

TABLE 1.1 List of interviews

Interviewee	*Description*	*Age*	*Gender*
Albert	Developer, artist	25	Male
Alfred	Strong identification as gamer, highly involved	26	Male
Ander	Not identified as gamer, loosely involved	33	Male
Carl	Strong identification as gamer, highly involved	28	Male
Conan	Youtuber, games, and films critic	23	Male
Dante	Head of a video game website	31	Male
Darius	Developer, game designer, indie	28	Male
Edward	Head of a Masters' on video games	54	Male
Elisabeth	Not identified as gamer, loosely involved	25	Female
Emmett	Head of video game cultural site	48	Male
Federico	Head of community management department, online games	31	Male
George	Developer, level designer, AAA games	42	Male
Iker	Not identified as gamer, loosely involved	43	Male
Jack	Coordinator of two degree programs on video games development	46	Male
Javier	Developer, game designer, big company	32	Male
Jill	Mild identification as gamer, loosely involved	26	Female
John	Former pro gamer, manager of pro gamer team	32	Male
Karla Zimonja	Co-founder of Fullbright, game artist, *Gone Home*	37	Female
Laura	Developer, artist, indie games	26	Female
María	Translator, player experience, online games	39	Female
Marta	Mild identification as gamer, highly involved	24	Female
Noel	Developer, programmer and game designer	24	Male
Pablo	Developer, programmer, AAA games	35	Male
Patxi	Developer, programmer and game designer, indie, and AAA	38	Male
Pawel Miechowski	Co-founder of 11 bit studios, senior writer, *This War of Mine*	40	Male
Robert	Head of video game cultural site	47	Male
Víctor Somoza	Director of a documentary on video games, *Memories: Beyond the Game*	27	Male
Zelda	Mild identification as gamer, highly involved	25	Female

This research then involved the use of play as a method of research (see Mäyrä, 2008; Bizzocchi and Tanenbaum, 2011; Karppi and Sotamaa, 2012; van Vught and Glas, 2017). In this sense, and following actor–network theory, video games are also seen as active 'participants' in this research. Frans Mäyrä (2008: 165) argues that playing games is the 'most crucial element in any methodology of game studies'. Hence, it is argued by several authors that in order to fully understand video games, it is essential that the researcher plays them. However, how a researcher plays and analyzes a game can vary greatly. It is not our intention here to set out a full consideration of the value, limitations, and use of play as a research tool, as others, such as Jasper van Vught and René Glas (2017) already offer an excellent overview of this method; nevertheless, it is important here to at least briefly highlight some of the main features of what is still a largely new and innovative research method, as well as setting out our own particular approach here.

In particular, van Vught and Glas (2017) set out a categorization of ways of using play as a research method, organized around the two axes: focus and style. In terms of focus, van Vught and Glas suggest that researchers can adopt what they term an 'object' or 'process' focus. They categorize an object approach as research that focuses on games as a specific object or a text that are analyzed to understand their structure or content. This can then draw on a more literary tradition, and consider a game's narrative or iconography, for example, or a more ludology-inspired approach and focus on aspects of the game such as its structure and rules. A process approach involves 'pushing the analysis past a focus on either the player or the game and towards the various forces and connections holding up the assemblage of games as processes' (van Vught and Glas, 2017: 3). This then provides a more contextual approach, which locates games, players, and the researcher within a wider socio-cultural framework and understanding.

Next, van Vught and Glas (2017) highlight, how the researcher chooses to play the game, matters. Here they contrast 'instrumental' and 'free' styles of play. Instrumental play is where the researcher seeks to survey the full range of possibilities in the game, such as exploring all game areas or styles of play. In contrast, free play is where the researcher seeks to subvert the preferred reading of the game, and instead engages in 'transgressive play' (Karppi and Sotamaa, 2012), such as cheating, and pushing the boundaries of the game to see what is possible.

Of course, the model set out by van Vught and Glas (2017) is largely an analytical tool, and many researchers combine or blur the lines between different styles of play; and, as with most game scholars, our particular approach does not necessarily neatly fit into one particular type. As sociologists, and also given the particular focus of this book and our theoretical approach to this, we do mostly adopt a *process* orientated approach, which seeks to analyze games as actors within a wider social framework. However, in doing so, we also often seek to focus on the narrative, structure, or content of particular games, where these are relevant. Similarly, our styles of play varied greatly. Sometimes, this involved little more than what Aarseth (2003) refers to as 'superficial play', where we merely dipped into a game for a few minutes. Other times, this involved a much more detailed and systematic playing of games to explore as many avenues and play possibilities as we could; while at others, we tried to stray from our, and others', usual styles of play, and experiment, and see what was possible with particular games.

Hence, all of the games listed in this book have been played by at least one of the authors, and most by both during the course of researching and writing this book; sometimes at length and to completion, or sometimes more superficially. At the beginning of this project we began with a list of different kinds and genres of games, on various platforms, we intended to play, and over the course of the project added many more titles, as they become available or we became aware of them. This included AAA games, indie games, games on personal computers, on various consoles, old and new, on mobile devices, on web-browsers, online, offline, alone, with others, and much more. Some were the kinds of games we might normally play, and these we often played to completion, such as *The Witcher 3: Wild Hunt* (CD Projekt RED, 2015); some we had not played in a while and we revisited in a more focused and analytical way, such as *Assassin's Creed* (Ubisoft, 2007); some we played with others, such as with our children, like the *CBeebies Playtime* app (BBC Media, 2015); while some we played merely to push the boundaries of the kinds of games we would normally encounter, such as trying our hand at *Pokémon GO* (Niantic Labs, 2012). This then gave us a long and diverse range of games, many of which we reference in this book, but the list of those we played analytically extends many times beyond those referred to here. Though of course the list of games played in this research and referenced in this book is far from exhaustive, and tends to include mostly very contemporary games, this is far more lengthy and diverse than that typically seen in most video game studies.

In addition to playing many more games than we normally would have, and doing so in a much more focused and analytical way, we also chose to try and engage with wider video game culture, in a deeper and more meaningful way. This mostly involved much more regular and focused non-participant observation of online and offline game culture than we would have normally engaged in; such as regularly reading and watching video games magazines, blogs, reviews, message boards, and YouTube and Twitch channels. For example, magazines, websites, and blogs such as *Rock, Paper, Shotgun*,[3] *Polygon*,[4] *Kotaku*,[5] *GiantBomb*,[6] *Gamasutra*,[7] *Edge*,[8] *Waypoint*,[9] *PC Gamer*,[10] *Eurogamer*,[11] *Kill Screen*,[12] *AnaitGames*,[13] *Zehngames*,[14] *Deus Ex Machina*,[15] *AntiHype*,[16] *Presura*,[17] and *FS Gamer*,[18] to name but a few. In relation to YouTube and Twitch, we regularly followed channels such as *PewDiePie*,[19] *Feminist Frequency*,[20] *TotalBiscuit – The Cynical Brit*,[21] *The Syndicate Project*,[22] *Pushing Up Roses*,[23] *PBS Game Show*,[24] *Markiplier*,[25] *Jim Sterling*,[26] *Scanliner*,[27] *DayoScript*,[28] *Bukku qui*,[29] *SonyaTheEvil*,[30] *Fremily*,[31] *Littlemisspiss*,[32] and *Silentsentry*.[33] We also looked into comments made on social network sites such as Twitter, Facebook, and Reddit. Daniel Muriel also made the decision that it would be useful to participate in this culture in a more active way, and hence, decided to create a blog (The Three-Headed Monkey[34]), on which he could engage with an online gamer community, test out ideas, and explore their validity. He too contributed to media outlets specialized in video games.[35] Additionally, we also undertook specific case studies where observations were made around following various video game titles (including *Gone Home*, *This War of Mine*, *Titan Souls*, *Papers, Please*, *Gods Will Be Watching*, *Watch Dogs*, *Life is Strange*, *Skyrim*, and *Bloodborne*) online, and what was said in relation to them by three main communities of actors: video gamer communities on online forums and social media, media professionals on specialized websites, and developers on websites. In a social context traversed by a preeminent digital culture, what happens on the Internet is crucial to understanding the social realities that are forming around it. Among other things, Twitter, Facebook, Reddit, Instagram, YouTube, websites, and blogs form a social space where social relations are established, and social reality takes shape. This is particularly important for video game culture.

Book structure: X marks the spot

At the beginning of *The Secret of Monkey Island* (LucasArts, 1990), its protagonist, Guybrush Threepwood, had to appear before the three pirate leaders of Mêlée Island in order to fulfill his wish of becoming a pirate. In order to show his worth, the pirate leaders set Guybrush three trials: sword fighting, thievery, and treasure hunting. In relation to the treasure hunting trial, the bold, but not so brilliant, Guybrush – his only skill, remarkable nonetheless, consists of holding his breath for ten minutes – asked the pirate leaders if he needed a map to find the treasure. 'Ye can hardly expect to find a treasure without a map!' answered one of the pirate leaders with undisguised disdain. And they added: 'X marks the spot!'.

If the aim of this book is to map the different ways in which video game culture intertwines with important aspects of contemporary social life and culture, then before we progress on this task, it is necessary to pause for a moment to set out the latitudinal and longitudinal lines that this book will follow; and where necessary, throughout the book, signpost them again.

This book is intended for a wide range of potential readers; from game studies, social science, and media and cultural studies scholars, to PhD, Masters, and higher-level undergraduate students, including anyone interested in the study of video games, its culture, and wider issues that affect contemporary society. *Video Games as Culture* is a book that offers original, novel, and significant insights into different areas, topics, and notions that are relevant to contemporary society such as: video game culture, video gamers, video game experiences, identity, agency, experience, empathy, digital and participatory cultures, and neoliberalism, to name but a few.

Chapter 2 considers a few key examples of how and why video games are becoming a growing cultural phenomenon that is contributing to wider social transformations. After proposing a definition of video game culture within the context of the rise of the (video)ludic century and digital culture, the chapter explores different cases that help us to understand the emergence and consolidation of video game culture. Among them, the gamification of reality, the growing interest of video games amongst the general public, a flourishing video game industry, the links between video games, education and work, video game audiences, video games in academia, and video games as a cultural product.

Chapter 3 approaches the contemporary nature of agency and its sociopolitical constraints and possibilities in the context of video games. Building mainly on actor–network theory and also the work of Michel Foucault, the chapter understands the notion of agency as the multiple, distributed, and dislocated production of transformations that can take a multitude of forms. Thus, agency is defined as what transforms reality one way or another within the framework outlined by the political rationalities linked to the neoliberal dispositifs and assemblages. Although the notion of agency in video games seems to be dominated by the referents of neoliberalism, it is still possible to imagine ways in which agency heads towards more promising outcomes.

Chapter 4 argues that video games can be understood as postphenomenological experiences. In this sense, video games help to channel different experiences in order to connect with other realities, game experiences are often recounted as any other lived experience, video games are necessarily enacted and embodied experiences, and video games are linked to a wider social tendency that sees reality in terms of a set of experiences. Furthermore, not only can video games be understood as experiences, they are also helpful in shedding new light on our understanding of the contemporary nature of experience. Hence, experience can be described as, at the same time, individual, unique, and contingent, but also collective, shared, and stable.

Chapter 5 further explores how video games can create different experiences of play, focusing here specifically on those that promote social empathy and processes of identification, and challenge the idea of video games as exclusively an escapist activity. Not only are video games self-contained universes designed to escape to, but they are also a medium to connect with different aspects of reality. The key to understanding the fundamental and interrelated mechanisms of empathy and identification as ways to connect with other social realities rests on the idea that video game experiences do not necessarily substitute the experiences they are based on, but rather, mediate between them and video game players.

Chapter 6 focuses on the contemporary nature of identity in relation to video gamers. In particular, it suggests that video games provide a useful vantage point from which to observe the process of identity formation in contemporary society. In particular, it is argued that video game culture anticipates and helps us to understand new modes of meaning and processes of identity construction. The chapter reviews some of the theoretical discussions on identity that have taken place in recent years, and looks at the different conceptualizations of the video gamer and its communities that emerge from our research. Finally, here we envisage the rise of a post-identity scenario, in which the processes of identity formation change radically and the very notion of identity is jeopardized.

Chapter 7 sets out the conclusions of the book, summarizing its main findings and the theoretical debates that were discussed. This includes, first and foremost, the main idea of the book: that key aspects of contemporary society can be understood through the lens of video game culture, which not only mirrors those fundamental dimensions of social reality but also, within its limits, takes part in them. The chapter then navigates the many ways in which video game culture represents and affects society: video games and their culture then appear as the beta version of a society to come, a video game culture that helps us visualize the ontological and sociopolitical articulations of agency in contemporaneity, the fundaments of video games that anticipate a society that is progressively becoming an assemblage of technologically mediated experiences that connects different realities, situations, and cultures, and the video gamer identity as the epitome of identity construction in contemporary society.

Hence, the 'x' we are seeking to place on the map is added knowledge and a deeper understanding of an extremely significant, though still under-researched, culture. However, we cannot forget that in research, as in the *Monkey Island* game, we find a big X already inscribed on the land in front of us, which always raises the same questions: What x was carved first? The 'x' on the ground, or is this big 'x' merely replicating what was on the map first, or were they created simultaneously? And can one exist without the other? In any case, the 'x' always marks the spot, because the real treasure is that 'x' and not what is buried below. We hope this book points you toward the relevant 'x's' of video game culture and its relation to contemporary society and culture.

Notes

1 'Video games' is our preferred term to refer to all games played on electronic devices, such as video games consoles, personal computers, mobile telephones, and tablet computers.
2 https://www.youtube.com/playlist?list=PL6th9XqkD_C19K_eSPbcVvV4VL9fTa-TH
3 https://www.rockpapershotgun.com/
4 https://www.polygon.com/
5 http://kotaku.com/
6 https://www.giantbomb.com/
7 http://www.gamasutra.com/
8 http://www.gamesradar.com/edge/
9 https://waypoint.vice.com/en_us
10 http://www.pcgamer.com/
11 http://www.eurogamer.net/
12 https://killscreen.com/
13 http://www.anaitgames.com/
14 http://www.zehngames.com/
15 http://deusexmachina.es/
16 http://antihype.es/
17 http://www.presura.es/
18 http://www.fsgamer.com/
19 https://www.youtube.com/user/PewDiePie
20 https://www.youtube.com/user/feministfrequency
21 https://www.youtube.com/user/TotalHalibut
22 https://www.youtube.com/user/TheSyndicateProject
23 https://www.youtube.com/user/pushinguproses
24 https://www.youtube.com/user/pbsgameshow
25 https://www.youtube.com/user/markiplierGAME

26 https://www.youtube.com/user/JimSterling
27 https://www.youtube.com/channel/UCWz51s7gd-p55UXY_xm69FQ
28 https://www.youtube.com/user/DayoScript
29 https://www.youtube.com/channel/UCGO1Jl3yFtHJbTnoZgeoKZg
30 https://www.twitch.tv/sonyatheevil
31 https://www.twitch.tv/fremily
32 https://www.twitch.tv/littlemisspiss
33 https://www.twitch.tv/silentsentry
34 http://the3headedmonkey.blogspot.co.uk
35 To access the complete list of contributions, see: https://danielmuriel.com/other-contributions/

References

Aarseth, Espen (2001). 'Computer Game Studies, Year One', *Game Studies*, 1 (1), [http://www.gamestudies.org/0101/editorial.html] [Last Accessed: 10/07/2017].

Aarseth, Espen (2003). 'Playing Research: Methodological Approaches to Game Analysis', Paper presented at *Digital Arts and Culture (DAC)*, 28–29 August 2003, Melbourne, [http://www.bendevane.com/VTA2012/wp-content/uploads/2012/01/02.GameApproaches2.pdf] [Last Accessed: 10/07/2017].

Agamben, Giorgio (1993). *The Coming Community*. Minnesota: University of Minnesota Press.

Antonelli, Paola (2013) (video). 'Why I bought Pac Man to MoMA', *TED Talk*, [https://www.ted.com/talks/paola_antonelli_why_i_brought_pacman_to_moma] [Last Accessed: 23/05/2017]

Bauman, Zygmunt (2004). *Identity*. Cambridge: Polity Press.

Bizzocchi, Jim and Tanenbaum, Joshua (2011). 'Well Read: Applying Close Reading Techniques to Gameplay Experiences', in *Well Played 3.0: Video Games, Value and Meaning*, Drew Davidson (editor) Pittsburgh, ETC Press, [http://press.etc.cmu.edu/content/well-read-jim-bizzocchi-joshua-tanenbaum] [Last Accessed: 07/07/2017].

Bourdieu, Pierre; Chamboredon, Jean-Claude; Passeron, Jean-Claude (1991). *The Craft of Sociology*. Berlin: Walter de Gruyter.

Castells, Manuel (2010). *The Information Age: Economy, Society and Culture. The Rise of the Network Society Vol 1*. Oxford: Wiley-Blackwell.

Chatfield, Tom (2011). *Fun Inc.: Why Gaming Will Dominate the Twenty-First Century*. New York: Pegasus.

Chhina, Gagun (2016). 'The Emerging Field of Video Gaming in India', unpublished PhD thesis, Manchester: University of Manchester.

Crawford, Garry (2012). *Video Gamers*. London: Routledge.

ESA (2016). *Essential Facts About the Computer and Video Game Industry*, [http://essentialfacts.theesa.com/Essential-Facts-2016.pdf] [Last Accessed: 11/05/2017].

ESA (2017). *Essential Facts About the Computer and Video Game Industry*, [http://essentialfacts.theesa.com/mobile/] [Last accessed: 30/05/2017].

Gere, Charlie (2008). *Digital Culture*. London: Reaktion Books.

Giddens, Anthony (1991). *Modernity and Self-Identity*. Cambridge: Polity Press.

Hine, Christine (2000). *Virtual Ethnography*. London: Sage.

Jenkins, Henry (2006). *Fans, Bloggers, and Gamers. Exploring Participatory Culture*. New York: New York University Press.

Juul, Jesper (2010). *A Casual Revolution: Reinventing Video Games and Their Players*. Cambridge, MA: MIT Press.

Karppi, Tero and Sotamaa, Olli (2012). 'Rethinking Playing Research: DJ Hero and Methodological Observations in the Mix', *Simulation & Gaming*, 43, (3): 413–429.

Kerr, Aphra (2006). *The Business and Culture of Digital Games. Gamework/Gameplay*. London: Sage.

Kerr, Aphra (2017). *Global Games: Production, Circulation, and Policy in the Networked Era*. London: Routledge.

Kirby, Alan (2009). *Digimodernism*. New York: Continuum.

Kirkpatrick, Graeme (2015). *The Formation of the Gaming Culture: UK Gaming Magazines, 1981–1995*. London: Palgrave.

Latour, Bruno (2007). *Reassembling the Social. An Introduction to Actor-Network-Theory*. Oxford: Oxford University Press.

Law, John (2004). *After Method. Mess in Social Science Research*. London: Routledge

Law, Ying-Ying (2016). 'The Travelling Gamer: An Ethnography of Video Game Events', PhD dissertation, University of Salford.

Mäyrä, Frans (2008). *An Introduction to Game Studies. Games in Culture*. London: Routledge.

Mäyrä, Frans (2017). 'Pokémon GO: Entering the Ludic Society', *Mobile Media & Communication*, 5(1):1–4.

Newman, James (2008). *Playing with Videogames*. London: Routledge.

Raessens, Joost (2010). *Homo Ludens 2.0. The Ludic Turn in Media Theory*. Utrecht: University of Utrecht.

Rose, Nikolas (1999). *Politics of Freedom. Reframing Political Thought*. Cambridge: Cambridge University Press.

Simmel, Georg (1964) [1917]. *The Sociology of Georg Simmel*. New York: Free Books.

Simmel, Georg (2004) [1900]. *The Philosophy of Money*. London: Routledge.

Taylor, T. L. (2012). *Raising the Stakes. E-Sports and the Professionalization of Computer Gaming*. Cambridge, MA: MIT Press.

Thornham, Helen (2011). *Ethnographies of the Videogame. Gender, Narrative and Praxis*. Surrey: Ashgate.

Ukie (2017). *UK Video Games Fact Sheet (20 March)*, [http://bit.ly/2q92Mpd] [Last Accessed: 11/05/2017].

van Vught, Jasper and Glas, René (2017). 'Considering Play: From Method to Analysis', *Proceedings of DiGRA 2017 conference*, Melbourne, 2–6 July 2017, [http://digra2017.com/static/Full%20Papers/56_DIGRA2017_FP_Vught_Considering_Play.pdf] [Last Accessed: 10/07/2017].

Walz, Steffen P. and Deterding, Sebastian (2014) (editors). *The Gameful World. Approaches, Issues, Applications*. Cambridge, MA: MIT Press.

Wolf, Mark J. and Perron, Bernard (editors) (2015). *The Routledge Companion to Video Game Studies*. London: Routledge.

Zimmerman, Eric (2014). 'Manifesto for a Ludic Century' in Walz, Steffen P. and Deterding, Sebastian (2014) (editors). *The Gameful World. Approaches, Issues, Applications*. Cambridge, MA: MIT Press, 19–22.

Ludography

11 bit studios (2014). *This War of Mine*.
Acid Nerve (2015). *Titan Souls*.
Activision, Infinity Ward (2003–to date). *Call of Duty* series.
BBC Media (2015). *BBC CBeebies Playtime*.
Bethesda (2011). *The Elder Scrolls V: Skyrim*.

Blizzard Entertainment (2004). *World of Warcraft*.
CD Projekt RED (2015). *The Witcher 3: Wild Hunt*.
Deconstructeam (2014). *Gods Will Be Watching*.
Dontnod Entertainment (2015). *Life is Strange*.
FromSoftware (2015). *Bloodborne*.
Fullbright (2013). *Gone Home*.
King (2012). *Candy Crush Saga*.
LucasArts (1990). *The Secret of Monkey Island*.
Niantic Labs (2016). *Pokémon GO*.
Pope, Lucas (2013). *Papers, Please*.
Ubisoft (2007). *Assassin's Creed*.
Ubisoft (2014). *Watch Dogs*.

2
THE EMERGENCE AND CONSOLIDATION OF VIDEO GAMES AS CULTURE

Introduction

The fundamental premise on which this book is based is that there is a growing and consolidating video game culture, which permeates contemporary society. This, for example, makes it possible to think in terms of a process of (what we term) the *videoludification*[1] of society. Obviously, this culture is also part of broader social phenomena and transformations, with which game culture intertwines in complex ways; such as the emergence and rise of digital culture (Castells, 2010), neoliberal political rationalities (Rose, 1999), participatory culture (Jenkins, 2006), risk society (Beck, 1992), expert culture (Giddens, 1991; Knorr Cetina, 1999), new cultural logics (Gere, 2008), liquid modernity (Bauman, 2000), post-humanism (Haraway, 1991), an age of simulacra (Baudrillard, 1994), staged authenticity (MacCannell, 2011), and many other aspects of the changing nature of social reality in late capitalism. Thus, it is our central argument that video game culture is both a consequence of, and key contributor to, complex contemporary social and cultural transformations – which we will explore in more detail throughout this book.

In this chapter, we consider a few key examples of how and why video games are becoming an established and growing cultural phenomenon that is contributing to wider social transformations. First, we set out the framework of these processes by proposing a definition of video game culture within the context of the rise of (video)ludic century digital culture. Then, we consider different cases that help us explore the emergence and consolidation of video game culture, such as the gamification of reality (including ideas of gamification, serious games, and augmented reality), the growing importance of video games among the general public, a thriving video game industry, the links between video games, education, and work, the construction of a video game audience, the growing importance of video games in academia, and the consolidation of video games as a cultural product.

Defining video game culture

The rise of digital culture

Walking through the *Museum of Science and Industry*[2] in Manchester (UK), the visitor is invited to witness some of the magnificent – yet terrible and monstrous – industrial machinery that was behind the origins of the Industrial Revolution. A revolution that, indeed, changed the world. In the same museum, there is also an area dedicated to our computer's ancestors. One of them is a replica of the famous Small Scale Experimental Machine (SSEM), nicknamed 'Baby', which was built at the University of Manchester in 1948. 'Baby' is credited with the achievement of storing and running a programme for the first time. Everything in it feels more analogical than digital, but it is still one of the first expressions of the digital tsunami that was to come. Unlike the formidable engines that powered the industrial revolution, it seems difficult to understand how that rudimentary computer could also give birth to a new revolution that transformed the world. Nonetheless, a huge transformation was on its way. The digital age was born.

In the introduction of his book *Digital Culture*, Charlie Gere (2008) recalls the generalized paranoia that overran the last months of 1999 due to the fears surrounding the 'Millennium bug' or 'Y2k bug' that was predicted to corrupt all of our computers as they failed to deal with the year date of '00. Although we know that nothing of particular significance happened – as far as we know – with our computerized systems and electronics, the infamous Y2k bug had an (unintended) consequence of making us all much more aware that we now lived in a fully digitalized world:

> Like a lightning flash over a darkened scene, it made briefly visible what had hitherto been obscure; the almost total transformation of the world by digital technology.
>
> *(Gere, 2008: 13)*

Digital technology has transformed reality at all levels. There are few areas that have not been changed by digitalization. This vast transformation includes the fields of media (new and old), work, government, economy, welfare, education, law, leisure, and almost every aspect of our everyday life activities:

> It is hard to grasp the full extent of this transformation, which, in the developed world at least, can be observed in almost every aspect of modern living. Most forms of mass media, television, recorded music, film, are produced and, increasingly, distributed digitally. These media are beginning to converge with digital forms, such as the Internet, the World Wide Web, and video games, to produce a seamless digital mediascape. When at work we are also surrounded by such technology, whether in offices, where computers have become indispensable tools for word processing and data management, or in, for example, supermarkets or factories, where every aspect of marketing

and production is monitored and controlled digitally. Much of the means by which governments and other complex organizations pursue their ends rely on digital technology. Physical money, coins and notes, is no more than digital data congealed into matter. By extension, information of every kind and for every purpose is now mostly in digital form, including that relating to insurance, social services, utilities, real estate, leisure and travel, credit arrangements, employment, education, law, as well as personal information for identification and qualification, such as birth certificates, drivers licences, passports and marriage certificates.

(Gere, 2008: 13–14)

Every aspect of our social and personal lives is starting to become digitally mediated, and even though it may still be possible to partially escape the digital world, 'it is becoming increasingly difficult to do so every day' (Tredinnick, 2008: 22).

However, while digital culture has more generally become the dominant cultural logic in contemporary societies, it could be said, according to Kirby (2009: 168), that video games are specifically the central cultural product of this epoch:

the figure of the computer game player, fingers and thumbs frenetically pushing on a keypad so as to shift a persona through a developing, mutating narrative landscape, engaging with a textuality that s/he physically brings – to a degree – into existence, engulfing him or herself in a haphazard, onward fictive universe which exists solely through that immersion – this is to a great extent the figure of digimodernism itself. And as computer games have spread in their appeal across age-ranges, classes, and genders, they have become a synecdoche for an entire new form of cultural-dominant.

The video game is, therefore, the prototypical cultural form of digital culture; it is – so to speak – its purest form. Video game and video gamers are thus seen as (at least) one of the main products and driving forces of our contemporary society. Though we might not go as far as Kirby, it is obvious that, even if video games are not *the* most important product of a digital culture, they are certainly still an essential one – and along with this, comes a video game culture.

A definition of video game culture

Before entering into a more detailed discussion of what video game culture encompasses, and why it is becoming an important, if not an essential, part of our social and cultural landscape, let us offer a practical definition of video game culture as: *the institutionalization of video game practices, experiences, and meanings in contemporary society, which places video games and video gaming as an important part of our social imaginary*.

First then, this definition incorporates Crawford's (2012: 143) argument that video gaming should be understood, not as an isolated activity, but rather as a 'culture which extends far beyond the sight of a video game machine or screen'. Drawing on authors such as Newman (2004) and Burn (2006), Crawford (2012: 143) argues that 'video gaming is not just the act of playing a game, but also a source of memories, dreams, conversations, identities, friendships, artwork, storytelling and so much more'. Undoubtedly, video games 'are about more than just the act and moment of play itself' (Newman, 2004: 153). This then, is the first understanding of video game culture we would like to apply here; as 'a system of meaning' (Mäyrä, 2008: 13), as well as a set of social practices, located within a wider social context.

In this sense, the definition of 'culture' we are utilizing here can be situated between the traditional holistic anthropological approach to the notion – almost everything that is produced by humankind – and the more restrictive humanistic one – a particular aspect of a society, usually what is understood as high culture and within the field of arts. That is to say, it is our intention to consider both the specific practices of video game culture, and also, how video game culture is embedded within a wider cultural landscape.

If we focus on its etymology, 'culture' has always been linked to acts of caring or rearing; in short, culture is the product of what is cultivated. Then, in its most restrictive, humanistic sense, culture can be understood as that which is possessed after the efforts made to create it. Moreover, in this definition, culture distinguishes between those who are seen to possess it and those who do not. This conceptualization of culture then, is not particularly useful to us, because it is too restrictive and discriminating; however, it is an argument we will at least briefly revisit when it comes to analyzing some forms of elitist or strongly demarcated formulations of video game culture and video gamer identity (see Chapter 6).

The second, more inclusive anthropological usage of the term 'culture' is defined by Edward B. Tylor (1973: 4–5) in the following terms:

> Culture or Civilization, taken in is wide ethnographic sense, is that complex whole which includes knowledge, belief, art, morals, custom, and any other capabilities and habits acquired by man as a member of society.

The problem with Tylor's approach to culture is what Clifford Geertz (1973: 4–5) highlights: it is a definition so broad that it forces us to take all directions at the same time, and makes the concept impracticable from both a theoretical and practical position. Even though we might feel inclined to theorize video game culture in a broad sense, we would agree with Frans Mäyrä, that we probably cannot equate this culture to those typically studied by traditional anthropology. As Mäyrä (2008: 23) writes:

> If the concept of culture is taken in this broad and general sense, and applied as such directly into game studies, this can lead into a rather heavy-handed way to conceptualize 'game culture'. […] One could also certainly argue that games do not define our existence or place in a society in a way that belonging to a traditional ethnic culture, say Bantu or Inuit culture, defines

the way of life and identity for those people. But games and game playing practices do have some significance for those people who are actively engaged with games.

Hence, Mäyrä helps delimit the notion of culture we would like to attach to video games and the group of people who play them. Video game culture is for us then, as with Mäyrä, the phenomenon that is 'built upon layers of learning and experience among all the previous games that the particular group of individuals sharing this culture have interacted with before' (Mäyrä, 2008: 19). In sum, Mäyrä defines culture as a set of shared experiences – and, in particular, this notion of 'experience' we explicitly seek to explore in more detail in Chapter 3. In a similar, but slightly different, vein, and again drawing on the work of a variety of anthropologist and social theorists, Celia Pearce (2009: 51–54) approaches the idea of culture, as a network of shared meanings; essentially, employing the Weberian definition of culture given by Geertz (1973: 5):

> Believing, with Max Weber, that man [sic.] is an animal suspended in webs of significance he himself has spun, I take culture to be those webs, and the analysis of it to be therefore not an experimental science in search of law but an interpretive one in search of meaning.

If we then blend these descriptions of culture, as shared experiences and meanings, with the ideas highlighted above of other game studies scholars, such as by Crawford (2012), which emphasizes the importance of certain practices, we then come to the definition of video game culture we set out at the beginning of this chapter, as consisting of a collection of practices, experiences, and meanings, which is located within a wider cultural landscape.

Exploring (video)ludification

Video games have been portrayed as the medium of the twenty-first century (Pearce, 2009: 51); a 'prototypical cultural form of digital culture' (Kirby, 2009: 167), which has become hegemonic and culturally dominant (Pearce, 2009: 168). We would not go as far as to suggest that video game culture is *the* most important cultural medium of the present century, but it would be difficult to understand contemporary society without it. Above all, it is our central argument that video game culture provides the opportunity to study social issues of great importance, such as: agency (Chapter 3), culture (Chapter 2), identity (Chapter 6), experience (Chapter 4), politics (Chapter 3), social practices (Chapter 2), the process of identification and empathy (Chapter 5), and community formation processes (Chapter 6). In particular, video game culture allows us to do this in a neatly framed and bounded way, which is almost like an ideal sociological living laboratory.

In this sense, the definite evidence that video game culture is permeating (almost) all areas of our society can be found in those aspects of video games that go beyond the limits of their own culture. This happens when everyday life is colonized by the logic and mechanics of video games; when different social contexts, such as those in the fields of economy, work, leisure, education, health, and consumption, are permeated by the rationale that governs video games. The expansion of video game culture, as we will show in this chapter, inexorably brings about the videoludification of culture.

In particular, we would suggest that this process of videoludification of social reality is visible in the spheres of: gamification (the use of game elements – particularly from video games – applied to education, labour, therapy, business, or social relationships), virtual reality (proliferation of domestic virtual reality devices through video games), augmented reality (with paradigmatic cases like *Pokémon GO*, where public spaces become playgrounds), social networks (Twitter, Facebook, Instagram, or Tinder, which transform social relations into an activity that resembles video gaming in terms of achievements and scores through their accounting of 'likes', 'followers', 'reach', 'milestones', and so on), production of knowledge (the existence of wikis and 'open access' as part of a participatory culture – typical of video game practices, but also through the assessment of publications and research using the logics of 'impact factor', 'accreditations', funding based on a competitive basis and scoring, and gamified social networks – such as Academia.edu or ResearchGate), commercial relations (fidelity programmes and consumption patterns' control through a system of points, discounts, gifts, and badges), media (assessed by the number of clicks, visitors, and rankings, along with enabling and fostering the interactivity with their audience), politics (polling as high score tables, participatory democracy using apps and websites, affiliation working as clans in MMOGs, and social networks' activism), warfare (the use of game technology applied to the military such as drones and robots using video game-like interfaces and controllers), and many other areas.

This is a trend that some game scholars have labelled as the 'gameful world' (Walz and Deterding, 2014), 'the ludic century' (Zimmerman, 2014), the 'ludification of culture' (Raessens, 2006; Raessens, 2010), or the 'ludic society' (Mäyrä, 2017). In particular, in the *Manifesto for a Ludic Century*, Eric Zimmerman (2014: 20) argues that the twenty-first century is an era where, increasingly, the ways people 'spend their leisure time and consume art, design, and entertainment will be games – or experiences very much like games'. Digital technology, Zimmerman (2014: 19) suggests, is what has given games a new relevance. Hence, digitally mediated games will become the primary mode for the design and consumption of social experiences (see Chapters 4 and 5). According to Zimmerman (2014: 21–22), games literacy – the ability to create and understand meaning in and through games – will be central in the Ludic century. Mastering the languages, procedures, and systems of games will be gradually more important for those individuals who seek to navigate the new tides of employment, personal development, training, social relationships, and conviviality. It is about thinking and acting in terms of games. Therefore, it is not surprising that Zimmerman (2014: 22) suggests that 'everyone will be a game designer'; in the sense that individuals will be required to *play* the *game of the social*, in a deep active manner, using the possibilities of game design, which involve 'systems logic, social psychology, and culture hacking'.

Similarly, Joost Raessens (2010: 6) argues that we are immersed in a relentless process of ludification of culture, in which play 'is not only characteristic of leisure, but also turns up in those domains that once were considered the opposite of play', such as education, politics, and warfare. Mäyrä (2017) suggests that we are entering a 'Ludic Society' or an 'Era of Games', defined by a process of the ludification of culture and society that 'relates to play and playful elements emerging in different areas of culture and society' and 'where play and associated ludic literacies become culturally dominant'. Or as Steffen Walz and Sebastian Deterding (2014: 7) argue, we live in a 'gameful world', where practices 'and attitude, patterns and tropes, materials and tools, languages and concepts from (digital) games and play increasingly pervade all arenas of life'. This *ludification of culture* is indelibly linked to a *cultivation of ludus*, in which 'artists and businesses, scholars and technologists, institutions and subcultures in turn attempt to harness and shape games and play for their own purposes'. Building on Caillois (2001), Walz and Deterding (2014: 7) describe a *gameful world* that includes 'serious games' (games designed for non-entertainment purposes), 'serious toys' (toys designed for non-entertainment purposes), playful design (non-toy objects and experiences designed to afford playful experiences), and gamification (non-game objects and experiences designed to afford gameful experiences).

These authors mostly refer to games in general, not necessarily or specifically, video games. But it is obvious that in their analyses and examples, video games play a very significant, if not central, role. For example, as stated above, Zimmerman (2014: 19) argues that it is digital technologies that have given games a new and increased social and cultural relevance. Hence, accordingly, we would like to suggest that video games and their culture are what is, *de facto*, pervading society, and therefore, we are mainly experiencing a specific process of *video*-ludification of society, rather than just a less specific process of ludification or gamification of the real. This development is undoubtedly about games and what is playful, but the translation of that gamified culture into our everyday practices comes primarily and essentially from video games; their logics, aesthetics, languages, practices, and relations. The Ludic century will be, more specifically, a *VideoLudic* century.

Hence, the videoludification of society would be the ultimate evidence of an emerging and consolidating video game culture, which is pervading many aspects of our society and wider culture. In the following sections we will explore this videoludification of reality as the expression of a video game culture, which reflects and drives wider social changes, by means of a series of examples. These do not exhaust all the possibilities in which video game culture impacts on or reflects contemporary society, but rather, introduce some key illustrative examples of this process. Among other things, we will see how reality is gamified, how the spaces of work, education, and play blur, how video gaming pervades all demographics, and how video games become a major cultural product and object of study and consumption.

Gamifying reality: gamification, serious games, and augmented reality

Gamification

As Fuchs *et al.* (2014) suggest, gamification can have, at least, two meanings. On the one hand, gamification can be seen as a central part of a process of ludification of society. In this case, gamification would be the 'general process in which games and playful experiences are understood as essential components of society and culture' (Fuchs *et al.*, 2014: 7). On the other, gamification can be defined as a more limited practice, typically 'brought forward by marketing gurus and designers' (Fuchs *et al.*, 2014: 8). In this second definition then, gamification can be seen as a tool to obtain specific outcomes in the fields, for example, of education (Markopoulos *et al.*, 2015), work (Dale, 2014), health (Maturo and Setiffi, 2016), or leisure (Xu *et al.*, 2016). Since we consider below some of the wider social changes implicated in the rising importance and centrality of video game culture within our society, here we will instead focus on the latter meaning that Fuchs *et al.* identify: the use of game elements to design gameful experiences in various social environments.

Simplifying the different approaches to gamification, we find two principal lines of thought: the critical and the celebratory. In this, gamification is seen as either a perverse tool for dominating individuals – typical of neoliberal rationalities (see Chapter 3) – or as a creative and empowering instrument linked to ideas of a participatory culture (see also Chapter 3). For those interested, a panorama of these opposing views can be found in Deterding (2014b).

On the one side, amongst the critics of gamification, we find Ian Bogost (2014: 67), who in his 'gamification is bullshit' thesis, likens gamification to a 'party trick'. It is a trick that entails two parts: the 'game', as a way of appealing to potential customers, and 'the "-ification" suffix', to make the process look like something 'easy and achievable'. Thus, gamification is not a style of games design but rather 'a style of consulting that happens to take up games as its solution' (Bogost, 2014: 68). Bogost (2014: 72) suggests substituting the term *gamification* for *exploitationware*; since the final goal of gamification is not primarily about producing playful experiences, but rather, gamification seeks the production of 'compliance'.

This representation of gamification as exploitation is in line with some critical approaches to ideas of (neo)liberal political rationalities (Rose, 1999). For example, drawing on Thaler and Sunstein (2008), Niklas Schrape (2014: 35) considers gamification as part of the methods intended to regulate societies in today's world, which follows an extreme version of liberalism, the *libertarian paternalism*:

> Libertarian paternalism implies that, for example, the state grants its subjects the freedom of choice, but designs all possible options in such a way that they will decide in an intended way. The subjects should feel free but their behaviour is regulated. This principle is familiar to all players of computer games.

Schrape suggests that gamification practices belong to a new form of governmentality (Foucault, 2003); one that implies the 'fulfilment of liberalism' thanks to the fact that gamification 'makes it possible to effectively motivate intended behaviour in a pleasant way, without the need to appeal to the mind or reason' (Schrape, 2014: 43). This argument represents probably the most solid case of the generalization of video game culture and, along with it, the success of neoliberal rationalities – and in Chapter 3 we explore this subject in more detail. In this depiction of gamification, the final end is profit maximization, where rewards only benefit the few and not the many, and individuals participate actively and willfully in their own exploitation. It is the neoliberal mentality at its best.

However, there is of course, another side to this argument, one that praises the use and value of gamification. One of the most celebratory accounts of gamification can be found in the works of Gabe Zichermann and Joselin Linder (2010; 2013). They define gamification as the process of implementing elements of game design, loyalty programmes, and behavioural economics, in order to engage employees and customers. Zichermann and Linder (2013: 18) believe that when governments, businesses, and organizations embrace 'game thinking and mechanics, they are better able to engage their audiences, cut through the noise, drive innovation, and ultimately increase their revenue'. According to this argument, gamification is about finding and delivering enjoyment in a wide range of contexts through game mechanics: points, badges (achievements), levels, leaderboards, and rewards (Zichermann and Linder, 2013: 18–22). These authors offer gamification as a tool to raise 'employee engagement, satisfaction, performance, and tenure' (Zichermann and Linder, 2013: 70), along with heightening 'customer engagement' (Zichermann and Linder, 2013: 156). In sum, Zichermann and Linder (2013: 216) openly and shamelessly embrace the mechanisms by which gamification is criticized as the ultimate resource for (self-)exploitation in the context of neoliberalism:

> We are moving rapidly toward a future where 'fun' is the new 'work'. Fun is also the new buying, selling, attention grabbing, and health achieving. [...] Gamification is leading the charge to radically change industries by making it more fun and ultimately more effective at building a strong, happy, and better engaged community.

This appraisal of gamification seeks to promote it as an instrument to obtain more profit and productivity from employees, customers, and citizens, by turning work, consumption, and well-being into a game where they are responsible for their own achievements, care, and regulation. Nevertheless, there are other 'positive' approaches to gamification that distance themselves from this framework imbued with neoliberal rationalities. For example, Linehan, Kirman, and Roche (2014: 101) seek to distance themselves from those entrepreneurs and businesses that have seized upon gamification 'as a way to increasing engagement with products', and the scholars and game designers that perceive it 'as a desecration of their craft'. In particular, Linehan *et al.* propose using 'applied behavior analysis' as a way of gaining a better understanding of the processes at work when a player is engaged in gamified scenarios. In doing so, they suggest that the designers and professionals implicated in this process 'have the ability to create measurably better-gamified experiences for the benefit of their players' (Linehan et al., 2014: 101). But the use of this analysis will depend on the aims sought by the creators of the gamified experience; whether that is to extract more resources (money, labour power, obedience) from individuals for the creators' own profit, or it is benefiting the group of individuals that 'play' the experience. Hence, for Linehan et al. gamification in itself, is not necessarily a negative or exploitative process, but rather one we need to analyze to understand its different uses and values.

It is also suggested that gamification can be an educational and communitarian tool for social intervention, collaboration (Williams, 2014), and the improvement of people's lives. In this sense, gamification should move from a 'change in the system' to 'change *of* the system', that is, 'from designing games as interventions deployed within certain contexts to designing contexts as interventions, informed by game design' (Deterding, 2014a: 325). Therefore, gamification is something that 'realizes, furthers, or is at least congruent with living a good life with others' (Deterding, 2014a: 321). In this line of argument, the aim then, is the growth of the community; individuals are only rewarded if the group benefits from the actions taken.

Regardless of the stand taken on gamification and its relative merits or detriments, gamification as a generalized practice within businesses, workplaces, and other organizations is quickly pervading the social fabric of contemporary society. As Miguel Sicart (2014b: 239) suggests, 'gamification is just a symptom of a cultural trend: the vindication of play as a legitimate way of living, creating, and expressing'.

Serious games

Another, closely linked, example of video games' colonization of wider culture can be found in 'serious games'. The syntagm 'serious games' describes a tension between the terms that are part of it; the notion of 'games', which are usually associated with ideas of fun, leisure, triviality, and superficiality, is attached to 'serious', a word typically linked to ideas of boredom, importance, work, and solemnity. 'Serious games' then is, somehow, an oxymoron, and yet the concept has gained traction over the last years.

Serious games entail video games and digital simulations that are used in a 'wide range of educational and training environments' (Sanford et al., 2015: 91) to address educational, social, medical, labour, and political issues. For instance, serious games include examples such as: *Immune Attack* (Federation of American Scientists and Escape Hatch Entertainment, 2008),[3] a game that teaches immunology to middle school and high school students in the biology class; *PeaceMaker* (Impact Games, 2007),[4] inspired by the Israeli–Palestinian conflict, which lets players take the role of the political leader in both sides; *Re-Mission* (Realtime Associates and HopeLab, 2006) and *Re-Mission 2* (HopeLab, 2013)[5] are games aimed at helping children and young adults with cancer to encourage treatment adherence; and *Dragon Box*

(2012–2016),[6] a series of games that are oriented to teaching mathematics to children. Of course, these are just a few of the many examples, and a longer list of serious games in different sectors (military, government, educational, corporate, healthcare, political, religious, and arts) can be found in the work of David Michael and Sande Chen (2006: 45–228).

Serious games are therefore 'games that do not have entertainment, enjoyment, or fun as their primary purpose', even though they might still be 'entertaining, enjoyable, or fun' (Michael and Chen, 2006: 21). These kinds of games could be seen as part of a wider process of gamification – and the two are certainly linked – but, the distinction is that serious games tend to be more typically about using specific games as a particular kind of tool, rather than applying aspects of games to another context. Although the notion of 'serious games' can be traced back to the 1970s with its usage in relation to board games (Abt, 2002), it is a term that has been more fully developed in relation to the use of video games for 'serious' purposes. Hence, when video games begin to colonize other spheres of culture, making games something serious and turning what is serious into a game, it makes even more obvious the existence of a growing *videoludification of society*.

Augmented reality

Augmented reality (AR) provides another example of gamified reality. According to Azuma *et al.* (2001: 34), augmented reality is a system that 'supplements the real world with virtual (computer-generated) objects that appear to coexist in the same space', and can be defined by three main properties: 'combines real and virtual objects in a real environment; runs interactively, and in real time; and registers (aligns) real and virtual objects with each other'. Thus, augmented reality is the outcome of a process of hybridization between virtual and real objects; an articulation of humans, digital technologies, and spaces. Although AR technology has been in development for decades, with the capacity of offering AR experiences already existing in the 1980s (Hofmann and Mosemghvdlishvili, 2014: 266), it is the proliferation and wide adoption of smartphones among the general public that has made augmented reality much more widespread.

Some of the most popular AR smartphone applications ('apps') and games include: *Layar* (Lens-FitzGerald *et al.*, 2009), an app to watch videos, reviews, and additional information on the pages of magazines and posters; *IKEA Catalog* (IKEA, 2013), which allows users to place furniture in their rooms using AR functionality; *Invizimals* (Novarama, 2009), developed for the PlayStation Portable (PSP), which requires players to capture creatures using a camera attachment for the PSP in order to use them later on in battles against other players; *Ingress* (Niantic, 2013), an AR game that requires players to be physically close to the objects represented on the map to interact with them; and – probably, to date, most famously – *Pokémon GO* (Niantic, 2016), the AR version of the popular Nintendo video game, where players chase and capture creatures (Pokémon) and items for battles against other players.

In particular, we would like to explore *Pokémon GO* in more detail, as it represents an example of how video games are leading the process of the (video)ludification of culture. *Pokémon GO*, released in July 2016, triggered an unprecedented reaction from the media and the general public for a video game. It became news all around the world, and in the months following its release, one of the most downloaded video games of all time. Along with this, thousands of people started wandering the streets, squares, parks, and many other public spaces in search of Pókemon. Groups of people gathered around certain spots; *PokeStops*, special places to acquire in-game items, or *Gyms*, places to train Pokémon or engage in battle with other players. The use of a well-known franchise among gamers and smartphone capabilities, including augmented reality features, recontextualized how individuals 'engage with different forms of media' (Keogh, 2017: 40), and in particular, video games. This recontextualization transformed, according to Keogh (2017: 40–41), a core video game 'franchise into a ubiquitous pop cultural icon, a niche videogame experience into an accessible casual experience attractive to a broader player base'. *Pokémon GO*, thus, resulted in an assemblage of software, technology, individuals, space, and distributed agency. As Giddings (2017: 61) argues, the game 'is played out in its distribution across smartphones as mobile devices, images and mediated action, software algorithms, and actual bodies and spaces'.

Pokémon GO was therefore capable of articulating and mobilizing several agents successfully: the app, camera, GPS, players, locations, buildings, maps, and so forth. This articulation of software and hardware, of human and non-humans, and of real and virtual, turns reality into a game field (and not just the limited spaces of a 'magic circle' – see Chapter 5). *Pokémon GO* generated a level of social interaction mediated by technology, including the axes local–global and offline–online, hardly seen until then. The massive attention that the game attracted from the media is evidence of the cultural and social 'shock' that entailed. When thousands, if not millions, of individuals – more diverse (and older) than expected – occupied public spaces playing *Pokémon GO*, they helped make visible something that was already going on, but probably not in such an explicit way; that gaming culture is now widely extended throughout society. As Sicart (2017: 32) claims, reality 'has always been augmented' and what *Pokémon GO* did was to give us 'a new language and a new technology to access, experience, and most importantly play in and with this augmented world'. Hence, we agree with Mäyrä (2017: 49), who suggests that if 'we take seriously the hypothesis that we are entering the "Ludic Society," or an "Era of Games"', then, 'it is exactly phenomena like Pokémon GO that we should be paying close attention to'.

The growing importance of video games among the general public

One of the most notable indications that video game culture is no longer, if it ever was, a strongly bounded subculture, is the increasing number of people playing video games. It seems that more and more individuals of different backgrounds, ages, and gender are becoming video game players; or at least, occasionally play video games. For example, Egenfeldt-Nielsen et al. suggest that the number of 'people who have never played a video game, from first graders to retirees, seem to be inexorably dwindling' (2008: 134). They illustrate this affirmation with an article from *The New York Times* in which the author (Schiesel, 2007) explains how video games are being regularly played in retirement homes. A generation of people who did not grow up in a world where video games existed, at least not as a culturally relevant phenomenon, is now part of the wider video game playing population.

As Egenfeldt-Nielsen et al. (2008: 139) point out, in 2001 'the movement from subculture to mass-market' was already well advanced when the three major video game console companies launched their new generation consoles (Sony's PlayStation 2, Microsoft's Xbox and Nintendo's GameCube), which 'for the first time directly targeted the up to then reluctant "general public"'. By the turn of the new century, left far behind were the days when 'the subculture of gamers was born' in the 1980s (Egenfeldt-Nielsen et al., 2008: 52). Similarly, drawing on data from various market research companies and video game industry associations, Pierce concluded that the 'fact that video games are part of the mass media landscape can no longer be sufficiently argued against in light of the data' (2009: 51). Among the statistics mentioned by Pierce, there were noteworthy findings, such as the suggestion that two-thirds of all Americans play video games, or that almost half of American households have a game console.

The spread of video games into more and more households seems to be confirmed year-on-year by various industry surveys. For example, the *Essential Facts about the Computer and Video Game Industry* annual report, which is produced by the Entertainment Software Association (ESA), the most important video game industry association in the United States,[7] suggests that in 65% of United States households there is at least one person who plays video games regularly (3 hours or more per week) (ESA, 2017). This report also suggests that 67% of American households own a device that plays video games, and that 48% own a dedicated game console (ESA, 2017: 6). Other data here of interest indicates that the average game player is 35 years old, with 45% of video gamers over 35, and that 42% of gamers are women (ESA, 2017: 7).

Likewise, data gathered by the Association for UK Interactive Entertainment (Ukie), the principal video game industry organization in the UK, shows similar figures for British households. In their *UK Video Games Fact Sheet* (Ukie, 2017), Ukie estimates that 57% of the United Kingdom population plays video games, and that the gender breakdown of gamers here is 58% male and 42% female. These findings are also echoed in research published by Karol Borowiecki and Hasan Bahkshi (2017), based upon data gathered from the UK's government *Taking Part* survey. In their report, Borowiecki and Bahkshi (2017: 12) assert that a video gamer's average age is 43.2 years and 'the average gamer is more likely to be female'; although, amongst those who play, women tend to play less often.

These findings are similar to those published by The Interactive Software Federation of Europe (ISFE), which comprises video game publishers and trade associations in the European Union. According to their 2012 survey *Video Games in Europe: Consumer Study* (ISFE, 2012), in which participants from 16 European countries responded to online and offline questionnaires, 48% of Europeans played video games at least once in that year. The Swedish appeared to be the population who played the most (62%), and the British, Spanish, and Portuguese the least (40%). When taking into account those who play most frequently, the data shows that, on average, a quarter of Europeans play video games at least once a week. In relation to gender and age, the report indicates that 55% of European gamers were male and 45% female, while a 27.5% of those between 55 and 64 played video games. Also, the ISFE *GameTrack* survey (ISFE, 2016) conducted in the UK, France, Germany, and Spain (along with the US and Russia, but that information is not included in their digest) shows similar results in the last quarter of 2016: 47.5% of the population between 6 to 64 years played video games at least once in 2015, and 53% of gamers were male and 47% female.

All the data point to the same suggestion, that around half of the population in Western countries appear to play video games, that the number of women who play video games has increased to levels similar to men, and even those not born in an era of video game culture have started to play them. This would then be the general portrait of the contemporary nature of video gamers, which quantitatively corroborates the hypothesis of a wide and growing video game culture. However, these broad brushstrokes are so vaguely defined that there is still a great deal of detail missed in the data. Most commonly they tend to miss information about, for example, who plays what video games on what devices, or how often. For instance, in some cases these surveys define a video gamer as anyone who has played any game, even once, in the last six months, or even the previous year. This approach then assumes that anyone who has played any type of video game, even once, relatively recently, is a gamer. This, of course, raises important questions about who and what a gamer is – a topic we will return to in Chapter 6, but it is important to highlight here at least, that how these surveys typically categorize gamers does not equate to how most of the general public would typically define a gamer.

In any case, those are not the only concerns that can be raised in relation to these data. The fact that sometimes, in these reports, the 'original sources are often poorly referenced' (Crawford, 2012: 51), and that they seem to mix information from different sources without taking into account methodological differences, undermine their reliability. Furthermore, as data of this nature is often produced and published by representatives of the video game industry, these organizations often seek to 'convey a very particular image of video gaming as normal, social and healthy pursuit' (Crawford, 2012: 51).

However, even if the information selected is biased in order to give a certain impression of video games and gamers, it is still valid as information that points towards how video game culture has burst into contemporary society. Whether this is caused by the rise of new kinds of video games and platforms (so-called 'casual games', like those played on web browsers, smartphones, and tablets) as it has been suggested by authors like Jesper Juul (2010), or by other wider social processes, the fact is that the normalization of video games and video gaming in our society is now an unavoidable reality:

> Video games are becoming normal [...]. The rise of casual games is the end of that small historical anomaly of the 1980s and 1990s when video games were played by only a small part of the population.
>
> *(Juul, 2010: 20)*

This is what Juul considers a *casual revolution* in video games, which in recent years has reached – and is increasingly reaching – a broader audience. Categorizations, such as *hardcore gamers* and *casual gamers*, will be dealt with in more detail in Chapter 6 where we explore how video gamers identities are constructed and maintained, but it is important to recognize that the expansion of the universe of video games and gamers is fundamental to understanding the constitution of video game culture: 'Video games are fast becoming games for *everyone*' (Juul, 2010: 152).

In short, the emergence and consolidation of video game culture in contemporary society may be best reflected, though not solely, by the significant growth in more – and different types of – people playing video games. This is one of the most noticeable characteristics of contemporary video game culture and its normalization in today's world.

A thriving video game industry

Considering the rapid increase in the number of people playing video games in recent years, the spectacular growth of the video game industry should not be surprising. One process could not exist without the other. In this sense, Jon Dovey and Helen Kennedy (2006: 2) argue that the 'computer games industry is the most established of all sectors of the emergent new media landscape' commanding a 'mass mainstream market', while Egenfeldt-Nielsen *et al.* (2008: 88) assert that 'the business of video games is booming'. They estimate that the 'U.S. sales have more than doubled in less than a decade, rising from $3.2 billion in 1995 to $7.0 billion in 2005'. Similarly, Tom Chatfield (2011: 27) considers that at a 'time when most global media are either shrinking or static, perhaps the most noteworthy fact about the video games industry is its growth'. He also describes the rapid growth of global video gaming sales from a few billion dollars a year at the end of the 1970s, to the more than $40 billion by the end of 2008. Chatfield claims that it is 'already fair to call video games the world's most valuable purchased entertainment medium'.

The data provided by the authors above is surely impressive, but it is important to look at more recent statistics. Hence, despite their potential drawbacks, here we must turn again to data provided by the video game industry, as it possesses probably the most comprehensive and up-to-date information currently available.

In the US, the ESA suggests that consumers spent $30.4 billion on video game-related products[8] in 2016 (ESA, 2017: 15). In the period 2006–2009, where only new physical content at retail outlets was taken into account, the total amount in sales rose from $7 billion in 2006 to over $10 billion in 2009 (ESA, 2016: 12). Figures for the period 2010–2016, which also included digital distributed video games, saw total spend increased from $17.5 billion in 2010 to $24.5 billion in 2016 (ESA, 2017: 15). Hence, put simply, between 2006 and 2016 sales of video games in the US tripled.

Ukie (2017: 2) suggests that global video game revenue was $91 billion in 2016, and is expected to reach $118.6 billion by 2019. According to a report by Newzoo[9] (Ukie, 2017: 3), the biggest market in 2016 was the Asia–Pacific region, representing 47% of the global market with $46.6 billion. The six largest video game markets in 2015 in terms of consumer revenues were, in order, China, the US, Japan, South Korea, Germany, and the UK (Ukie, 2017: 16). In 2016, according to the Entertainment Retailers Association,[10] video games sales in the UK generated a revenue of £2.96 ($3.81) billion (ERA, 2017).

Hence, if we accept as accurate that the global market revenue in 2016 was $91 billion, then video games surpass the Gross Domestic Product (GDP) of numerous sizable countries such as Bolivia ($32.9), Croatia ($48.7 billion), Uruguay ($53.4 billion), and Ukraine ($90.6 billion).[11] If the video game industry was a nation, it would be the 59th largest economy in the world.

It is difficult to predict whether video games are close to reaching their peak in economic or cultural terms or if they have just started to take off, but it is clear that the video game industry is becoming hegemonic. There are now several well-known video game franchises such as *Grand Theft Auto* (Rockstar Games, 2001–2013), *Call of Duty* (Activision, Infinity Ward, 2003–to date), *The Sims* (Maxis, 2000–to date), *Assassin's Creed* (Ubisoft, 2007–to date), *World of Warcraft* (Blizzard Entertainment, 2004–to date), and many others, which are played by millions of people all around the world. Probably, one recent and prominent example of the global cultural status of video games was the release of *Destiny* in 2014 (Activision Blizzard, 2014). According to Bobby Kotick, CEO of Activision, the development and marketing of *Destiny* cost $500 million (Webster, 2014). This investment even exceeds the already impressive numbers of Rockstar's *Grand Theft Auto V* (2013), which cost around $267 million (McLaughlin, 2013) and earned $800 million in the first 24 hours (Webster, 2013). In comparison, the production of the (generally acknowledged as) most expensive film ever made (to date), the fourth installment of *Pirates of the Caribbean, On Stranger Tides* (Marshall, 2011), cost around $410 million (Sylt, 2014).

Even many games that are considered to be part of the *indie* scene, as opposed to those AAA games mentioned above, have been a resounding financial as well as cultural success in recent years. One notable example here is *Minecraft* (Mojang, 2011). In September 2014, Microsoft bought out Mojang for $2.5 billion (Stuart and Hern, 2014), and according to Mojang, *Minecraft* had sold 122 million copies across all platforms by February 2017 (Sarkar, 2017a). Additionally, there are other indie titles that similarly sold millions of copies in recent years, such as: *Fez* (Fish, 2012), *Don't Starve* (Klei Entertainment, 2013), *Limbo* (Carlsen, 2010), *The Stanley Parable* (Wreden, 2013), *No Man's Sky* (Hello Games, 2016), *Bastion* (Supergiant

Games, 2011), *Super Meat Boy* (Team Meat, 2010), *Braid* (Blow, 2010), *Hotline Miami* (Dennaton Games, 2012), and *The Binding of Isaac* (McMillen and Himsl, 2011), to name but a few prominent examples.

Beyond the universe of video consoles and personal computers, there is also an immense field of mobile platforms in which the video game industry has rapidly grown in recent years. Popular examples here include *Candy Crush Saga* (King, 2012) and *Angry Birds* (Rovio Entertainment, 2009), which had by 2013, been installed on mobile platforms 500 million and 2 billion times, respectively (Dredge, 2013). More recently, *Pokémon GO* (Niantic Labs, 2016), according to its developers, was downloaded more than 650 million times in the first seven months of its release (Sarkar, 2017b). Furthermore, although these kinds of video games are often based on a 'free-to-play' model, in which their profitability comes from microtransactions and advertisement, they are among the world's most profitable video games. For example, *Candy Crush Saga*'s players spent $2.37 billion between June 2013 and December 2014 (Dredge, 2015), and King, the developers of the game, were acquired by Activision-Blizzard for $5.9 billion in 2016 (Rundle, 2016).

Regardless of the platform (personal computer, video game console, mobile device), the kind of production (AAA, medium-sized, indie) or the business model (retail, digital purchase, microtransaction), it is apparent that video games are part of a large and booming industry. This then helps to corroborate our argument of the importance of a growing video game culture. Nevertheless, though significant, the most important thing for this research is not video games' economic impact, but rather their social and cultural importance.

Video games: blurring the lines between play, education, and work

Traditionally, video games have often been seen as *merely* entertainment, primarily aimed at children or, at best, adolescents (Kowert *et al.*, 2012; Kirkpatrick, 2015; Bergstrom *et al.*, 2016). Things have changed: as we saw above, video games are increasingly played by a diverse range of individuals; video games are part of a buoyant cultural industry; and beyond this, an increasingly important part of wider contemporary culture. Video games are no longer, if they ever were, simply a form of *mere* entertainment. In particular, there are two further areas we wish to highlight where we are starting to see the influence of video games: work and education.

When it comes to considering the importance and role of the video game in education and work there are at least two main ways of doing this. The first is to show the impact video games have had on the traditional structures of work and education. This approach then, takes into account the number of video game-related jobs that have been created in recent years and the amount of different courses, degrees, and any other training activities focused on developing video game skills. The second course of action is to assess the extent and ways video game culture and practices have blended with, and blurred, the boundaries between, work, education, and play. We will briefly explore both courses of action in this section.

The work of play

It is evident that the video games industry is a large and growing sector. It was suggested that in 2013 'the UK video game sector […] supported 23,900 FTEs [full time equivalent]' jobs (Ukie, 2017), while the ESA suggests that there are now 65,678 workers employed in game software development and publishing in the US (ESA, 2017). In addition to this, there are of course, amateur bedroom coders producing game mods and hacks, beta testers (see Bulut, 2014) – who are the individuals that work testing games before they are launched – and numerous other unpaid workers contributing to the continued success and profitability of this industry. For a fuller discussion of the nature of the video game industry we would refer you to the work of Kerr (2006, 2017), Weststar and Legault (2014, 2016), Prescott and Bogg (2014), Zackariasson and Wilson (2014), and Weststar (2015).

Although there has been a significant rise in the number of people directly employed in making and selling video games, it is important to note that in recent years the rising popularity of video games has also facilitated the potential for individuals to make a career out of playing video games as well. The job of the professional gamer is to play video games. This can involve playing competitively, such as in esports tournaments, working as a games reviewer, or simply just to entertain an audience via uploaded videos on YouTube or streaming sites like Twitch.

In relation to competitive gaming, the number of tournaments and prizes has increased significantly in recent years. For instance, Valve's documentary film *Free to Play* (2014) reports on the esports scene surrounding the adventures and misfortunes of some of the contestants in a *Dota 2* (Valve, 2013) tournament known as *The International* in 2011. This was, at the time, the biggest ever prize pool totaling $1.6 million, with $1 million for the winning team. Only five years later, in 2016, the prize pool had surpassed the $20 million mark, with more than $9 million for the winner (Van Allen, 2016). One of our interviewees, John, a 32-year-old, former pro-gamer and now manager of a pro-gaming team, explained the partially unexpected, rapid ascension of professional gaming:

> We assumed we would get to this point, like where we are now, selling out stadiums, getting millions of viewers watching online. We knew we'd get there. We just didn't think we'd get there this quick. That we'd get here during the recession.

Video gaming, both in terms of production and play, is now starting to seem like a viable career option for many. Although we may not necessarily share Valve's enthusiastic prediction made in *Free to Play* that esports will soon overtake established sports such as football and basketball, in terms of widespread popularity, there are signs, however, to suggest that the popularity of esports is certainly on the rise. For example, it is suggested that esports is already regarded as the 'national pastime' in South Korea (Mozur, 2014), where, according to sources from the Federal Game Institute of South Korea, 10 million South Koreans follow esports on a regular basis. Moreover, Taylor (2012: 17) writes that in South Korea the 'number of people who go spectate pro basketball, baseball and soccer put together is the same as the number of people who go watch [esports] pro game leagues'. Certainly, the audience of esports is growing worldwide: in 2016, there was a global audience of 323 million people and it is estimated that this audience will be almost 600 million people by the end of 2020 (BBC, 2017). Esports already is a significant part of video game culture, and has the potential to reach a much wider audience, and possibly one day may challenge the hegemony of sports such as football as the world's favourite game. However, we do not have the time or space here to consider the phenomenon and scene of esports in any detail, and hence, we would point you towards the work of others, such as T.L. Taylor (2012), for a more thorough consideration of this activity and its culture.

Nonetheless, not all those who game professionally do so competitively. As highlighted above, online video channels, such as YouTube and Twitch, provide the opportunity for gamers to upload videos of themselves playing or reviewing games, which can, in some cases, attract millions of viewers and followers. The economies of this are based on advertising, subscriptions, and donations, which can in some cases, be very large. Thus, there appears to be a whole, and growing, economy based around a model of 'play and pay', which turns gameplay into work (Postigo, 2016). Though figures for the personal income of professional YouTube and Twitch gamers are very hard to come by, it is likely that some of the most followed, like *PewDiePie* or *Markiplier*, are making a very sizable income from this;[12] though for most, this is, at best probably supplementing their income from their regular jobs. For example, one professional YouTuber we interviewed, Conan (23, male, video game critic, and youtuber), highlighted how he, and many others he knew of, make very little income from their game-related videocasts: 'my content is what it is, and I survive thanks to things like Patreon or because someone notices me and decides to hire me for something else'.

In this world, as with any other aspect of social life, there are different levels in professional gaming careers. Away from the star system of top-level professional esports players and the most famous videocasters, there are also the day labourers who are struggling to make a career as a professional gamer, or even those who are exploited as 'gold farmers';[13] where teams of gamers are employed, often in terrible work conditions for very little pay, to generate in-game items and sell these for profit via 'real money trade' (see Castronova, 2005; Dibbell, 2007; Lee and Lin, 2011).

Education in/by video games

Related closely to the rise in video gaming as a legitimate career avenue is an associated increase in the number of courses, degrees, and masters for the study, creation, design, and production of video games that have emerged in recent years. Jack, a 46-year-old coordinator of two degree programmes on video game development, suggests that in the near future, in Europe alone, thousands of new jobs in the video game industry will be created. Hence, he does not believe that the explosion of video game-related courses and degrees is 'a fashion', that 'people are teaching video games because it's cool to do it now', rather for him, 'it's because it's a need'. Edward, a 54-year-old head of a Masters' programme on video games, goes beyond the mere *the video game industry is growing* argument. For him, there is 'an increasing acceptance of video games as a cultural medium', and video games are transitioning from merely 'a software product into a part of the cultural industries'. The rapid rise of video game-related courses is therefore linked to a wider acceptance of video games as part of our contemporary cultural landscape, while in turn, the proliferation of video games in the field of education is also helping legitimize video games as an established part of our wider culture.

Possibly more surprising though, is the introduction of activities at schools specifically oriented to encourage children and teenagers to play more video games. Here, not only are we alluding to the use of the *serious games* (discussed above) in classrooms, we are also seeing increasing examples of 'regular' – that is to say, commercial games, not specifically created for educational purposes – video games being used for educational purposes. For example, in places like GlassLab[14] (known as the 'Institute of Play') they use video games, such as *Minecraft*, to teach mathematics. According to Jessica Lindl, the general manager of GlassLab, children who play 'the game are exercising mathematical functions, solving problems, and collaborating, concepts teachers have been struggling to get kids to learn in the classroom' (Pitts, 2014: online). But she goes even further to suggest that the main problem in education is the current nature of formal (which is largely summative) assessment, and that the use of video games could help to change how we assess children in classrooms. As she suggests, with video games there is 'little or no lag between instructing the kids to do a thing and determining how well they learnt the lesson' (Pitts, 2014: online). Therefore, video games seem to be a more efficient way to cover the entire educational process of teaching, learning, and assessment.

This is what Paul Darvasi, a high school English and media studies teacher, serious games/educational games designer, and consultant, seems to believe. He developed a method to use *Gone Home* (Fullbright, 2013) in the classroom with an extensive list of activities for the students.[15] This video game then was used in the context of the classroom to teach different issues, such as how narratives are created, to carry out an archeology of mundane objects of the 1990s, to gather data systematically, and to trace signs of determined musical, artistic, and literary subcultures linked to feminism and queer movements, among other issues.

Moreover, the integration of video gaming within every step of education is going deeper. Some esports video game companies, such as Riot Games (developers and promoters of *League of Legends*), are offering university scholarships to those students who perform well in high school leagues (Warr, 2014). In a similar fashion to traditional college sports scholarships, the people responsible for these video games within the competitive scene are selecting future esports stars inside the educational system to help launch them into a professional career in video gaming.

Blurring the boundaries between play, labour, and education

There is a sequence in Valve's film, *Free to Play* (2014), in which one of the professional gamers' mothers starts her sentence with 'I was the typical parent' followed by a 'you're spending too much time playing computer games' (Valve, 2014). She refers to the fact that, as a mother, she tried to encourage her son, Clinton, to invest more time in his education in order to make a career in a viable profession. For her, playing video games was a distraction from more important matters: like education and work. In no way did she foresee that video games would lead to a valid and profitable career. Another participant in the film subscribes to the main hypothesis articulated here, that video gaming, including professional gaming, will increasingly become something normal, part of our accepted culture: 'it's going to go from a niche to becoming accepted in societies' (Valve, 2014). She closes the dilemma established by Clinton's mother, because, for her, the definite turning point will be achieved when gamers become parents and they start to encourage their children to play video games: 'When the gamers now become parents, we will be supportive of our kids playing' (Valve, 2014).

Video games have been traditionally seen as diversions from the important things in life, like education and work. But now, instead, video games are becoming a professional area of interest, as well as educational tools. Video games are, therefore, increasingly integrated into core aspects of our society to the point that distinguishing between aspects of play and work becomes increasingly difficult. As Kerr (2006: 7) argues:

> It would appear that distinguishing between production and consumption and between work and play in contemporary Western societies is increasingly problematic.

The invasion of video games into spaces of work and education is helping to melt well-established dichotomies of the now old industrial societies. The emergence of phenomena like 'playbour' (Kücklich, 2009; Frelik, 2016; Hjorth, 2017) or 'edutainment' (Charsky, 2010; Egenfeldt-Nielsen, 2011; Ma, Oikonomou, and Jain, 2011; Katsaliaki and Mustafee, 2015), where the boundaries between play, work, and education blur, is evidence of a world in which everything is becoming 'just a game' (Taylor *et al.*, 2015: 383).

Max Weber's (2001) classic work on the key role of the Protestant work ethic in the origins of modern capitalism (understood as the individual accumulation of capital as an end in itself) stresses the importance of the 'separation of business from the household' (Weber, 2001: xxxv); that is, the differentiation between the domestic and professional spheres. According to Boltanski and Chiapello (2005: 155), this has changed radically in the new spirit of capitalism: it now 'becomes difficult to make a distinction between the time of private life and the time of professional life'. As Boltanski and Chiapello suggest, the 'ethic of toil' that had permeated the original spirit of capitalism has been affected under the new spirit: there is no 'clear distinction between personal or even leisure activity and professional activity'. This has, as a consequence, that the time devoted to work and leisure is more and more difficult to distinguish, and the aim is to 'blur the boundaries between these different states, which were hitherto clearly separated' (Boltanski and Chiapello, 2005: 456). This is in line with what neoliberal political rationalities seek (as we will see in Chapter 3), which foster the construction of individuals willing to govern themselves in a way that self-imposed discipline and responsibility are actively pursued by citizens, and in doing so, the 'neoliberal programme penetrates not only the political and economic realms but also our intimate lives' (Winch and Hakim, 2017: 40).

Our lives have become a set of open tasks that happen at the same time. We continually multitask, jump from one to another in the same fashion as we do between open tabs on a computer screen. We do not need to finish one task to initiate another or to continue with others that are already in progress, whether it is leisure, work, or education time. Time itself seems to have lost its linearity and usefulness as a tool for organizing people's lives. Even our dead time is gamified: when users lose their Internet connection while using *Chrome* (Google, 2008), they can play a mini-game until the signal comes back. As Maffesoli (2001: 68) notes, presentism in contemporary society means that it is not possible to consider 'there are things that are more important than others'. In everyday life, if everything is equally important, then nothing is important. Individuals cannot differentiate between spaces, times, and activities anymore. They play while working, they work while playing. It is even difficult to discern what belongs to the fields of work and education and what is supposed to be playful. As Maffesoli (2001: 20) writes, a ludic conception of society has been generalized: 'The game of the world, or the world as a game. Life as a game is the acceptance of a world as it is'. Education and work are making their way into the world of video games, but video game culture is also increasingly pervading and transforming those areas. We are closer to a *videoludic society* than ever before.

The construction of a video gaming audience

Another sign of video games' growing cultural significance is their increasing presence in the other media. Not only is this notable in new media forms, such as the massive number of specialized websites dedicated to video games, but also more traditional media has, for some time now, covered and incorporated video games in the same way that it does with other cultural products such as films, music, and television shows. In this regard, well-regarded newspapers such as *The Guardian* and *The New York Times* are pioneers, with a regular focus on video games since the early 2000s. As Keith Stuart (2017: online), *The Guardian's* former games editor, writes: 'We publish reviews, analyse the industry, consider trends and controversies – in other words, we treat games in the same way as films and music'. Stuart argues that there has been a shift in games criticism, where video games are analyzed as an 'art form rather than a product' and that reviewers seek to 'examine and convey the experience of playing, the feel of the world, the pull of the narrative, the emotional connection with characters, or the intelligence of the mechanics [...] rather than providing a clear guide on whether or not you should buy a consumer item'.

Magazines have historically played an important role in the formation of early gaming culture, as Kirkpatrick (2015) argues in his Bourdieusian analysis of UK video game magazines in the 1980s and 1990s. Though the death of traditional print media has been foretold for some time, it is evident that video game-related magazines continue to be numerous and popular, including those that focus more generally on all aspects of video game culture, such as *EDGE* (1993–to date), those that concentrate on specific companies or consoles, like *Official Xbox Magazine* (2001–to date), or those which cover particular genres or enthusiasms, such as *Retro Gamer* (2004–to date). Also, as highlighted above, it is notable that video game reviews and related features are now a common part of the majority of mainstream print newspapers in many countries. There is also a fairly long history of television shows revolving around, or featuring, people playing video games. An early example of which was *TV Powww* that debuted in the US in 1978, one of the more successful was the Channel 4 show *GamesMaster*, which was broadcast in the UK between 1992 to 1998, and from 2017 the BBC started regularly showing esports on its online channel BBC3.

As we will discuss in Chapter 6, in relation to the prototypical representation of the gamer, it is through the development of a common and shared discourse of game evaluation that the act of playing video games acquires the status of a cultural practice. When this discourse is broadened, and inserted into general-interest newspapers, magazines, and other media, a specific gaming culture starts to blur its boundaries and to affect larger portions of society, generating a multitude of video game-related cultures and practices. Nevertheless, if there is a medium on which video games have naturally proliferated, that would, undoubtedly, be the Internet.

To a large extent, the Internet and video games grew together as largely symbiotic new media forms, each supporting and helping the other grow (Crawford *et al.*, 2011); and today, that strong relationship remains well intact. YouTube, for instance, is packed with gaming channels. In fact, the YouTube channel that has more subscribers than any other is a gaming-related one, which is owned by the user *PewDiePie*[16] — the *nom de guerre* of the Swedish YouTube personality Felix Arvid Ulf Kjellberg. As of August 2017, his channel had more than 56 million subscribers. According to Google Trends, 'searches for *PewDiePie* on YouTube are on par with stars such as Eminem and Katy Perry' (Ramdurai, 2014). Among the top 100 YouTube channels worldwide more than 20 are video game-related, and 'YouTube data shows that six of the top ten most-viewed channels in the U.S. are about gaming' (Ramdurai, 2014: online). In this regard, Conan, a male 23-year-old game critic and youtuber, believes that in the field of video games 'there are youtubers that have greater audience than most video game media' and 'not only do they have a greater audience, but that audience listen to them more carefully'. It seems therefore, that video games are a central part of today's YouTube generation (Google, 2013).

Maybe equally relevant is the fairly recent creation of Twitch, a specific Internet-based broadcast platform for video games content. Twitch was launched on June 2011 and was purchased by Amazon in August 2014 for $970 million (Gittleson, 2014). According to Twitch,[17] they have an average of 10 million active users per day. Twitch primarily consists of people watching other people playing video games. A user creates a channel, starts playing a video game, and broadcasts it live. Then, other people can join the channel and watch the broadcaster playing, while they comment on this with other viewers, and in turn, the person playing the game might respond to these comments. These viewers have the opportunity to follow, subscribe, or donate to the broadcaster.

All of these examples suggest that an audience exists for watching (others') video game play. Of course, there is an argument for considering video game players as an audience in themselves. When Eskelinen and Tronstad (2003: 196) claim that video games are *audienceless*, this is explicitly stated because they wish to argue that video games do not 'need audiences as an integral part of their "communication" structure'. This reluctance to admit the existence of a video game audience is based upon a rather narrow ludological approach that refuses to conceive video games as media, or to admit that video games have any characteristic that can be associated with (older) media such as television, cinema, music, or literature. This approach ignores common aspects of video games that are not ergodic or purely interactive, such as 'map screens, score or lap-time feedback screens and so on' (Newman, 2002). Furthermore, Crawford (2012: 34) expands Newman's argument to suggest in the normal mode of play, video gamers are primarily spectators to the 'visual- and audio-scapes present in standard video game play'. Players watch at least as much as, but probably more than, they direct the game.

There is also a long history of video games that have verged on, or even blurred the boundary between game, interactive fiction, and film. For example, text-based adventure games, such as William Crowther's 1976 classic *Adventure*, blur the boundaries between game and literature, while there are others, such as those developed by Quantic Dream, like *Heavy Rain* (2010) and *Beyond: Two Souls* (2013), which are very film-like. Moreover, there has been a notable rise in popularity in recent years of a genre of games frequently referred to as 'walking simulators'.

In a walking simulator game, the player usually spends a good deal of time walking around, having conversations, seeking clues, and following a predetermined narrative. Titles typically included in this genre include *Proteus* (Key and Kanaga, 2013), *Dear Esther* (The Chinese Room, 2012), *Gone Home* (Fullbright, 2013), *Everybody's Gone to the Rapture* (The Chinese Room, 2015), and *What Remains of Edith Finch* (Giant Sparrow, 2017). Initially, 'walking simulator' was a pejorative term used to discredit certain types of video games in order to highlight the fact that they did not have the typical elements and mechanics that usually define a video game. In this sense, these games were also often tagged as 'non-games', 'no-games', or 'not-games'.

These works then raise important questions about game-ness, ideas of interactivity, and storytelling, and the role of contemplation, exploration, and observation in

FIGURE 2.1 The rise of the walking simulators: screenshot from *Firewatch* (Campo Santo, 2016).

video games. These titles lay their cards on the table about the act of watching and gazing within a video game. Video games specifically designed to be watched and heard, experiencing their audio- and visual-scapes. This even brings a common cultural practice to video games: the gamer as a tourist, an observer, a witness. Something that could be seen beyond the 'walking simulator' label, extending to games like *The Elder Scrolls* (Bethesda, 1994–to date), *Grand Theft Auto* (Rockstar Games, 2001–2013), or *Assassin's Creed* (Ubisoft, 2007–to date) franchises, where players can forget about the missions and just start exploring and observing the in-game universe. A video game turned into spectatorship, where undoubtedly the gamer is also the audience.

Of course, video games have also always had an audience in the more traditional sense of this word. As long as people have been playing video games, from the early days of computer laboratories and arcades, there have always been other gamers, friends, colleagues, and even complete strangers, who were interested in peering over the current player's shoulder to watch the action unfolding onscreen. And certain authors have highlighted the important and interactive role onlookers can have in game play and culture, particularly with certain genres of games or in specific settings. For example, Lin and Sun (2008) highlight the role that onlookers play in the culture of *Dance Dance Revolution* in gaming arcades, while Conway (2010) discusses how players of *Pro Evolution Soccer*, along with those watching, all communally work together to help maintain a 'flow' state (Csikszentmihalyi, 1988) and the rhythms of the game experience.

There is however, little doubt that the Internet, YouTube game channels, and video platforms like Twitch, have massively increased the opportunity for watching others play video games. This is what Ander (male, 33, not identified as a gamer, and loosely involved with gaming culture) conveys when he recalls how he used to watch football on television, but having lost interest in this, now prefers to watch *Starcraft II* (Blizzard Entertainment, 2010) games online: 'Now I only follow a channel of esports on YouTube, I only watch *Starcraft II*'. This is of course, an example of just one individual who switched from watching a traditional and well-established activity (football) to an emerging interest (video games), but what makes this interesting is that this individual does not particularly identify with gaming culture. Ander does not see himself as a gamer, or even a big gamer fan, but still, he avidly watches others playing video games online. In particular, this seems to be a growing trend, as for example, a *Google Consumer Survey* in 2014 suggested that only 37% of a group of people watching gaming videos on YouTube consider themselves gamers (Ramdurai, 2014). This, and other examples then, adds to our central argument concerning the growing social and cultural importance of video game culture; as even those not directly involved as participants in this culture, may also increasingly be implicated in gaming culture as an audience member. Video game culture is starting to reach a much wider audience.

Video games and academia

In July 2001, Espen Aarseth (2001) inaugurated the first issue of the first peer-reviewed journal in, what he stated to be, the newly created discipline of 'computer game studies'. The journal *Game Studies* was born and, according to Aarseth, it signaled the arrival of a new academic field of study that was dedicated to video games. Espen Aarseth (2001) stated that 2001 could be seen 'as the Year One of Computer Game Studies as an emerging, viable, international, academic field'. Similarly, two years later, Mark Wolf and Bernard Perron (2003), in the introduction of the first anthology edited on the matter, asserted that the idea of video game theory was starting to be accepted in academia. One year on from that, Aarseth (2004: 45) insisted that the idea of academically studying video games had gone from 'non grata to a recognized field of great scholarly potential, a place for academic expansion and recognition'. Video games were already an emerging area of study towards the end of the twentieth century, but it was in the early 2000s that this began to develop more notably into a recognized field of video games studies.

In 2009 Wolf and Perron (2009: 1) published the second volume of their video game theory reader. This new anthology begins with the following assertive statement:

> It need not be said that the field of video game studies is now a healthy and flourishing one. An explosion of new books, periodicals, online venues, and conferences over the past decade has confirmed the popularity, viability, and vitality of the field, in a way that perhaps few outside of it expected. The time has come to ask not only how the field is growing, but in what directions it could or should go.

According to these authors, the relevance of a field dedicated to the study of video games was, by the end of the 2000s, no longer in question. Seldom is it possible to witness the emergence of a topic into the academic world at such a rapid pace as video game studies did in those early years. In the years that followed, we began to see an explosion of publications and the creation of a number of research centres specializing in the study of video games. By 2015, when Wolf and Perron published the *Routledge Companion to Video Game Studies*, there was noticeably less evidence of the editors seeking to justify and legitimize this field. Instead, here we see more of a declaration of an evolving discipline:

> Naturally, we realize that a single volume, substantial as it may be, can give only a sampling of the many topics and lenses through which video games can be considered and studied; and as time passes the field of game studies will grow broader and deeper, just as its object of study continues to expand and evolve.
>
> *(Wolf and Perron, 2015: xxiv)*

Video game studies – or as it is sometimes known: digital game studies, computer game studies or, more commonly, simply game studies – encompass a wide range of influences and draw on numerous other disciplines, such as: anthropology, artificial intelligence, communication theory, economics, computer science, cultural studies, game theory, history, gender studies, education, law, literature, medicine, philosophy, political science, psychology, semiotics, sociology, and many others.

It is worth noting that some efforts to introduce and define this emerging field of studies have already been made. Along with the texts by Perron and Wolf (2003, 2009, 2015) highlighted above, this includes the works of Newman (2004), Juul (2005), Raessens and Goldstein (2005), Egenfeldt-Nielsen, Smith and Pajares Tosca (2008), Mäyrä (2008), Taylor (2009), Hjorth (2011), Crawford (2012), Sicart (2014a), Goldberg and Larsson (2015), Bogost (2015), and Kowert and Quandt (2016). However, these are only a small sample of the great number of titles published on the subject. A *Google Books* search (in mid-2017) for 'Video Games' finds 445,000 works, and 329,000 when searching for 'Computer Games'; providing a combined result of over 744,000 books, which is comparable to the number of volumes addressing other, much more well-established subjects, such as for example, 'cultural heritage' (729,000 books).

The growing number of international academic peer-reviewed journals in this area also pays testament to the developing importance of this field, and currently includes (but is not limited to), the journals of *Game Studies* (since 2001), *Games and Culture* (2006), *Eludamos* (2007), *Loading...* (2007), *International Journal of Computer Games Technology* (2007), *Entertainment Computing* (2009), *Journal of Gaming and Virtual Worlds* (2009), and *ToDIGRA* (2013). And of course, this does not include the plethora of other, less specific journals, which accept and publish video game-related research; the list of which is far too extensive to set out here. As Pearce (2009: 51) wrote:

> [J]udging by the fact that there are now sufficient peer review-quality academic papers to justify the publication of a journal titled Games and

Culture, it is safe to say we have arrived at a point where the previous debates about whether these two terms can coexist in the same phrase can be put to rest.

A number of key research groups and centres focusing on, or incorporating the study of video games, have also been set up; including, but in no way limited to, the *Center for Computer Games Research* (IT University of Copenhagen, 1999), *DIGAREC – Digital Games Research Center* (University of Potsdam, 2008), *The Singapore-MIT GAMBIT Game Lab* (Massachusetts Institute of Technology, 2007), *The Mobile VINN Excellence Centre* (Stockholm University, 2007), *Technoculture, Art and Games* (Concordia University, Montreal, 2008), *NYU Game Center* (New York University, 2008), and *The Utrecht Center for Game Research* (Utrecht University, 2014). In addition, the international *Digital Games Research Association* (DiGRA) was formally established in 2003, and since then a number of countries or regions have established their own national chapters for the study of video games, including those in Australia, China, the Netherlands, Finland, Germany, Israel, Italy, Japan, Turkey, and the UK.

However, it is important to note that game studies, although a rapidly developing research field, are still an area that does not yet share the same status of other similar areas of study, such as those of literature, film, or even television studies. Game academics are very much like the modern game critics described by Stuart (2017) as, 'like their film equivalents in the 1920s; they are still wrestling with this vast new medium, which is undergoing seismic shifts in form and meaning – but the biggest changes are yet to come' (Stuart, 2017: online). The struggle to place video game studies as a central and fully accepted area of academic study is still on. For example, the fact there is still currently only a handful of full professors working in the area of game studies is evidence that this area may not yet have fully matured.

Overall, it appears then, that though the study of video games is a very recent area of research, and still has not reached the same level of recognition that other many related areas of study have, it has over its short life undergone a very rapid expansion, and has quickly established itself as a valid area of academic interest. This, in many ways has happened because of the growing significance of video games in wider society, and the development of video game culture; however, in turn, the legitimization of video games studies has helped establish this as a non-trivial area of social and cultural life.

Video games and culture

In her book *Global Games: Production, Circulation, and Policy in the Networked Era*, Aphra Kerr (2017) seeks to locate and understand the video game industry within a wider social, cultural, and economic landscape. In particular, here, Kerr, adopts a 'cultural industries' approach to studying the video game sector. This approach has its origins in the work of Adorno and Horkheimer (1979) on the culture industry. In this thesis, the industry that produces culture, such as film and popular music, is seen as producing cultural goods, not based upon their artistic merits, but rather on their ability to maximize profit. Hence, what gets made by the culture industry are anti-intellectual, standardized, and formulaic products; based upon what capitalism knows will sell and can reach the largest audience. Certainly, the argument could be made that the contemporary video game industry is the pinnacle of the culture industry, as understood by Adorno and Horkheimer. In particular, Crawford and Rutter (2006) suggest that the market dominance of video game sequels and remakes of existing games could be seen as an industry's tendency to churn out products that are not necessarily innovative or original, but rather, produced merely to generate guaranteed profit.

Kerr highlights the value of this approach, as it allows us to understand the unequal power relations that exist with the cultural sector and its industries. However, Kerr (2017) adopts a slightly less critical position, by utilizing the work of Miége (2011), who adapts this term to the 'cultural industries', to suggest that commodification may not always have wholly negative consequences. In particular, Kerr suggests that the video game industry has many similarities to other cultural industries, such as film, television, and music, as, for example, they all share similar high risks in producing content, and have similar internal tensions between profit and creativity. However, Kerr suggests that the video game industry is also different, or certainly at the forefront of many of the other cultural industries, as the games industry has led on harnessing the networking potential of the Internet and 'embraced digital distribution, Internet intermediaries and amateur content creation' (Kerr, 2017: 6).

Video games are becoming one of the most relevant cultural and artistic products of our time. It is not unusual to find video games in art galleries or museums, like in the Museum of Modern Art (MoMA) in New York, where video games have been part of its permanent collection since 2012; and includes works such as *Tetris* (Pajitnov, 1984), *The Sims* (Maxis, 2000), *Myst* (Cyan Worlds, 1993), *Eve Online* (CCP Games, 2003), *Flow* (Thatgamecompany, 2006), *Pac-Man* (Namco Ltd., 1980), and *Street Fighter II* (Capcom, 1991). Paola Antonelli (2013: online), the MoMA's senior curator of architecture and design, who is responsible for the inclusion of video games in the museum, seeks to 'preserve and show artifacts that will more and more become part of our lives in the future'. She also claims that video games are useful for highlighting how interaction is part of our life; as video games could be portrayed as 'the purest form of interaction'. For Antonelli, video games 'can be truly deep even when they are completely mindless', and can be considered as 'an experience' that might 'seem weird to many' but 'are very educational'. Antonelli concludes that 'design is truly everywhere', and moreover, suggests that video games can be understood as the quintessence of design and interaction, and 'because of its centrality to our lives', more people are coming to it 'as part of their own culture'. Thus, according to this argument, video games deserve to be in a museum because they are becoming a fundamental part of our culture.

Moreover, not only are video games becoming part of the collections and exhibitions of already established museums and galleries, but a number of video game-specific museums, galleries, and archives have also emerged in recent years such as the *Computerspielemuseum* [Computer Games Museum] in Berlin (founded in 1997), the *Video Game Art Gallery* in Chicago (2013), *The National Videogame Arcade* in Nottingham (2015), the *National Videogame Museum* in Frisco, Texas (2016), and *The Video Game History Foundation* in Oakland, California (2017). In this sense, Emmett, a 48-year-old head of a video game museum, explains why they decided to set up the museum in which he works: 'we were all convinced back then that computer games are more than a toy and we are convinced that they are a very important part of culture'. He also adds that the main aim they would like to achieve with their museum is to raise 'awareness of the cultural importance of computer games', because video games are, in his opinion, 'a kind of an early indicator for things and developments which will come in the future'. This argument then, is very similar to that given by Antonelli (above) concerning bringing video games to the MoMA; video games are important and are an ineludible part of our culture that can help us gain a better understanding of current (and coming) society. As Robert, a 47-year-old head of another video game museum states in an interview 'we think that games and the people who make games are interesting'.

In relation to this, the *Guidelines for the Preservation of Digital Heritage* that the National Library of Australia (2003) prepared for UNESCO advocates preserving digital elements and the technical equipment for their reproduction such as 'word processing, email, websites, relational databases, computer models and simulations, digital audio and video, space imagery, and computer games' (National Library of Australia, 2003: 29), to name but a few. Video games therefore become objects of interest for institutions that curate cultural elements, and video games then become cultural heritage.

Hence, video games now fall under the dominion of spaces like museums and art galleries, which are usually represented as 'high culture' institutions. However, video games are, undoubtedly and principally, part of popular culture.[18] For example, their presence and importance in television series has grown in recent years. *The Big Bang Theory* (Lorre and Prady, 2007–to date) often portrays the protagonists playing and speaking about video games, linking gaming practices to a wider stereotyped 'geek culture', and some of its episodes primarily revolve around video games. In the more recent American version of *House of Cards* (Willimon, 2013–to date), the main character – Francis Underwood – is a regular gamer, and the show makes references to a number of titles, which hints that politics and (video) games have much in common. *The Guild* (Day, 2007–2013) is a comedy series that follows the lives of a group of gamers who are part of a guild in a (fictional) Massively Multiplayer Online Game (MMOG) called *The Game*. There are also several series that have aired video game themed episodes or depict situations in which the characters play or speak about video games, including (but not limited to) *Black Mirror* (Brooker, 2011–to date), *CSI Miami* (Zuiker, Donahue, and Mendelsohn, 2002–2012), *Law and Order* (Wolf, 1990–2010), *Seinfeld* (David and Seinfeld, 1989-1998), *The X-Files* (Carter, 1995–2002, 2016), *Star Trek: The Next Generation* (Roddenberry, 1987–1994), *Breaking Bad* (Gilligan, 2008–2013), *The Walking Dead* (Darabont, 2010–to date), *Mr. Robot* (Esmail, 2015–to date), and many more. Also, at the time of writing this book there are proposed, or in development, a number of television series based on video game licenses such as *Battlefield*, *The Witcher*, and *Castlevania*. There is also a long and expanding history of films that are adaptations of video games, for example, *Super Mario Bros.* (Morton and Jankel, 1993), *Street Fighter* (de Souza, 1994), *Mortal Kombat* (Anderson, 1995), *Tomb Raider* (West, 2001; de Bont, 2003; Uthaug, 2018), *Resident Evil* (Anderson, 2002; Witt, 2004; Mulcahy, 2007; Anderson, 2010; Anderson, 2012; Anderson, 2016), *Silent Hill* (Gans, 2006), *Max Payne* (Moore, 2008), *Prince of Persia: The Sands of Time* (Newell, 2010), *Doom* (Bartkowiak, 2005), *Hitman* (Gens, 2007), and *Assassin's Creed* (Kurzel, 2016), to name but a few of the most popular. Besides this, there are also films that involve, or revolve around video games, such as *Tron* (Lisberger, 1982), *WarGames* (Badham, 1983), *eXistenZ* (Cronenberg, 1999), *Avalon* (Oshii, 2001), *Wreck-It Ralph* (Moore, 2012), *Pixels* (Columbus, 2015), and *Ready Player One* (Spielberg, 2018) – the latter which is significantly based on a novel (Cline, 2011) that represents how video game culture is hegemonic, and leads and drives popular culture.

There is little doubt that cinema and television have heavily influenced the nature and design of video games over the years. This most clearly includes the vast number of video games that have been developed that directly draw on, or tie into, a particular film, including, *Star Wars: Knights of the Old Republic* (Bioware, 2003), *Mad Max* (Avalanche Studios, 2015), and *Alien: Isolation* (The Creative Assembly, 2014). However, other notable influences include how many videos games include cinematic style cut scenes, or there are numerous video games that are very film-like, such as can be seen in games like *Heavy Rain* (Quantic Dream, 2010), *The Order: 1886* (Ready at Dawn, 2015), *Uncharted* (Naughty Dog, 2007–to date), and *Metal Gear* (Konami, Kojima Productions, 1987–to date) series.

However, the influence of television and film on video games is far from one-directional, and certainly as video games have become increasingly successful in recent decades, more and more we have seen older media forms looking towards video games, not just as subject matter to include in their products, but also in terms of influencing their design, presentation, and style. For example, there are many films that very notably, and often quite knowingly, draw on the style and tropes of video games, including, *Crank* (Neveldine and Taylor, 2006), *Speed Racer* (Wachowski and Wachowski, 2008), and *Sucker Punch* (Snyder, 2011). Also, certain film directors openly acknowledge the influence of video games on their films, such as *Drive* director Nicolas Winding Refn, who stated in an interview the key influence of *Metal Gear Solid* (Konami, 1998) and its creator Hideo Kojima on his 2013 film *Only God Forgives* (Winding Refn, 2013). Furthermore, Refn also adds how his 2016 film *The Neon Demon* was 'designed like a video game in that it has different levels. It's designed for a futuristic audience who will potentially see entertainment in different ways. Its colour palette has an artificialness to it which isn't dissimilar to a video game's' (Golby, 2016: online). Video games are becoming an established, and highly influential, part of audiovisual culture.

Furthermore, there is also an established but growing relationship between video games and popular music. Video game music is becoming less of an incidental aspect of the game, and much more central in creating and maintaining the gaming experience. Many video games now have originally composed cinematic-like soundtracks, such as *The Witcher 3: The Wild Hunt* (CD Projekt Red, 2015), which features 35 original tracks, with a total running time of over 81 minutes. Serious artists are now recording original soundtracks for games, such as Chvrches who provided an original song for the game *Mirror's Edge Catalyst* (EA Dice, 2016). Moreover, Ying-Ying Law (2016) writes of how concerts playing video game music are becoming increasingly popular, and are now being held in serious and sizable music venues, such as the Royal Albert Hall in London. It is also evident that video games are having a notable influence on the music industry. For example, The Cardigans 1998 album was named *Gran Turismo* after their favourite video game; and the album also features a track called *My Favourite Game*. Also, the R&B singer Gallant stated in an interview how video games had shaped his music: 'Video games have influenced my music, for sure. My song *Weight in Gold* has an 8-bit thing going on. I really fell in love with that sound making it. That, and the beautiful strings and minor chord changes you get in game music. It's like the world's ending, but everyone's accepted it' (Golby, 2016).

The importance of video games as a relevant cultural manifestation of contemporary society is undoubtedly linked to the rise of digital culture and, particularly, *digimodernism*. Drawing on Frederic Jameson's (1992) definition of postmodernism, Alan Kirby (2009: 1–2) characterizes *digimodernism* as the dominant cultural logic or hegemonic norm of the twenty-first century. Having appeared in the second half of the 1990s, 'digimodernism has decisively displaced postmodernism to establish itself as the twenty-first century's new cultural paradigm' (Kirby, 2009: 1). According to Castells (2010: 403), every 'cultural expression, from the worst to the best, from the most elitist to the most popular, comes together in this digital universe'. Not only is the digital mediating almost every aspect of our lives, but it has become the hegemonic cultural logic. A digital revolution that affects how 'we think of ourselves and the planet' (Creeber and Martin, 2009: 5). In this sense, *digitality* – a concept used by authors such as Gere (2008) in a similar way to digimodernism – 'can be thought of as a marker of culture because it encompasses both the artefacts and the systems of signification and communication that most clearly demarcate our contemporary way of life from others' (Gere, 2008: 16).

Digitality is an essential feature of our reality and, probably, as Gere suggests, one of the most important defining elements in our contemporary societies, including the 'ways of thinking and doing' (Gere, 2008: 17). This intertwines with a wider set of processes:

> The last 30 years have seen both the rise of globalization and the domination of free market capitalism, the increasing ubiquity of information and communications technologies, and the burgeoning power and influence of techno-science. Digital technology is an important and constitutive part of these developments, and has, to some extent, determined their form.
>
> *(Gere, 2008: 14)*

Accordingly, García Selgas lists a series of historic-material transformations that partially explain these changes in our basic understanding of reality – an ontological transition. García Selgas (2003: 30–36) identifies processes usually linked to globalization or *glocalization* (Robertson, 1995), such as the substitution of the industrial capitalism by Post-Fordism or financial capitalism, the revolution of the technologies of information and communication, and the rise of a dominant virtual-media culture. In all of them, digital technology is an essential ingredient to understand their expansion. It is in this context that video game culture emerges as a sociocultural phenomenon that condenses and promotes all these changes.

There are, of course, numerous other ways in which we can see that video games are infiltrating and influencing our cultural landscape. For instance, the number of conferences, festivals, and other video game-related events has significantly grown over the previous decades. According to Ying-Ying Law (2016: 5), in her ethnography study of attendees at video game events in the UK, these events 'have vastly increased in number and popularity'. For example, Law highlights how the *Tokyo Game Show* had around 160,000 visitors in 1999 and almost 270,000 in 2015, while the first LAN event organized by *Multiplay* in the UK had only 20 participants in 1995 but over 25,000 by 2013 (an event called *Imsonmnia50*). There are numerous video game events all around the world, such as *E3* (Los Angeles, US), *Gamescom* (Cologne, Germany), *Penny Arcade Expo* (the PAX series of video game events in the US and Australia), *QuakeCon* (Dallas, US), *Barcelona Games World* (Barcelona, Spain), *Fun and Serious Festival* (Bilbao, Spain), *EGX* (Birmingham, UK), *Distant Worlds* (concerts featuring music from *Final Fantasy* on a world tour), *Tokyo Game Show* (Tokyo, Japan), *Paris Games Week* (Paris, France), *China Digital Entertainment Expo and Conference* (*ChinaJoy*, Shanghai, China), and many others. There are also other popular culture conventions that include video games, along with comic books, collectible card games, television series, films, anime, and manga, like *Comic-Con* (San Diego, US) and *Supanova* (in different cities in Australia), amongst others. Therefore, these video game events 'have become a popular and meaningful form of social activity' (Law, 2016: 6).

These video game events are still, to a certain degree, a niche activity; however, they are becoming increasingly more popular. As Law (2016: 196) suggests: 'we can no longer identify an "average gamer"', and those who attend these events are becoming increasingly diverse. Hence, we are starting to see the spread of video game-related practices, such as going to conventions or concerts, beyond their traditional association with 'geek' culture, while at the same time, noticing a new coolness and popularity attached to geek and its associated cultural practices; a kind of *geek chic*, typified in the popularity of television shows such as *The Big Bang Theory* and *GEEK* t-shirts (Harrison, 2013).

In this sense then, video game-related practices become more intertwined with wider culture, such as like buying video game-related merchandising. Merchandising relating to video games has exponentially increased in recent years, including t-shirts, posters, figurines, cups, keyrings, purses, caps, doormats, notebooks, books, music, and much more. Consuming these objects is a way to extend the video game experience beyond the act of playing the game, by bringing it (more) into everyday life. Accordingly, Zelda, a female, 26-year-old, regular video gamer, believes that people purchase merchandise and attend video game-related events in order to keep the game alive: 'They have these figurines to remind them how good they [the video games] are: you have posters, you have signings, you have photographs'. This also affects the processes of identity and community formation amongst gamers, which we explore further in Chapter 6. However, it is important to highlight here how video game merchandise, icons, and symbols are pervading society beyond the limits of video game culture.

All of this has a consequence of melting video game culture (more) into general culture; when something becomes implicated in other broader culture forms, such as arguably video games have, then its cultural importance and influence can no longer be in any doubt.

Conclusions

Contemporary society can be defined by the interrelated association of several logics, dynamics, forces, practices, discourses, agents, and cultures that weave the shape of its seams and, amongst them, we find video game culture. In this way, video game culture is the result of broader social and cultural processes, but it is also a driving force that intensively participates in the (re)production of the dominant cultural, political, social, and ontological questions that define social reality.

In this chapter, we have set out how video game culture is more than an emerging process; it is a growing, and in process of consolidation, reality. Thus, video game culture is important in today's society for various reasons. First, video games are part of a flourishing cultural industry, where statistics show that it is reaching more and more people from different backgrounds. Second, video games are becoming one of the most relevant cultural and artistic products of our time, as the proliferation of exhibitions, conferences, festivals, events, and museums about video games demonstrates. Third, in the field of media, the number of websites, video platforms, and content focused on video games has increased considerably, and similarly, video games have become a regular topic for older media forms, such as television and print media. Fourth, video games are becoming an important sector in the fields of education and work, as the exponential growth of courses, degrees, Masters, and jobs related to video games indicates. Fifth, video game studies are now an established area within academia, and an interest in studying video games and their culture is growing in other disciplines. Sixth, video games, digital by birth, are seen as the essential cultural product of the digital era, which can be considered a purely native reality of contemporaneity, given that it is a phenomenon only relevant – from a sociological point of view – since the 1980s. Finally, and more generally, an ongoing process of *videoludification* of society is evident, through which video game culture appears as the testing ground of things to come.

Video games as culture means that video games are both an expression of the contemporary nature of our culture, but also increasingly, an established part of this. Video games both reflect, and help drive, wider social changes and processes, and hence, crucial facets of our culture are intertwined with video games and their structures. That is why studying video games can help us understand important issues in our contemporary society; as increasingly their presence or influence can be seen as pervading a growing number of areas in our social and cultural world.

Notes

1 The prefix of 'video' to describe games played on electronic devices Newman (2014) attributes to their rise in popularity around the same time as the emergence of other televisual-related technologies, such as the video cassette recorder (VCR). Hence, these new technologies were often categorized together as 'new TV toys', which were 'changing television for the better' (Newman, 2014: 29).
2 http://www.mosi.org.uk/
3 http://www.sciencegamecenter.org/games/immune-attack
4 http://www.peacemakergame.com/
5 http://www.re-mission.net/
6 http://dragonbox.com/
7 Among its members are companies such as Activision Blizzard, Capcom, Electronic Arts, Epic Games, Microsoft, NVIDIA, Square Enix, Ubisoft, Nintendo, Sony, or SEGA.
8 This comprises content (video games), hardware, and accessories. Their source is The NPD Group and Games Market Dynamics: U.S.
9 https://newzoo.com/insights/articles/global-games-market-reaches-99-6-billion-2016-mobile-generating-37/
10 The Entertainment Retailers Association is a UK trade organization that represents the majority of retailers and digital services offering music, video, and games. Among its members are Amazon, Spotify, Tesco, Sainsburys, Asda, Morrisons, HMV, Game, Sky, etc.
11 GDP in 2015. Data extracted from the World Bank: http://bit.ly/2prWtA7
12 Both *PewDiePie* and *Markiplier* appear in the Forbes' list of *The Highest-Paid YouTube Stars* in 2016, earning between June 2015 and June 2016 $15 million and $5.5 million, respectively. To access the full list, see Berg (2016).
13 However, Dibbell and Eikenberry in the podcast *Geek's Guide to the Galaxy* suggest that the decline of certain games/online worlds like *Second Life*, and the introduction of anti-cheat mechanisms into many games, has made the phenomenon of gold farming and real money transactions much less common than it once was (Wired, 2017).
14 http://www.instituteofplay.org/
15 He documented the whole process in his blog. The first entry is as follows: http://www.ludiclearning.org/2014/03/26/launch-codes-info-bulbs-and-inventories-prepping-to-teach-gone-home/
16 https://www.youtube.com/user/PewDiePie/
17 https://www.twitch.tv/p/about
18 Nevertheless, divisions such as those between high and low culture have been widely challenged by many theorists and professionals (Jameson, 1991).

References

Aarseth, Espen (2001). 'Computer Game Studies, Year 1', *Game Studies*, 1 (1), [http://www.gamestudies.org/0101/editorial.html]

Aarseth, Espen (2004). 'Genre Trouble: Narrativism and the Art of Simulation', in Wardrip-Fruin, Noah and Harrigan, Pat (editors). *First Person: New Media as Story, Performance, and Game*. Cambridge, MA: MIT Press, 45–54.

Abt, Clark C. (2002). *Serious Games*. Lanham, MD: University Press of America.

Adorno, Theodor and Horkheimer, Max (1979). *Dialectic of Enlightenment*. London: Verso Books.
Antonelli, Paola (2013) (video). 'Why I brought Pac-Man to MoMA', *TED Talk*, [https://www.ted.com/talks/paola_antonelli_why_i_brought_pacman_to_moma] [Last Accessed: 23/05/2017]
Azuma, Ronald; Baillot, Yohan; Behringer, Reinhold; Feiner, Steven; Julier, Simon; MacIntrye, Blair (2001). 'Recent Advances in Augmented Reality', *IEEE Computer Graphics and Applications*, 21 (6): 34–47.
Baudrillard, Jean (1994). *Simulacra and Simulation*. Ann Arbor, MI: University of Michigan Press.
Bauman, Zygmunt (2000). *Liquid Modernity*. Cambridge: Polity Press.
BBC (2017). 'Esports "Set for £1bn Revenue and 600 Million Audiences by 2020"', *BBC Sport*, [http://www.bbc.com/sport/39119995] [Last accessed: 05/06/2017].
Beck, Ulrich (1992). *Risk Society: Towards a New Modernity*. London: Sage.
Berg, Madeline (2016). 'The Highest-Paid YouTube Stars 2016: PewDiePie Remains No. 1 With $15 Million', [https://www.forbes.com/sites/maddieberg/2016/12/05/the-highest-paid-youtube-stars-2016-pewdiepie-remains-no-1-with-15-million] [Last accessed: 21/06/2017].
Bergstrom, Kelly; Fisher, Stephanie; Jenson, Jennifer (2016). 'Disavowing "That Guy": Identity Construction and Massively Multiplayer Online Game Players', *Convergence*, 22 (3): 233–249
Bogost, Ian (2014). 'Why Gamification Is Bullshit' in Fuchs, Mathias; Fizek, Sonia; Ruffino, Paolo; Schrape, Niklas (2014) (editors). *Rethinking Gamification*. Lüneburg: Meson Press, 65–79.
Bogost, Ian (2015). *How to Talk about Videogames*. Minneapolis, MN: University of Minnesota Press.
Boltanski, Luc and Chiapello, Ève (2005). *The New Spirit of Capitalism*. New York: Verso.
Borowiecki, Karol J. and Bakhshi, Hasan (2017). 'Did you Really Take a Hit? Understanding How Video Games Playing Affects Individuals', *Nesta*, [http://www.nesta.org.uk/sites/default/files/did_you_really_take_a_hit_understanding_how_video_games_playing_affects_individuals.pdf] [Last Accessed: 03/08/2017].
Bulut, Ergin (2014). 'Playboring in the Tester Pit: The Convergence of Precarity and the Degradation of Fun in Video Game Testing', *Television and New Media*, 16 (3): 240–258.
Burn, Andrew (2006). 'Reworking the Text: Online Fandom', in Carr, Diane; Buckingham, David; Burn, Andrew; Schott, Gareth (editors). *Computer Games: Text, Narrative and Play*. Cambridge: Polity, 103 –118.
Caillois, Roger (2001). *Man, Play, and Games*. Urbana-Champaign, IL: University of Illinois Press.
Castells, Manuel (2010). *The Information Age: Economy, Society and Culture. The Rise of the Network Society Vol 1*. Oxford: Wiley-Blackwell.
Castronova, Edward (2005). *Synthetic Worlds. The Business and Culture of Online Games*. Chicago: The University of Chicago Press.
Charsky, Dennis (2010). 'From Edutainment to Serious Games: A Change in the Use of Game Characteristics', *Games and Culture*, 5 (2): 177–198.
Chatfield, Tom (2011). *Fun Inc.: Why Gaming Will Dominate the Twenty-First Century*. New York: Pegasus.
Cline, Ernest (2011). *Ready Player One*. New York: Random House.
Conway, Steven (2010). 'It's in the Game and Above the Game', *Convergence*, 16 (3): 334–354.
Crawford, Garry (2012). *Video Gamers*. London: Routledge.
Crawford, Garry. and Rutter, Jason (2006). 'Cultural Studies and Digital Games', in J. Bryce and J. Rutter (editors.). *Understanding Digital Games*. London: Sage.

Crawford, Garry, Gosling, Victoria K. & Light, Ben (2011). 'The Social and Cultural Significance of Online Gaming', in G. Crawford, V.K. Gosling & B. Light (editors). *Online Gaming in Context: The Social and Cultural Significance of Online Gaming*. London: Routledge.

Creeber, Glen and Martin, Royston (2009). *Digital Cultures. Understanding New Media*. Maidenhead: Open University Press.

Csikszentmihalyi Mihaly (1988). *Optimal Experience: Psychological Studies of Flow in Consciousness*. Cambridge: Cambridge University Press.

Dale, Steve (2014). 'Gamification: Making Work Fun, or Making Fun of Work?', *Business Information Review*, 31 (2): 82–90.

Deterding, Sebastian (2014a). 'Eudaimonic Design, or: Six Invitations to Rethink Gamification', in Fuchs, Mathias; Fizek, Sonia; Ruffino, Paolo; Schrape, Niklas (editors). *Rethinking Gamification*. Lüneburg: Meson Press, 305–331.

Deterding, Sebastian (2014b). 'The Ambiguity of Games: Histories and Discourses of a Gameful World' in Walz, Steffen P. and Deterding, Sebastian (editors). *The Gameful World. Approaches, Issues, Applications*. Cambridge, MA: MIT Press, 23–64.

Dibbell, Julian (2007). *Play Money: Or, How I Quit My Day Job and Made Millions Trading Virtual Loot*. New York: Basic Books.

Dovey, Jon and Kennedy, Helen W. (2006). *Game Cultures. Computer Games as New Media*. Maidenhead: Open University Press.

Dredge, Stuart (2013). 'Candy Crush Saga Reaches 500m Installations on Mobile and Facebook', *The Guardian*, [http://www.theguardian.com/technology/2013/nov/15/candy-crush-saga-reaches-500m-installs-mobile-facebook] [Last accessed: 25/05/2017].

Dredge. Stuart (2015). 'Candy Crush Saga Players Spent £865m on the Game in 2014 Alone', *The Guardian*, [https://www.theguardian.com/technology/2015/feb/13/candy-crush-saga-players-855m-2014] [Last accessed: 26/05/2017].

Egenfeldt-Nielsen, Simon (2011). *Beyond Edutainment: Exploring the Educational Potential of Computer Games*. Raleigh, NC: Lulu.com.

Egenfeldt-Nielsen, Simon; Smith, Jonas Heide; Pajares Tosca, Susana (2008). *Understanding Video Games: The Essential Introduction*. New York: Routledge.

ERA (2017). 'Entertainment Sales Reached £6.3bn in 2016', [http://www.eraltd.org/news-events/press-releases/2017/entertainment-sales-reached-63bn-in-2016/] [Last Accessed: 12/05/2017].

ESA (2016). *Essential Facts About the Computer and Video Game Industry*, [http://essentialfacts.theesa.com/Essential-Facts-2016.pdf] [Last Accessed: 11/05/2017]

ESA (2017). *Essential Facts About the Computer and Video Game Industry*, [http://essentialfacts.theesa.com/mobile/] [Last accessed: 30/05/2017].

Eskelinen, Markku and Tronstad, Ranghild (2003). 'Video Games and Configurative Performances', in Wolf, Mark J. and Perron, Bernard (editors). *The Video Game Theory Reader*. New York: Routledge, 195–220.

Foucault, Michel (2003). 'Governmentality' in Rabinow, Paul and Rose, Nikolas (editors). *The Essential Foucault*. New York: The New Press, 229–245.

Frelik, Pawel (2016). 'The Master's Digital Tools: Cognitive Capitalism and Non-normative Gaming Practices', *Journal of Gaming and Virtual Worlds*, 8 (2): 163–176.

Fuchs, Mathias; Fizek, Sonia; Ruffino, Paolo; Schrape, Niklas (2014) (editors). *Rethinking Gamification*. Lüneburg: Meson Press.

García Selgas, Fernando J. (2003). 'Hacia una ontología de la fluidez social', *Política y Sociedad*, 40 (1): 27–55.

Geertz, Clifford (1973). *The Interpretation of Cultures*. New York: Basic Books.

Gere, Charlie (2008). *Digital Culture*. London: Reaktion Books.

Giddens, Anthony (1991). *Modernity and Self-Identity*. Cambridge: Polity Press.

Giddings, Seth (2017). '*Pokémon GO* as Distributed Imagination', *Mobile Media & Communication*, 5 (1): 59–62.

Gittleson, Kim (2014). 'Amazon Buys Video-game Streaming Site Twitch', *BBC News*, [http://www.bbc.co.uk/news/technology-28930781].

Golby, Joel (2016). 'How Video Games Made You the Man You are Today', *Shortlist*, [http://www.shortlist.com/tech/gaming/how-video-games-changed-your-life] [Last accessed: 21/06/2017].

Goldberg, Daniel and Larsson, Linus (2015) (editors). *The State of Play: Creators and Critics on Video Game Culture*. New York: Seven Stories Press.

Google (2013). 'Introducing Gen C. The YouTube Generation', *Think with Google*, [https://ssl.gstatic.com/think/docs/introducing-gen-c-the-youtube-generation_research-studies.pdf] [Last accessed: 26/05/2017].

Haraway, Donna (1991). *Simians, Cyborgs, and Women: The Reinvention of Nature*. New York: Routledge.

Harrison, Andrew (2013). 'Rise of the New Geeks: How the Outsiders Won', *The Guardian*, [https://www.theguardian.com/fashion/2013/sep/02/rise-geeks-outsiders-superhero-movies-dork] [Last accessed: 22/06/2017].

Hjorth, Larissa (2011). *Games and Gaming: An Introduction to New Media*. Oxford: Berg.

Hjorth, Larissa (2017). 'Ambient and Soft Play: Play, Labour and the Digital in Everyday Life', *European Journal of Cultural Studies*, [https://doi.org/10.1177/1367549417705606].

Hofmann, Sebastian and Mosemghvdlishvili, Lela (2014). 'Perceiving Spaces through Digital Augmentation: An Exploratory Study of Navigational Augmented Reality Apps', *Mobile Media & Communication*, 2 (3): 265–280.

INE (2016). 'Estadística sobre las actividades en investigación científica y desarrollo tecnológico (I+D)', [Statistics on R+D Activities], *INEbase*, [http://www.ine.es/dyngs/INEbase/en/operacion.htm?c=Estadistica_C&cid=1254736176754&menu=ultiDatos&idp=1254735576669] [Last Accessed: 12/05/2017].

ISFE (2012). *Video Games in Europe: Consumer Study*, [http://bit.ly/1DiiRKh] [Last Accessed: 11/05/2017].

ISFE (2014). *GameTrack Survey (Quarter 4 2016)*, [http://www.isfe.eu/sites/isfe.eu/files/attachments/gametrack_european_summary_data_2016_q4.pdf] [Last Accessed: 11/05/2017].

Jameson, Frederic (1991). *Postmodernism, or, The Cultural Logic of Late Capitalism*. Durham: Duke University Press.

Jenkins, Henry (2006). *Fans, Bloggers, and Gamers. Exploring Participatory Culture*. New York: New York University Press.

Juul, Jesper (2005). *Half-Real. Video Games between Real Rules and Fictional Worlds*. Cambridge, MA: MIT Press.

Juul, Jesper (2010). *A Casual Revolution: Reinventing Video Games and Their Players*. Cambridge, MA: MIT Press.

Katsaliaki, Korina and Mustafee, Navonil (2015). 'Edutainment for Sustainable Development. A Survey of Games in the Field', *Simulation and Gaming*, 46 (6): 647–672.

Keogh, Brendan (2017). 'Pokémon GO, the Novelty of Nostalgia, and the Ubiquity of the Smartphone', *Mobile Media & Communication*, 5 (1): 38–41.

Kerr, Aphra (2006). *The Business and Culture of Digital Games. Gamework/Gameplay*. London: Sage.

Kerr, Aphra (2017). *Global Games: Production, Circulation, and Policy in the Networked Era*. London: Routledge.

Kirby, Alan (2009). *Digimodernism*. New York: Continuum.

Kirkpatrick, Graeme (2015). *The Formation of the Gaming Culture: UK Gaming Magazines, 1981–1995*. London: Palgrave.
Knorr Cetina, Karin (1999). *Epistemic Cultures*. Cambridge, MA: Harvard University Press.
Kowert, Rachel and Quandt, Thorsten (2016) (editors). *The Video Game Debate. Unravelling the Physical, Social, and Psychological Effects of Video Games*. London: Routledge.
Kowert, Rachel; Griffiths, Mark D.; Oldmeadow, Julian A. (2012). 'Geek or Chic? Emerging Stereotypes of Online Gamers', *Bulletin of Science, Technology and Society*, 32 (6): 471–179.
Kücklich, Julian Raul (2009). 'Virtual Worlds and Their Discontents. Precarious Sovereignty, Governmentality, and the Ideology of Play', *Games and Culture*, 4 (4): 340–352.
Law, Ying-Ying (2016). '*The Travelling Gamer: An Ethnography of Video Game Events*', Unpublished PhD thesis, University of Salford.
Lee, Yu-Hao and Lin, Holin (2011). '"Gaming is My Work": Identity Work in Internethobbyist Game Workers', *Work, Employment and Society*, 25 (3): 451–467.
Lin, Holin and Sun, Chuen-Tsai. (2008). 'Invisible Gameplay Participants: The Role of Onlookers in Arcade Gaming', *Conference Paper Presentation to the Under the Mask, University of Bedfordshire*, 7 June, [http://underthemask.wikidot.com/linandsun] [Last accessed: 19/06/2017].
Linehan, Conor; Kirman, Ben; Roche, Bryan (2014). 'Gamification as Behavioral Psychology', in Walz, Steffen P. and Deterding, Sebastian (2014) (editors). *The Gameful World. Approaches, Issues, Applications*. Cambridge, MA: MIT Press, 81–105.
Ma, Minhua; Oikonomou, Andreas; Jain, Lakhmi (2011) (editors). *Serious Games and Edutainment Applications*. Berlin: Springer.
MacCannell, Dean (2011). *The Ethics of Sightseeing*. Berkley and Los Angeles: University of California Press.
McLaughlin, Marty (2013). 'New GTA V Release Tipped to Rake in £1bn in Sales', *The Scotsman*, [http://www.scotsman.com/lifestyle/gadgets-gaming/new-gta-v-release-tipped-to-rake-in-1bn-in-sales-1-3081943] [Last accessed: 10/05/2017].
Maffesoli, Michel (2001). *El instante eterno* [The Eternal Instant]. Buenos Aires: Paidós.
Markopoulos, Angelos P.; Fragkou, Anastasios; Kasidiaris, Petros D.; Davim, Paulo J. (2015). 'Gamification in Engineering Education and Professional Training', *International Journal of Mechanical Engineering Education*, 43 (2): 118–131.
Maturo, Antonio and Setiffi, Francesca (2016). 'The Gamification of Risk: How Health Apps Foster Self-confidence and Why This is Not Enough', *Health, Risk, and Society*, 17 (7–8): 477–494.
Mäyrä, Frans (2008). *An Introduction to Game Studies. Games in Culture*. London: Routledge.
Mäyrä, Frans (2017). '*Pokémon GO*: Entering the Ludic Society', *Mobile Media & Communication*, 5 (1): 1–4.
Michael, David and Chen, Sande (2006). *Serious Games: Games That Educate, Train, and Inform*. Boston: Thomson.
Miége, Bernard (2011). *The Capitalisation of Cultural Production*. New York: International General.
Mozur, Paul (2014). 'For South Korea, Esports is National Pastime', *The New York Times*, [https://www.nytimes.com/2014/10/20/technology/league-of-legends-south-korea-epicenter-esports.html] [Last accessed: 31/05/2017].
National Library of Australia (2003). 'Guidelines for the Preservation of Digital Heritage', *UNESCO*, [http://unesdoc.unesco.org/images/0013/001300/130071e.pdf] [Last accessed: 22/06/2017].
Newman, James (2002). 'The Myth of the Ergodic Videogame. Some Thoughts on Playercharacter Relationships in Videogames', *Game Studies*, 2 (1).
Newman, James (2004). *Videogames*. London: Routledge.

Newman, Michael Z. (2014). *Video Revolutions. On the History of a Medium*. New York. Columbia University Press.

Office for National Statistics (2017). 'UK Gross Domestic Expenditure on Research and Development: 2015', *Statistical Bulletin*, 16 March 2017, [https://www.ons.gov.uk/economy/governmentpublicsectorandtaxes/researchanddevelopmentexpenditure/bulletins/ukgrossdomesticexpenditureonresearchanddevelopment/2015] [Last Accessed: 12/05/2017].

Pearce, Celia (2009). *Communities of Play. Emergent Cultures in Multiplayer Games and Virtual Worlds*. Cambridge, MA: MIT Press.

Pitts, Russ (2014). 'How Video Games Can Change the World, One Child at a Time', *Polygon*, [http://www.polygon.com/features/2014/4/24/5636832/glasslab] [Last accessed: 15/03/2016].

Postigo, Hector (2016). 'The Socio-technical Architecture of Digital Labor: Converting Play into YouTube Money', *New Media and* Society, 18 (2): 332–349.

Prescott, Julie and Bogg, Jan (2014). *Gender Divide and the Computer Games Industry*. Hershey, PA: IGI Global.

Raessens, Joost (2006). 'Playful Identities, or the Ludification of Culture', *Games and Culture*, 1 (1): 52–57.

Raessens, Joost (2010). *Homo Ludens 2.0. The Ludic Turn in Media Theory*. Utrecht: University of Utrecht.

Raessens, Joost and Goldstein, Jeffrey (editors) (2005). *Handbook of Computer Game Studies*. Cambridge, MA: MIT Press.

Ramdurai, Gautam (2014). 'Think Gaming Content is Niche? Think Again', *Think with Google*, [https://www.thinkwithgoogle.com/articles/think-gaming-content-is-niche-think-again.html] [Last accessed: 17/03/2016].

Robertson, Roland (1995). 'Glocalization: Time-Space and Homogeneity-Heterogeneity', in Featherstone, Mike; Lash, Scott; Robertson, Roland (editors). *Global Modernities*. London: Sage, 25–44.

Rose, Nikolas (1999). *Politics of Freedom. Reframing Political Thought*. Cambridge: Cambridge University Press.

Rundle, Michael (2016). 'Activision Completes $5.9 Billion Purchase of Candy Crush Makers King', *The Wire*, [http://www.wired.co.uk/article/king-candy-crush-activision-acquisition] [Last accessed: 26/05/2017].

Sanford, Kathy; Starr, Lisa; Merkel, Liz; Kurki, Sarah Bonsor (2015). 'Serious Games: Video Games for Good?', *E-Learning and Digital Media*, 12 (1): 90–106.

Sarkar, Samit (2017a). 'Minecraft Sales Hit 122M Copies', *Polygon*, [https://www.polygon.com/2017/2/27/14755644/minecraft-sales-122m-copies] [Last accessed: 13/08/2017].

Sarkar, Samit (2017b). 'Pokémon Go Hits 650 Million Downloads', *Polygon*, [https://www.polygon.com/2017/2/27/14753570/pokemon-go-downloads-650-million] [Last accessed: 26/05/2017].

Schiesel, Seth (2007). 'Video Games Conquer Retirees', *The New York Times*, [http://nyti.ms/1FYOIjx] [Last accessed: 22/05/2016].

Schrape, Niklas (2014). 'Gamification and Governmentality" in Fuchs, Mathias; Fizek, Sonia; Ruffino, Paolo; Schrape, Niklas (editors). *Rethinking Gamification*. Leuphana, Germany: MIT Press, 21–45.

Sicart, Miguel (2014a). *Play Matters*. Cambridge, MA: MIT Press.

Sicart, Miguel (2014b). 'Playing the Good Life' in Walz, Steffen P. and Deterding, Sebastian (editors). *The Gameful World. Approaches, Issues, Applications*. Cambridge, MA: MIT Press, 225–244.

Sicart, Miguel (2017). 'Reality has Always been Augmented: Play and the Promises of *Pokémon GO*', *Mobile Media & Communication*, 5 (1): 30–33.

Stuart, Keith (2017). 'Game Changers: How the Increasing Cultural Significance of Video Games is Reflected in our Coverage', *The Guardian*, [https://www.theguardian.com/membership/2017/jul/21/game-changers-how-the-increasing-cultural-significance-of-video-games-is-reflected-in-our-coverage] [Last Accessed: 28/07/2017].

Stuart, Keith and Hern, Alex (2014). 'Minecraft Sold: Microsoft Buys Mojang for $2.5bn', *The Guardian*, [http://www.theguardian.com/technology/2014/sep/15/microsoft-buys-minecraft-creator-mojang-for-25bn] [Last accessed: 14/08/2016].

Sylt, Christian (2014). 'Fourth Pirates of The Caribbean is Most Expensive Movie Ever with Costs Of $410 Million', *Forbes*, 22 July, [https://www.forbes.com/sites/csylt/2014/07/22/fourth-pirates-of-the-caribbean-is-most-expensive-movie-ever-with-costs-of-410-million/] [Last Accessed: 12/05/2017].

Taylor, T. L. (2009). *Play between Worlds. Exploring Online Game Culture*. Cambridge, MA: MIT Press.

Taylor, T. L. (2012). *Raising the Stakes. E-Sports and the Professionalization of Computer Gaming*. Cambridge, MA: MIT Press.

Taylor, Nicholas; Bergstrom, Kelly; Jenson, Jennifer; de Castell, Suzanne (2015). 'Alienated Playbour: Relations of Production in EVE Online', *Games and Culture*, 10: (4): 365–388.

Thaler, Rhichert and Sunstein, Cass (2008). *Nudge: Improving Decisions About Health, Wealth and Happiness*. New Haven: Yale University Press.

Tredinnick, Luke (2008). *Digital Information Culture: The Individual and Society in the Digital Age*. Oxford: Chandos Publishing.

Tylor, Edward B. (1871). *Primitive Culture: Researches into the Development of Mythology, Philosophy, Religion, Art, and Custom*. London: John Murray.

Ukie (2017). *UK Video Games Fact Sheet (20 March)*, [http://bit.ly/2q92Mpd] [Last Accessed: 11/05/2017].

Van Allen, Eric (2016). 'Millionaires in the Making: Record-setting $20M Esports Purse', *ESPN esports*, [http://www.espn.com/esports/story/_/id/17258717/20m-record-setting-esports-purse] [Last Accessed: 12/05/2017].

Walz, Steffen P. and Deterding, Sebastian (2014) (editors). *The Gameful World. Approaches, Issues, Applications*. Cambridge, MA: MIT Press.

Warr, Philippa (2014). 'Making the Grade: High School Starleague', *RedBull*, [http://win.gs/1JmBAKi]

Weber, Max (2001) [1905]. *The Protestant Ethic and the Spirit of Capitalism*. London: Routledge.

Webster, Andrew (2013). '"Grand Theft Auto V" Sets Record by Earning $1 Billion in Just Three Days', *The Verge*, [http://www.theverge.com/2013/9/20/4752458/grand-theft-auto-v-earns-one-billion-in-three-days] [Last accessed: 14/08/2016].

Webster, Andrew (2014). 'Activision is Spending $500 Million to Make 'Destiny' the Next 'Halo'', *The Verge*, [http://www.theverge.com/2014/5/6/5687160/destiny-will-cost-500-million] [14/08/2016].

Weststar, Johanna (2015). 'Understanding Video Game Developers as an Occupational Community', *Information, Communication and Society*, 18 (10): 1238–1252.

Weststar, Johanna and Legault Marie-Josée (2014). 'IGDA Developer Satisfaction Survey 2014. Employment Report', [http://c.ymcdn.com/sites/www.igda.org/resource/collection/9215B88F-2AA3-4471-B44D-B5D58FF25DC7/IGDA_DSS_2014-Employment_Report.pdf] [Last accessed: 31/05/2017].

Weststar, Johanna and Legault Marie-Josée (2016). 'IGDA Developer Satisfaction Survey 2016', [http://www.gameqol.org/s/IGDA-DSS-2016_Summary-Report_04Nov_FINAL.pdf] [Last accessed: 31/05/2017].

Williams, Peter (2014). 'Collaboration in the Gameful World', in Walz, Steffen P. and Deterding, Sebastian (editors). *The Gameful World. Approaches, Issues, Applications*. Cambridge, MA: MIT Press, 481–486.
Winch, Alison and Hakim, Jamie (2017). '"I'm Selling the Dream Really Aren't I?": Sharing Fit Male Bodies on Social Networking Sites', in McGillivray, D., McPherson, G. and Carnicelli, S. (editors). *Digital Leisure Cultures: Critical Perspectives*. London: Routledge.
Wired (2017). 'Remembering the Wild West Era of Videogame Gold Farming', *Wired*, [https://www.wired.com/2017/03/geeks-guide-gold-farming/] [Last accessed: 19/06/2017].
Wolf, Mark J. and Perron, Bernard (editors) (2003). *The Video Game Theory Reader*. London: Routledge.
Wolf, Mark J. and Perron, Bernard (editors) (2009). *The Video Game Theory Reader 2*. London: Routledge.
Wolf, Mark J. and Perron, Bernard (editors) (2015). *The Routledge Companion to Video Game Studies*. London: Routledge.
Xu, Feifei; Feng, Tian; Buhalis, Dimitrios; Weber, Jessika; Zhang, Hongmei (2016). 'Tourists as Mobile Gamers: Gamification for Tourism Marketing', *Journal of Travel & Tourism Marketing*, 33 (8): 1124–1142.
Zackariasson, Peter and Wilson, Timothy (2014). *The Video Game Industry: Formation, Present State, and Future*. London: Routledge.
Zichermann, Gabe and Linder, Joselin (2010). *Game-Based Marketing: Inspire Customer Loyalty Through Rewards, Challenges, and Contests*. Hoboken, NJ: Wiley.
Zichermann, Gabe and Linder, Joselin (2013). *The Gamification Revolution: How Leaders Leverage Game Mechanics to Crush the Competition*. New York: McGraw-Hill Education.
Zimmerman, Eric (2014). 'Manifesto for a Ludic Century' in Walz, Steffen P. and Deterding, Sebastian (2014) (editors). *The Gameful World. Approaches, Issues, Applications*. Cambridge, MA: MIT Press, 19–22.

Ludography

Activision Blizzard (2014). *Destiny*.
Activision, Infinity Ward (2003-2016). *Call of Duty* series.
Avalanche Studios (2015). *Mad Max*.
Bethesda (1994 to date). *The Elder Scrolls* series.
Bioware (2003). *Star Wars: Knights of the Old Republic*.
Blizzard Entertainment (2004). *World of Warcraft*.
Blizzard Entertainment (2010). *Starcraft II*.
Blow, Jonathan (2010). *Braid*.
Campo Santo (2016). *Firewatch*.
Capcom (1991). *Street Fighter II*.
Carlsen, Jeppe (2010). *Limbo*.
CCP Games (2003). *Eve Online*.
CD Projekt Red (2015). *The Witcher 3: The Wild Hunt*.
Creative Assembly (2014). *Alien: Isolation*.
Cyan Worlds (1993). *Myst*.
Dennaton Games (2012). *Hotline Miami*.
EA Dice (2016). *Mirror's Edge Catalyst*.
EA Sports (1993 to date). *FIFA* series.
EA Sports (1998 to date). *Madden NFL* series.
Federation of American Scientists and Escape Hatch Entertainment (2008). *Immune Attack*.

58 Video games as culture

Fish, Phil (2012). *Fez*.
Fullbright (2013). *Gone Home*.
Giant Sparrow (2017). *What Remains of Edith Finch*.
Hello Games (2016). *No Man's Sky*.
HopeLab (2013). *Re-Mission 2*.
Impact Games (2007). *PeaceMaker*.
Key, Ed and Kanaga, David (2013). *Proteus*.
King (2012). *Candy Crush Saga*.
Klei Entertainment (2013). *Don't Starve*.
Konami (1998). *Metal Gear Solid*.
Konami (2001 to date). *Pro Evolution Soccer* series.
Konami, Kojima Productions (1987–to date). *Metal Gear* series.
McMillen, Edmund and Himsl, Florian (2011). *The Binding of Isaac*.
Maxis (2000). *The Sims*.
Maxis (2000–2017). *The Sims* series.
Mojang (2011). *Minecraft*.
Namco Ltd. (1980). *Pac-Man*.
Naughty Dog (2007–to date). *Uncharted* series.
Niantic Labs (2013). *Ingress*.
Niantic Labs (2016). *Pokémon GO*.
Novarama (2009). *Invizimals*.
Pajitnov, Alexey (1984). *Tetris*.
Ready at Dawn (2015). *The Order: 1886*.
Realtime Associates and HopeLab (2006). *Re-Mission*.
Riot Games (2009). *League of Legends*.
Rockstar Games (2001–2013). *Grand Theft Auto* series.
Rockstar Games (2013). *Grand Theft Auto V*.
Rovio Entertainment (2009). *Angry Birds*.
Supergiant Games (2011). *Bastion*.
Team Meat (2010). *Super Meat Boy*.
Thatgamecompany (2006). *Flow*.
The Astronauts (2014). *The Vanishing of Ethan Carter*.
The Chinese Room (2012). *Dear Esther*.
The Chinese Room (2015). *Everybody's Gone to the Rapture*.
Ubisoft (2007–2016). *Assassin's Creed* series.
Valve (2013). *Dota 2*.
Variable State (2016). *Virginia*.
Wreden, Davey (2013). *The Stanley Parable*.

Other software

Google (2008). *Chrome*.
IKEA (2013). *IKEA Catalog*.
Lens-FitzGerald, Maarten; Boonstra, Claire; Van Der Klein, Raimo (2009–to date). *Layar*.

Films, television series, and music

Anderson, Paul W. S. (1995). *Mortal Kombat*.
Anderson, Paul W. S. (2002). *Resident Evil*.

Anderson, Paul W. S. (2010). *Resident Evil: After Life*.
Anderson, Paul W. S. (2012). *Resident Evil: Retribution*.
Anderson, Paul W. S. (2016). *Resident Evil: The Final Chapter*.
Badham, John (1983). *WarGames*.
Bartkowiak, Andrzej (2005). *Doom*.
Brooker, Charlie (2011 to date). *Black Mirror*.
Cardigans, The (1998). *Gran Turismo*.
Carter, Chris (1995–2002, 2016). *The X-Files*.
Chvrches (2016). *Warning Call*.
Columbus, Chris (2015). *Pixels*.
Cronenberg, David (1999). *Existenz*.
Darabont, Frank (2010–to date). *The Walking Dead*.
David, Larry and Seinfeld (1989–1998). *Seinfeld*.
Day, Felicia (2007–2013). *The Guild*.
De Bont, Jan (2003). *Lara Croft Tomb Raider: The Cradle of Life*.
De Souza, Steven E. (1994). *Street Fighter*.
Esmail, Sam (2015–to date). *Mr. Robot*.
Gans, Christophe (2006). *Silent Hill*.
Gens, Xabier (2007). *Hitman*.
Gilligan, Vince (2008–2013). *Breaking Bad*.
Kurzel, Justin (2016). *Assassin's Creed*.
Lisberger, Steven (1982). *Tron*.
Lorre, Chuck and Prady, Bill (2007 to date). *The Big Bang Theory*.
Marshall, Rob (2011). *Pirates of the Caribbean: On Stranger Tides*.
Moore, John (2008). *Max Payne*.
Moore, Rich (2012). *Wreck-It Ralph*.
Morton, Rocky and Jankel, Annabel (1993). *Super Mario Bros.*
Mulcahy, Russell (2007). *Resident Evil: Extinction*.
Neveldine, Mark and Taylor, Brian (2006). *Crank*.
Newell, Mike (2010). *Prince of Persia: The Sands of Time*.
Nolan, Jonathan and Joy, Lisa (2016). *Westworld*.
Oshii, Mamoru (2001). *Avalon*.
Roddenberry, Gene (1987–1994). *Star Trek: The Next Generation*.
Snyder, Zack (2011). *Sucker Punch*.
Spielberg, Steven (2018). *Ready Player One*.
Uthaug, Roar (2018). *Tomb Raider*.
Valve (2014). *Free to Play*.
Wachowski, Lana and Wachowski, Lilly (2008). *Speed Racer*.
West, Simon (2001). *Lara Croft: Tomb Raider*.
Willimon, Beau (2013–to date). *House of Cards*.
Winding Refn, Nicolas (2013). *Only God Forgives*.
Witt, Alexander (2004). *Resident Evil: Apocalypse*.
Wolf, Dick (1990–2010). *Law and Order*.
Zuiker, Anthony E.; Donahue, Ann; Mendelsohn, Carol (2002–2012). *CSI Miami*.

3
VIDEO GAMES AND AGENCY WITHIN NEOLIBERALISM AND PARTICIPATORY CULTURE

Introduction

Interactivity is a noun often associated with video games. In fact, the *interactive nature* of video gaming is one of the main arguments regularly used to differentiate video games from other cultural products or media. It is frequently argued that in video games, players 'do not merely consume a pre-established piece of media, but instead are active participants in the creation of their experience' (Calleja, 2011: 56). This is then commonly offered as definitive evidence, by which, video games should be considered as the purest form of a new paradigm of cultural consumption (Kirby, 2009: 167); one that requires the explicit participation of the player. This is often then opposed to a more vertical model, traditionally tied to 'older' media such as television, cinema, or literature; delineating a movement from social models mainly attached to 'spectatorship' (Debord, 1995) to those focused on 'participation' (Jenkins, 2006).

Of course, there are limitations to this argument. In particular, it can be argued that a binary division between 'active' and 'passive' media is deeply flawed, as there is no relationship with any cultural product that is unidirectional: a book or a film might be seen as closed works, but the multiple ways in which they are interpreted and transformed at all levels – individual, social, cultural – make it harder to sustain the vision of the uncritical subject who passively absorbs all that they receive. Furthermore, we are at risk of overlooking the limitations that video games impose on interactivity and players' agency (Crawford, 2012: 74). Players do not freely manipulate video games at their will; they are limited by the game's own restrictions and arc of possibilities. And yet, we would wish to argue, video games still occupy a privileged position from which to consider the contemporary nature of agency.

Video games have often been celebrated for being a medium that offers choices for those who play them, but we would suggest that in recent years this attribute has become even more central and explicit in certain games and genres; and there are several titles that explicitly explore the idea of player agency. For example, *Until Dawn* (Supermassive Games, 2015) and *Life is Strange* (Dontnod Entertainment, 2015) use the 'butterfly effect' metaphor and imagery to convey to the player that everything they do may affect the storyline and the characters' fate. In a similar vein, *Dreamfall Chapters* (Red Thread Games, 2014) warns players whenever a relevant choice has been made, by announcing that 'the balance has shifted'. Similarly, the recent oeuvre of Telltale Games such as *The Walking Dead* (season 1, 2012; season 2, 2013; season 3, 2016), *The Wolf Among Us* (2013), *Game of Thrones* (2014), *Tales from the Borderlands* (2014), and *Batman: The Telltale Series* (2016) let the player know that the story will be tailored by their choices. Other titles like Quantic Dream's *Heavy Rain* (2010), *Beyond: Two Souls* (2013), and *Detroit: Become Human* (2018) toy with the same ideas and, in their case, offer multiple endings depending on the decisions made. Moreover, most often this type of game offers statistics at the end of each chapter – as these tend to be presented in an episodic fashion – on the decisions made, allowing each player to compare their own choices with the rest of the population that have played the video game. The question of agency and the player's capacity to make significant changes are then at the centre of this trend in video games.

The idea of agency, or player control, is therefore central to many debates concerning the study or definitions of video games. However, in this context, the meaning and nature of agency is often taken as a given, and seldom has it been explicitly explored and defined in any real depth. This chapter then seeks to explore key aspects of player agency in video games, and in doing so, also argues that video games provide an important lens for considering the contemporary nature of agency in a social context of neoliberal political rationalities and ideas of a participatory culture. In particular, what has emerged from this research process is how relevant actors continually problematize agency. Here, we suggest that the medium of video games exposes different forms and examples of agency, which allows us the opportunity to examine this important notion and its meaning within video game practices and wider culture.

Building mainly on actor–network theory and also the work of Michel Foucault, the chapter begins by considering the notion of agency as the multiple, distributed, and dislocated production of differences and transformations that can take a multitude of forms. This then helps us to extend the definition of agency beyond its traditional limited scope of the human being, and also consider how video games, and the apparatuses in which they are produced, operate as agents as well as facilitators of action. In this sense, from an ontological point of view, agency is defined as what transforms reality in one way or another, and politically, how this operates within a framework outlined by contemporary neoliberal rationalities.

We then explore the rhetorical and practical tendencies that surround agency in video game culture. In particular, ideas of 'freedom', 'responsibility', and 'control' typically appear as indicators and expression of this agency. Video games present themselves as full of opportunities and choices to be made (even if these may actually be rather limited), and the responsibility to act is always bestowed on the player: which path to take, who should survive, what decision to make? Freedom is understood here in terms of a (neo-)Foucauldian approach, and as part of contemporary neoliberal political rationalities. The hegemonic discourse in video game culture, therefore, prioritizes the idea of the player as being *in control*; in control of their actions and the outcomes of these actions in the game. This makes the player responsible for both their achievements and failures, even though there are many other actors (not necessarily human) involved in the process. However, although the notion of agency in video games seems to be dominated by the referents of neoliberalism, it is still possible to glimpse ways in which agency can break through this 'wrapping' (Jameson, 1991) and head towards more promising outcomes, in particular, those described in the rise of a participatory culture.

Video games and the contemporary nature of agency

Primarily based on actor–network theory and the work of Michel Foucault, we will expound our approach to agency. In particular, the former will help us to shed light on the basic nature of agency, understood fundamentally as what produces change and transformation, while the latter will assist us in the definition of the parameters of what counts as change and transformation – and the alternatives that it offers – in a given political and cultural context.

Following an actor–network approach, there are three fundamental characteristics that define agency (see Muriel, 2016). These are: first, that agency produces differences and transformations; second, that the characteristics of agency are multiple and do not reside in any one prototypical actor; and third, that agency is distributed and dislocated.

First of all, then, agency is what produces differences and transformations. Agency exists because, in some way, it transforms reality. Agency, therefore, does not have to do with the intention, desire, or the will of an actor, but rather with the transformations that occur; which are effectively observable and traceable:

> Without accounts, without trials, without differences, without transformation in some state of affairs, there is no meaningful argument to be made about a given agency, no detectable frame of reference.
> *(Latour, 2007: 53)*

Thus, the core of all agency is that it produces some type of change or it does not exist. The agency of a specific actor can then only be defined 'through its action' (Latour, 1999a: 122). That is why video games – but also the hardware, connections, and peripherals that make the interaction possible – can be considered as actors. In that, their actions bring about change: 'The player does not act so much as he [*sic*] reacts to what the game presents to him, and similarly, the game reacts to his input' (Arsenault and Perron, 2009: 119–120). The language of our interviewees reflects the agency of video games by recognizing how they have an impact on reality, particularly on the people who play them. We see how video games 'can bring people together' (Carl, male, 28, dedicated, and self-identifying gamer), 'provide a sense of friendship' (Zelda, female, 25, highly involved in the culture but only mildly identified as a gamer), 'have an effect [on gamers]' (Jack, male, 45, coordinator of two degree programmes on video game development), or even 'overwhelm you or make you think twice' (Laura, female, 26, indie game developer/artist).

The second characteristic of agency is that it is multiple and does not reside in a prototypical actor. That is to say, action can be 'embodied' in very different formulas and does not necessarily entail any standard actor (Latour, 2007: 54). And in exploring the forms of actors and actions, we begin to see the multiplicity of agency (Latour, 2007: 55). Thus, we emphasize 'the open character of agency, which can be occupied by the most heterogeneous mix of humans and non-humans' (García Selgas, 2007: 144). This results in tremendous freedom to define what an actor is: from understanding it as an extremely complex and abstract entity (institutions, the rail network, the human body, for instance), to thinking of it as a concrete person or object (such as, the president of a government, God, the authors of this text, a particular video game). In short, it is a question of recognizing the *heteromorphism* of agency. In this sense, as Millington (2009: 622) contends, video games are paradigmatic for human and non-human transgression and hybridity, which blurs the distinctions between people and machines and demands 'reconsideration of the ontological status afforded to humans, and have created a need for renewed epistemological approaches'.

This can clearly be seen in those video games that explicitly seek to disempower the player. For example, *This War of Mine* (11 bit studios, 2014), where the player plays the roles of civilians in a city sieged by war. The lack of tutorial leaves players on their own; the game disorientates them, and they do not necessarily immediately know how things work. Or the *Dark Souls* (FromSoftware, 2011–2016) series, which punishes the mistakes that players make enormously, forcing them to repeat the same action several times, facing the same enemies, and passing through the same scenarios. Also, certain horror video games such as *Outlast* (Red Barrel Studios, 2013), *Amnesia* (Frictional Games, 2010), or *Alien: Isolation* (Creative Assembly, 2014) consist of putting the player in the shoes of an extremely vulnerable individual, who is only able to flee or hide from their enemies, with almost no means to defend themselves in a direct way. These are examples in which it is possible to see how video games are also viable actors, because they interfere in the course of the action of players.

Helen Thornham (2011: 82), who carried out an ethnographic study on video gamers in various households in the UK, similarly asserted that if video games have the power to cause interruptions and disruption to players' conversations and gameplay, they should then 'be afforded affective agency'. There are so many agents (human and not) that can condition and disrupt what the player is doing that it is difficult to disregard their influence.

Agency is also multiple in that it is configured relationally. For someone or something to be situated as a personification and act as a social agent, there must be an interaction among agents (García Selgas, 2007: 140). Thus, the fact that agencies appear in subject positions or as concrete personifications – assembled, institutionalized, stabilized – is an effect. Video games, video gaming platforms and networks, video gamers, developers, video game websites and broadcast channels, and artistic and social representations of video game culture are, in the end, the outcome of complex associations between different human and non-human actors. This is perfectly shown in the idea of video games as assemblages (another notion that is very important in actor–network theory; particularly in Latour's works):

> Games, and their play, are constituted by the interrelations between (to name just a few) technological systems and software (including the imagined player embedded in them), the material world (including our bodies at the keyboard), the online space of the game (if any), game genre, and its histories, the social worlds that infuse the game and situate us outside of it, the emergent practices of communities, our interior lives, personal histories, and aesthetic experience, institutional structures that shape the game and our activity as players, legal structures, and indeed the broader culture around us with its conceptual frames and tropes.
>
> *(Taylor, 2009: 332)*

The third and final characteristic of agency that we explore here describes it as distributed and dislocated. This notion of agency ignores 'the alternative between actor and system' (Latour, 2007: 216), dealing with the action–structure dualism that has limited the social sciences since its beginnings. Understanding that action is not born within an individual's consciousness, the fact that the individual can almost never do what they want to do is not explained by attributing this to an external social force, such as the habitus, society, the group, or any other specific aspect of reality that appropriates conduct (Latour, 2007: 43–46). The explanation lies in the idea that action is dislocated (Latour, 2007: 46), and not reducible to any predefined social categories such as those mentioned. Action, therefore, is not the direct product of the actor, but nor is it the product of the structure in which, in conventional terms, it occurs. Latour explains the origin of his approach as the necessity to address two problems:

- First, confronted with what is often referred to as the micro level (face-to-face interaction, or the local), social scientists realize that many of the things that they need to give meaning to a situation actually come from far away in time and space. This forces them to look on another level (such as, society, norms, values, culture, context, structure); 'to concentrate on what is not directly visible in the situation but has made the situation what it is' (Latour, 1999b: 17).
- Second, once this higher, macro level is reached, social scientists notice that they are missing something, as abstractions such as culture, society, values, and structure seem too large, so they return to looking at local situations, those of flesh and blood that they had previously left.

However, we can address these issues without attempting to overcome or resolve them. The social is, then, not made 'of agency and structure at all, but [is] rather a circulating entity' (Latour, 1999b: 17). Hence, this approach to agency allows a condensation of these dual paths: first, localizing the global, revealing the many concrete places where the structural is assembled; second, redistributing the local, exposing the distributed existence of action, and that all agency is invariably linked to other distant (in time and space) agencies. In both cases, neither structure nor action exist as specific places or substances, but only as movements, connections, associations, and mediations that may occasionally lead to the existence of concrete and contingent entities.

Moreover, we would suggest that the distributed nature of agency is clearly visible in video games and, as Giddings (2009: 148) argues, 'resist conceiving of the video game as a discrete and "whole" object'. A gaming experience is therefore an event in which human subjects, a set of technologies, and a media-cultural practice come together; an event that 'emphasizes the dynamic between the elements *in play*: entities coming together, material and aesthetic chains of cause and effect or feedback' (Giddings, 2009: 149), which can only 'be adequately addressed through acknowledgement of its bringing together of heterogeneous part(icipant)s' (Giddings, 2009: 150).

Hence, in summary, agency can be summarized as what produces changes and transformations in reality. However, having this definition of agency, how do we then define what should be considered as change and transformation in a particular social context? We find an interesting answer in Foucault's theory.

Video games as dispositifs

Apparatuses, or *dispositifs*, limit what happens inside of them, and are the principal manifestations and enactors of the conditions of possibility for a specific society and time. Foucault used the notion of *dispositif* (or apparatus in the most common translation of the term in English) in his works *Discipline and Punish* (1995) and the first volume of *The History of Sexuality* (1990). In a conversation with other intellectuals, he defined the concept as follows:

> What I'm trying to pick out with this term is, firstly, a thoroughly heterogeneous ensemble consisting of discourses, institutions, architectural forms, regulatory decisions, laws, administrative measures, scientific statements, philosophical, moral and philanthropic propositions – in short, the said as much as the unsaid. Such are the elements of the apparatus. The apparatus itself is the system of relations that can be established between these elements.
> *(Gordon, 1980: 194)*

We face again the conjunction of heterogeneous elements, an assemblage of actors, and, above all, the way in which they intertwine. Rather than defining a structure formed by a group of diverse pieces that fit together in a particular mode, it is about identifying the nature of the connection between those elements. The important part is the position that each element occupies in relation to the other and the transitoriness of that layout in an 'interplay of shifts of position' (Gordon, 1980: 195). It also should be pointed out that the *dispositif produces* and *is produced by* certain power–knowledge relations, which entail 'a certain manipulation of relations of forces, either developing them in a particular direction, blocking them, stabilising them, utilising them, etc.' (Gordon, 1980: 196). In this process, there is always a strategic function, that is, the *dispositif* is born to respond to 'an urgent need' (Gordon, 1980: 195). However, these are strategies that 'no one is there to have invented them, and few who can be said to have formulated them' (Foucault, 1990: 95). A *dispositif* may appear as a rational, coherent, and global strategy but is formed by multiple contradictory and dissimilar operations that oppose each other; it is intentional and, at the same time, non-subjective (Foucault, 1990: 95). As Latour notes, purpose is neither a property of humans nor of objects, but, precisely, it is an attribute of *dispositifs*, apparatuses, institutions, or, as we would like to suggest, assemblages:

> Purposeful action and intentionality may not be properties of objects, but they are not properties of humans either. They are the properties of institutions, of apparatuses, of what Foucault called dispositifs. Only corporate bodies are able to absorb the proliferation of mediators, to regulate their expression, to redistribute skills, to force boxes to blacken and close. Boeings 747 do not fly, airlines fly.
>
> *(Latour, 1999: 192–193)*

That is why Foucault spoke of a 'perpetual process of *strategic elaboration*' (Gordon, 1980: 195), or the way in which the *dispositif* can readjust itself in the presence of the contradictions and repercussions that stem from the different heterogeneous elements that emerge.

In video games, players' agency is delimited by the system – what they can see, say, and do – as in any other social interaction mediated by the *dispositifs* in which we live. Another question then, is to think that the system – *dispositif*, apparatus, or assemblage – has well defined contours: players are limited or enabled by the video game but also by the technology, the developers, other players, and many more social actors (human and not); some of them are close in time and space, others are acting at a distance (Latour, 1987: 219–232). This can be seen in how other agents are able to condition the player's agency, who, in some instances, feels that they are losing their ability to control the situation. This could be another person [...]:

> I like to play by myself and think by myself to see how I'm going to beat my opponent. But as soon as he looks around the shoulder, you think "Go away!", because he starts influencing the whole thing, which becomes quite annoying.
>
> *(Zelda)*

[…] the video game:

> Suddenly, something went wrong in the game. Then, you have to adapt, you can't control everything. So you have to make some decisions and adapt to those changes.
>
> *(Laura)*

[…] or even the Internet connection:

> But what really annoys me is actually the Internet that goes off. That annoys me most. […] The Internet went out and I couldn't do anything. Then when it finally reappeared I apparently lost [laughter]. […] I don't like it when I lose because of something beyond my control.
>
> *(Zelda)*

Thus, video games can be seen as devices that, at the same time, enable and condition the player's agency. Hence, we face a paradox that other theorists have previously found. For instance, Giddings (2009: 151) suggests that 'video game players are acted on as much as they act', and highlights the game event 'as one constituted by the playful translation of agency, the eccentric circuits of effect and affect, between human and non-human components'. There are also those who have approached this paradox by conceptualizing it in terms of balance (such as, Krzywinska, 2007) or even as an illusion: 'The illusion of interactivity sponsors a sense of agency – but this agency has been externally predetermined or pre-designed' (Charles, 2009: 286). Video games therefore offer a 'directed freedom' (Navarro-Remesal and García-Catalán, 2015). This apparent contradiction is perfectly summarized by Tulloch:

> The player is at the same time active agent and prisoner of the system, author of events, and slave to the game's authority, creative contributor and mindless automaton. Paradoxically, play is understood as being contingent upon both agency and compliance.
>
> *(Tulloch, 2014: 336)*

Nevertheless, Tulloch goes beyond this theoretical conundrum and offers a solution that tries to work around this trap. Drawing on Foucault's notion of power and agency, where both are (re)produced through each other instead of being in opposition, Tulloch (2014: 348) proposes that players' practices and expectations are 'shaped by the game, but at the same moment, the game only comes into being by their play'. Both are needed – along with other elements – in order to exist; they are part of the same productive force. Agency is thus constructed in that circulation of heterogeneous entities that are mutually influencing each other.

Agency and neoliberal political rationalities

We have seen so far what video games tell us about agency; as something that produces transformations in a multiple, distributed, and dislocated way. Video games help us to visualize the nature of agency in contemporary society as a post-human, assembled, and relational process. And they do this within *dispositifs*, apparatuses, and assemblages that regulate and give meaning to those transformations. However, a fundamental question is still pending: what are the political rationalities that define the contemporary *dispositifs* and the agency that they habilitate?

According to Miller and Rose (2008: 58), political rationalities can be understood as the regularities in the political discourse for 'the formulation and justification of idealized schemata for representing reality, analyzing it and rectifying it'. There are three main characteristics that define political rationalities (Miller and Rose, 2008: 58–59). First, political rationalities possess a moral form; they are based on principles that guide the tasks of government such as freedom, justice, equality, mutual responsibility, citizenship, common sense, economic efficiency, prosperity, growth, fairness, or rationality. Second, political rationalities have an epistemological character; they are articulated in relation to an idea of the nature of the objects governed, such as society, the nation, the population, or the economy. Third, political rationalities are expressed in a particular idiom; it is a language that works as an intellectual machinery for making reality thinkable under certain political deliberations. In sum, political rationalities are 'morally coloured, grounded upon knowledge, and made thinkable through language' (Miller and Rose, 2008: 59). In contemporary society, the hegemonic political rationalities are those associated with advanced-liberalism, or as it is more typically known, neo-liberalism.

Neoliberalism, McGuigan (2010: 117) suggests, 'is a truly hegemonic phenomenon of our time, concerning both political economy and ideological process in the broadest sense'. Neoliberalism is, at its core, concerned with *laissez-faire* economic policies and relations, which suggests that an open and free market that encourages competition offers the best model of economic success and prosperity for all. Neoliberalism was an idea and term first developed in the 1930s and 1940s, primarily as a response to growing concerns about the rise in totalitarian States, and how these were limiting individual expression and freedom. However, it is after the economic crises that gripped many Western nations in the mid- to late-1970s, that a neoliberalist agenda truly rose to prominence, replacing a more 'social-democratic' model that had dominated much of mid-twentieth century politics. In particular, this was most notably seen during the political reigns of Thatcher and Reagan in the UK and United States, respectively, which initiated widespread tax cuts for the rich, the undermining of union powers and rights, deregulation, privatization, and competition in the public sector (Monbiot, 2016).

Hence, in neoliberalism, the relationships between the public and private spheres are resignified as part of a progressive weakening of the State; what Gordon (1991: 36) calls 'modes of pluralization of modern government'. The power of the State is then devolved. The social and the question of governmentality do not exclusively rest on the so-called *L'Etat providence* (Donzelot, 2007: 176) anymore, but they rely on a network of agents that traverse it, transcend it, or appear in its periphery, such as sub- and supra-national organizations: NGOs, consultancy firms, think tanks, media networks, lobbies, and multinational corporations. It is a refocusing of the State's means of government, which uses the energy of those who are being governed. This creates a society of subjects responsible for their own government: 'Neoliberalism sees competition as the defining characteristic of human relations. It redefines citizens as consumers, whose democratic choices are best exercised by buying and selling, a process that rewards merit and punishes inefficiency' (Monbiot, 2016: online).

The powers of the State are then aimed at empowering entrepreneurial individuals capable of choosing for themselves. It is about 'turning the demand of sovereignty into a mandate of autonomy' (Donzelot, 2007: 177). This new post-Keynesian and post-Fordism reality requires self-regulated individuals, who can be defined as 'active, responsible, participative, and dynamic' (De Marinis, 2005: 25). It is the fundamental logic of neoliberalism in which citizens are governed through their 'freedom to choose' (Miller and Rose, 2008: 82). Thus, freedom and control, individual autonomy and government, are not opposing pairs; they are an inseparable part of a new formula of handling and defining realities. The discursive figures of freedom and control are, therefore, essential to understand agency in the context of advanced liberalism, which can be extended to the social universe that emerges around video games.

Control, freedom, and responsibility

Most representations of player's agency in video games revolve around the idea that they are the protagonist; the one in charge of manipulating the flow of what is happening on the screen. This leads to the common assumption in gaming cultures, also among our interviewees, that video games represent a (more) interactive cultural form:

> So reading is great, but reading, you're always an observer to it. Whereas in video games, it's the same story, however, you are not an observer anymore, you're actually in that story.
>
> *(Alfred, male, 26, strong identification as a gamer)*

According to this discourse, players do not merely observe, they are *in* the story, they belong to and are an operational part of the narrative and mechanical processes of video games. Video games force players to engage with them: 'to think that you are the one who is playing, what happens to the character is happening to you' (Patxi, male, 38, games developer and programmer). This is a generalized feeling among the vast majority of the interviewees, which leads them to claim that 'you almost feel you are the one who is inside the screen' (Iker, male, 43, an infrequent gamer). Definitely, video games foster this view in explicit (as in the series of titles we alluded to in the introduction, which are continuously reminding the player that their choices will have an impact on the story) and implicit ways (using different camera points of view, filling the screen with dozens of missions and elements to be discovered, or allowing various forms of character and game universe customization). The player is then 'pushed' to become the central agent in the system (whether this is true or not). Agency is a multiple and distributed transformation of reality, but also part of the politically mediated *dispositifs* of neoliberalism.

In this sense, the rhetoric of neoliberalist freedom is also the cornerstone of video games. Players often feel that video games enable them to act and go where they choose inside the universe of the game. As expressed by some of our research participants:):

> *Shadow of the Colossus*. It's a huge world but you only need to go from point A to point B. However, you have the freedom to ride with your horse. [...] And you say to yourself: 'I am free to explore this land'.
> (*Víctor, male, 27, a director of a documentary on video games*)

> *Grand Theft Auto*. It may be an adventure game but it offers you a lot of freedom. I play some of its missions but in the end I realize that, instead of doing what I'm supposed to do, I just grab a car and I start wandering around.
> (*Iker*)

This is the idea that is behind what it is known in the field of video games as 'open worlds'; which are not only linked to MMOGs such *World of Warcraft* (Blizzard Entertainment, 2004) or *Eve Online* (CCP Games, 2003), but also include works – related to a *sandbox* genre – like *Grand Theft Auto* or *The Elder Scrolls V: Skyrim* (Bethesda, 2011) with vast maps to explore and a non-linear gameplay, enabling and fostering emergent narratives. These games are based on the idea of giving freedom to players in order to explore the universe of the game and act without following a pre-established script, allowing players to choose what missions they want to accomplish and in which order, and flooding the story with secondary tasks and mini-games. *The Elder Scrolls*, *The Witcher*, *Grand Theft Auto*, *Assassin's Creed*, *Fallout*, and *Mass Effect* series are some of the paradigmatic examples of this approach that articulates the gameplay experience around the idea of free will, which is nothing else but the maximization of the principle that rhetorically governs every video game: player's freedom (even if that freedom just consists of moving a pad vertically on a screen).

Every time players decide to ignore the main story missions and freely walk in Liberty City or Tamriel (the realms of, respectively, *Grand Theft Auto* and *The Elders Scrolls* series), choose the next dialogue line that will define their relationship with other characters, or follow all those spots that inundate maps with the tasks to do, they are reproducing the idea of freedom that neoliberalism supports, where individuals are not 'merely free to choose, but obliged to be free, to understand and enact their lives in terms of choice' (Rose, 1999: 87). Following in Foucault's footsteps, Nikolas Rose (1999) reframes 'freedom', not as the opposite of power, but as its condition of possibility. There is no power without freedom – the possibility to choose – in the same way there is no freedom that has not been born in the tension of complex power relations. In Foucault's (2003: 139) words, there is needed a 'field of possibilities in which several kinds of conduct, several ways of reacting and modes of behaviour are available'. This obligation, we would suggest, is translated to the universe of video gaming, in the shape of a demand to have an influence:

> Looking at computer games, you can clearly see for example our demand for [...] the idea that we have an influence, that we have the option to interact.
> *(Emmett, male, 48, head of a video game museum)*

Video games are therefore not detached from the dominant political rationalities, rather video games are shaped by the existing social forces as much as they contribute to mould them. The option to interact, choose, and decide is fundamental:

> It's a video game because I can make decisions about what is happening. I mean, I can affect this world or this thing I'm interacting with.
> *(Javier, male, 32, game developer and programmer)*

This conceptualization of video game players puts them in the centre of the discussion on agency, which enables the recognition of players as the most important social actors here (something that, as we saw above, this text questions). It is not surprising then that a dominant discourse exists that focuses on how players are *in control* of the situation. Video games can only be defined as such if you, as the player, 'are in charge' and, in addition to that, 'control what is happening' (Víctor). In the end, 'video games are about making decisions' (Patxi, male, 38, games developer and programmer) and 'choosing your own path' (Karla Zimonka, female, 37, games developer and artist). In this sense, video games are clearly looking for active individuals; they are promoting the production of participative agents because otherwise the articulation of these two elements (video game players and video games) would not be possible:

> It's what makes it an active thing as opposed to a passive thing. You actually have to go off and do something to make something happen, or if nothing will, nothing will happen.
> *(Albert, male, 25, developer and game artist)*

This is paradigmatic of how an active subject is fundamental to understanding agency when it comes to video gaming. For example, Taylor (2006: 159) compares video gamers with social labourers that 'act as central productive agents in game culture'. She even goes further to suggest that 'there is no culture, there is no game, without the labour of the player' (Taylor, 2006: 159). This is a similar point of view offered by Egenfeldt-Nielsen *et al.* (2008: 138–139), who consider that video games demand players to explicitly interact with them; requiring 'the user to engage in play'. Moreover, the involvement of the player with the video game seems to be essential: 'it's really you who win and lose' (Kirby, 2009: 169). In this context, video games are about 'power fantasies' (Peter, 54, male, and lead of a video game-related Master's degree programme) and being in control:

> The reason why games like *Candy Crush* are very popular is because they give you a sense of control of daily life that you don't normally have. [...] Things are like they should be in your real life. Hard work is rewarded, you have control of it.
>
> *(Darius, male, 28, video game designer and developer)*

This, then, is neoliberalism *par excellence*, which casts players as powerful subjects, who are able to control the outcome of their actions in ways they could only imagine in their daily lives. As Oliva, Pérez-Latorre, and Besalú (2016: 12) argue, paratexts around video game culture (such as the text on case video game boxes) urge the player 'to "choose", "collect", "manage" and "win", defining what we should expect of a good game or a good player experience'. Video games create an environment (rhetorical but also material) where players' agency is inflated and promotes a sense of achievement and empowerment. In a more or less explicit way, video games facilitate the notion that players, if they are accomplished enough or try hard enough, are able to succeed and triumph:

> You always have to be kind to players. You want to make them feel that they are winning.
>
> *(George, male, 42, game developer and programmer)*

> There's sometimes quite subtle and sometimes really explicit message to do with empowerment. You can do it. You can do this.
>
> *(Robert, male, 47, and head of a video game-related exhibition)*

Video games produce the opportunities for these (perceived) narratives of success, where the player is the winner, and the one who can do whatever she or he chooses to do. It is the projection of an empowered and determined individual who can overcome any obstacle in their way. This representation of agency falls into the classic identification of human beings as conscious, active, and intentional subjects, which celebrates 'the emancipation of the rational or working subject' (Lyotard, 1984: xxiii) of modernity – a notion deeply anchored in the philosophical and political thinking of neoliberalism.

At an ontological level, this approach to agency ignores the idea of agency as multiple, distributed, and dislocated that we saw above. It maintains the dualism that divides those types of entities considered to be active (the human, the subject, the social) and those that are seen to be passive (the non-human, the object, nature) – as if agency was not, in fact, everywhere (Law, 2004: 131–134).

At a more sociopolitical level, this perspective reflects and reinforces the political rationalities of neoliberalism, in which one of its central axioms is the construction of an active, autonomous subject who takes care of themselves or, at most, participates with similar others in order to solve their own specific problems (Rose, 1999: 137–166). Hence, video game culture is generally traversed with this idea that players are responsible for controlling the game, and, moreover, are willing to do so:

> Typically I wouldn't read a guide or a walkthrough, because I'd like to be able to do it myself.
>
> *(Alfred)*

> When you play by yourself, you mainly want to get through the story, get through the game, and try and work it out. But you want to work it out by yourself rather than relying on other people.
>
> *(Zelda)*

If, according to the apparatuses in which they dwell, the condition of the possibility of video gamers' agency is their freedom to choose, then both their achievements and failures are their responsibility. Hence, although there are many of our interviewees who acknowledge that there are several moments in which they are at the mercy of the video games they play or other external factors, there is still a tendency to reintroduce the importance of the player as the agent who is capable of overcoming these obstacles, even though they may continue to fail:

> They are very vulnerable, you know, one hit gets them killed. It is kind of like they have no real power, because they're so fragile. When you as a player become more skilled in it, you understand that you have all the power, because you control these titans and you can kill them.
>
> *(Noel, male, 24, developer and programmer)*

For this developer, who is speaking of his video game (renowned for its high difficulty), the loss of agency, the fragility, and the sense of powerlessness are seen as temporary: the player has the ability to succeed, and if they fail, it is because of their lack of skill or because they did not invest enough time perfecting their skills. As Juul (2013: 7) has asserted in his essay on video gaming failure, video games 'promise us a fair chance of redeeming ourselves', which 'distinguishes game failure from failure in our regular lives'. However, even if video games are more explicit about the redemption opportunities they offer, we see there are similarities between failures in video games and in our regular lives. In a neoliberal society, individuals, or at most particular groups or communities, are to be held responsible for their own situation without considering any structural conditioning that might be affecting them. The rhetoric here, in video games, as it is in wider society, is that should they exert themselves, they will be able to achieve their goals, or else they will fail due to their own deficiencies or lack of effort.

Video games therefore require the player to take control of what they have in front of them – in a literal sense most of the time, since the player has to typically use a physical game controller – and are usually made accountable for both their achievements and failures. No matter if, as we have shown, video games, developers, or other agents, may severely condition video gamers' agency, it is widely established within video game culture that outcomes are primarily determined by the player. This is similar to what Shaw (2014: 13–39) found in the options video games offer in terms of representation. In principle, video games seem to propose different alternatives of representation; gamers are often given the freedom to choose between various characteristics, including race, gender, physical appearance, and at times, even sexuality. However, in the end, the video game is placing the burden of representation on the video gamers: 'rather than include diversity in games with set characters, most representation of marginalized groups and identifiers is placed in the hands of players' (Shaw, 2014: 35).

Neoliberalism, after all, seeks to 'govern using the maximum amount of energy available from the people who are to be governed' (De Marinis, 2005: 22). This is something we repeatedly see in video games; the individual is understood as 'the entrepreneur of himself or herself' (Gordon, 1991: 44). The promotion of active, self-responsible, and participative individuals, then, cannot solely be reduced to a disposition in some subcultural forms, but rather it is connected to wider tendencies that affect society as a whole.

Beyond neoliberal political rationalities: participatory culture

So far, we have seen how agency in video games is mainly governed by neoliberal political rationalities. In this sense, freedom and interactivity are enclosed in a context that promotes them in a fashion that does not let agency break the hegemonic discourses, practices, and systems. According to Brookey and Booth (2006: 218), in most video games, 'the player is not given the agency to change the game's structure and design', and therefore limitations are imposed on the choices available to players, which 'not always allow for the kinds of changes that could be equated with ideological resistance'.

However, because these neoliberal rationalities foster the ideal of the autonomous self-governed subject, they are also creating the opportunity for agency to produce lines of breakage. Neoliberalism has been very successful in giving choices to individuals, and making them responsible for the decisions they make. But, it could be said, that the forces of neoliberalism have been so successful that they have planted the seed of its partial demise. Its rationalities have promoted so feverishly individual freedom and self-responsibility that they have created a largely autonomous subject, one that, to a certain extent, may be able to escape its rationalities. After all, Deleuze (1990: 165) considered that every *dispositif* had two sets of groups: 'lines of stratification or sedimentation and lines leading to the present day or creativity'. The latter includes among them the lines of 'splitting, breakage, fracture' (Deluze, 1990: 162); those that outline the movement from one *dispositif* to another (Deluze, 1990: 161). This points to the possibility of breaking the system; like when people look for glitches in video games, and ways to exploit them.

Moreover, there are those who argue that the rise in new digital technologies, far from facilitating and enabling an increasingly individualized society, has provided new tools and forms of communication and collaboration. In particular, Henry Jenkins (such as, for example in Jenkins, 2006; Jenkins *et al.*, 2005) argues that new media technologies, like the Internet and video games, along with associated changes in the nature of audiences, have led to a more collective, collaborative, and 'participatory culture'.

Participatory culture is understood as the culture that 'absorbs and responds to the explosion of new media technologies that make it possible for average consumers to archive, annotate, appropriate, and recirculate media content in powerful new ways' (Jenkins *et al.*, 2005: 8). In the report entitled *Confronting the Challenges of Participatory Culture: Media Education for the 21st Century*, written for The MacArthur Foundation, Jenkins *et al.* (2005: 7) defined participatory culture as follows:

> For the moment, let's define participatory culture as one: 1. With relatively low barriers to artistic expression and civic engagement 2. With strong support for creating and sharing one's creations with others 3. With some type of informal mentorship whereby what is known by the most experienced is passed along to novices 4. Where members believe that their contributions matter 5. Where members feel some degree of social connection with one another (at the least they care what other people think about what they have created).

The key idea of participatory culture revolves around the open possibility of anyone making a significant contribution to all sorts of collective cultural expressions. Hence, the authors here are describing a culture that makes production accessible to large parts of the population, in which the collaboration and interdependency between social actors is crucial for producing outcomes and the sustainability of this culture. According to these authors, all contributions are seen and experienced as relevant, allowing new ways to collaborate and participate beyond consumerism, as Emmet – one of our interviewees – suggests in relation to video games:

> We are living in a mass society and we are mainly treated as consumers and I think computer games and their popularity shows that there are other belongings and wishes in us. One of the strongest you can see in computer games is that we also like to participate again and not only to consume and not only to become an object.

It is important to highlight that not 'every member must contribute, but all must believe they are free to contribute when ready and that what they contribute will be appropriately valued' (Jenkins *et al.*, 2005: 7).

For Jenkins (2006: 2) 'participatory culture is anything but fringe or underground today'. Jenkins goes even further, implying that there is a change of paradigm within the interactions of media content, where '[consumption] becomes production; reading becomes writing; spectator culture becomes participatory culture' (Jenkins, 2006: 60). Jenkins' earlier work (most notably, Jenkins, 1992) emphasized fans as at the vanguard of a participatory culture. While ordinary audiences were typically happy to passively consume mainstream content, fans actively took from media texts and narratives to create their own stories or artwork. Jenkins (1992), drawing on the work of Michel de Certeau (1984), referred to this as 'textual poaching'. However, Jenkins in his later work suggests there has been a major cultural transformation, shifting from a culture previously dominated by a mainstream passive audience of consumers, to a current more active culture where the boundaries between production and consumption start to blur. For Jenkins, active participation becomes the dominant form of media engagement. Gere (2008: 213) makes a similar argument, emphasizing the important role of new technologies in transforming the relationship between consumers and producers:

> The transformations in the media brought about by new technologies are transforming how we think about ourselves. In particular we are no longer passive consumers of the media, but, increasingly, also actively producers.

In this sense, participatory culture and digital technology also transform the traditional ways cultural content is created from an economic point of view; such as, the rise of crowdfunding platforms like *Kickstarter* give birth to figures like the 'prosumer-investor' (Planells, 2015). However, for Jenkins, this process is not necessarily just top down. For Jenkins, the rise in participatory culture has been brought about by three key interrelated processes. First, there is the advent of new technologies and tools, such as the Internet, which 'enable consumers to archive, annotate, appropriate, and recirculate media content' (Jenkins, 2006: 135). Second, 'horizontally integrated media conglomerates encourage the flow of images, ideas, and narratives across multiple media channels and demand more active modes of spectatorship' (Jenkins, 2006: 136). Here, Jenkins is referring to the rise of 'transmedia', where media narratives increasingly crosscut, and sometimes require engagement with, different media forms. For Jenkins, transmedia requires the existence of a more active consumer, who will seek out and actively engage with narratives across a variety of media texts and forms. Hence, third, the rise of participatory culture is also the result of the changing nature of contemporary audiences. In particular, Jenkins suggests there has been a rise of a number of subcultures that promote Do-It-Yourself (DIY) media production, such as video game modders or Internet bloggers. These subcultures help initiate a more active and participatory form of media consumption, but in recent years this mode of engagement has spread from the margins to the mainstream.

These then are the basis of participatory culture; the series of events that unchained the new paradigm. The first trend refers to new technologies as enabling devices that make it possible for social actors to manipulate media content in ways previously not seen. Essentially, Jenkins points to the digital revolution that facilitates all those operations: easier forms of storing, commenting, appropriating, changing, and disseminating content. The second and third trends are linked to specific transformations directed at a more active disposition towards media content, changing the hierarchies between production and consumption, while making both categories more interrelated and problematic. The notion of authorship is challenged, giving way to 'multiple authorship' (Kirby, 2009: 1).

In particular, video games are for Jenkins one of the key examples and drivers of this participatory culture, which includes the production of walkthroughs, mods, fan art and fiction, new games, websites, hacks, game guides, reviews, interpretations, wikis, cosplaying, and a considerable list of other examples, which recognizes 'video gaming is so much more than simply the interaction of one or a few individuals with a video game machine' (Crawford, 2012: 120). Similarly, Dovey and Kennedy (2006: 123–124) consider video game cultures as 'empirical evidence into the shifting relationships between media producers and consumers at the beginning of the twenty-first century'. In particular, this is the central argument of James Newman's (2008) book *Playing with Videogames*; that gaming culture is a participatory culture, which extends far beyond the act of playing the video game:

> In this book, I hope to build on some of the emerging work on gaming fan cultures and practices [...] by highlighting the inherent creativity, productivity and sociality of these wider videogame cultures. The investigation of gamers' artistic and literary production, the creation of walkthroughs and FAQ texts, the modification of existing games and the development of entirely new games, speaks clearly of the complexity of engagements with videogames and the ways games are reconfigured to increase their life-span.
>
> *(Newman, 2008: 14)*

Newman is here giving a hint as to where to look for this participatory culture in video games: walkthroughs, modding, fan art and fiction, derivative creations, intertextuality, new games. His book is then divided into three main parts; each one exploring one aspect of these participative cultures and the practices of video gamers.

The first part of Newman's (2008: 21–88) book is dedicated to the textual qualities of video games, and explores how video gamers, far from being solitary individuals, share and construct collective experiences (see Chapter 4) about video games in different ways: talking (in-game and out-game conversations, on forums, discussion boards, and through comments in video game magazines), reading and writing (official novelizations, reviews, fan fictions), and performing (fan art, music interpretation, cosplay). In particular, in relation to this, one of our research participants, Zelda, explains how she occasionally cosplays along with other video game and anime enthusiasts: 'they [cosplayers] have a community online, they've got a Facebook group, and we all go online and collaborate [...] and try to get people to do different characters, rather than the same one, then we get a group photo of everyone'. Participatory culture fosters then an agency that is collectively articulated and, most typically, digitally mediated.

In the second part, Newman (2008: 89–148) explores the ludic aspects of video games. Among them, he considers the production of game guides, walkthroughs, and FAQs. These texts, he suggests, are aimed at encouraging new styles of engagement with video games, and the possibility of even regulating the way video games are played (2008: 93). For example, some of our interviewees spoke about searching for video tutorials on how to progress in a game:

> Then it's figuring out the quickest way of [...] then at that point if you don't know how to do it [...] just start looking up tutorials, watching a few videos on YouTube to figure out how to do it.
>
> *(Albert)*

Participatory culture enables an agency that is oriented to sharing knowledge, know-how, and information with others. If the neoliberal narrative on agency focuses on personal growth and individual success, participatory culture is seen to benefit group dynamics. In this sense, video game culture has the potential to direct agency towards forms of collective collaboration that, even though it might reproduce some of the celebratory aspects of the liberal rationale and the free individual who must take care of themselves, represents a way to extend the agency of video gamers in a more solidary way.

In the third part of his book, Newman (2008: 149–178) focuses on video games as technology, dealing with 'the ways in which gamers may modify the actual program itself' (2008: 151). There are the three main practices described by Newman here: *codemining, modding*, and *gamemaking*. In codemining, video gamers try to unveil hidden or redundant elements of the game, which were present in earlier iterations, but can still be found in the code. This then, presents an opportunity for the gamers to peer into how the game could have been, in order to extend its possibilities and its experience. Next, modding is where users modify existing games at different levels: from simple graphic enhancements to complete modifications of the game, resulting in some cases in totally new gamemaking. Here, Newman (2008: 167) argues, that even if just a minority have the technical knowledge to directly manipulate and modify the code and assets of a video game, 'the outputs of these endeavours exist within, and even help to create and sustain, the wider cultures, communities and rich contexts for criticism, review and gameplay'. In sum, then, Newman argues that this participatory culture contributes to maintaining an active and supportive community, not only for those who actively mod, codemine, or make games, but for the wider gamer community as well; as Alfred argues in relation to large-scale beta testing campaigns:

> But even if you're not actually interacting with the community, you're still benefitting from the community. [...] *Football Manager*, for example, do a beta testing. When you need to test something in a business, you get one or two people to test it. When you want to get a computer game to test something,

you give ten thousand of your fans the chance to play it for free and pick holes in it. Whoever plays that finished game, offline, without ever interacting with anyone else in the community, they benefit from mass testing on a scale I can't off the top my head compare.

Additionally, we would like to add that the availability of tools for developing games, without almost any programming abilities, such as *Game Maker, Construct 2, Rpg Maker, Stencil* and many others, have democratized the possibility of creating video games for the general public. Some of them may become even commercially successful games, while others will become part of the pool of products that may only ever be played by the person who made them. However, Aphra Kerr (2006: 123) warns about assuming that all gamers engage with a wider gamer community, or that the actions of a few, give any significant power to video gamers:

> While modding, cheating and artistic interventions are part of the wider game culture and provide interesting examples of player creativity and agency, it might be unwise to overstate their prevalence. For many game players game playing is a 'private' activity which takes place in the home with friends and family, or alone when there is nothing better to do. Many are content to keep trying until they succeed in overcoming an obstacle or to ask friends for advice rather than buying strategy guides or going online to look for hints.

It is also important to highlight that many use the potentialities of participatory culture to engage in far less positive and supportive actions, like harassment and abuse, such as the actions described by Mortensen (2016: 13–14) in the case of gamergate (see Chapter 6). This then, clearly highlights the limitations of ideas of productive agency. As, in the case of gamergate, this is collectively coordinated agency, multiplied and widened by digital technologies, but used in a destructive way.

However, whether we should praise the apparent endless possibilities of participatory culture for video gamers, or contain our celebratory fervour, and highlight the potential limits, or even dangers, of a participatory culture is not necessarily our focus here – and certainly, we can point to some of our other work where we have been far more challenging of the (largely positive) assumptions often associated with participatory culture (see for example, Crawford, 2012). What we wish to highlight here, is that all of these activities are part of a wider video game culture; one that is gradually becoming a fundamental aspect of our contemporary society and is changing the way we act collectively. Agency acts within neoliberalism, but this can at times be within more supportive and caring rationalities; of course, not always.

Conclusions

In this text, we have explored agency in video game culture. The obsession of the medium with offering an experience of freewill, difficult choices, actions with consequences, and a generalized discourse about the centrality of the video game player, leads us to argue that studying video games and their culture constitutes an optimal field in which to approach questions related to the contemporary nature of agency, interactivity, political rationalities, freedom, and power.

In particular, the rich variety of actors in video game culture leads us to question traditional ideas of agency, as we are dealing nowadays with more complex networks of actors, interactions, and power than before. Video games contribute to subverting the received theoretical status of agency, and indicate how it has changed over the last decades and how we need new approaches to it. Video game culture is proof of an ontologically promiscuous notion of agency that requires new epistemological lenses; new lenses that help us blur the generic face of humanity as a modernist figure and reconfigure it in the frame of a post-humanist landscape (Haraway, 2004: 47).

Similarly, video games show us that, today, agency is, at the same time, part of both emancipatory and alienating practices. Not only is agency linked to freedom, empowerment, and autonomy, but it is also connected to submission, disempowerment, and dependency. Limitations and potentialities are both part of the same uses of agency. The Foucauldian *dispositif* explains this duality, as Poltronieri (2015: 174) has noted: 'The player is free to take action to reach desired results as long as these actions are codified in the interior of the apparatus'. The *dispositif* limits and allows all that can be seen, said, and done within a regime of truth, but, as it is necessarily reproduced through the generative force of agency, it contains the potentiality to break itself and produce new ones. Video games and the agency they promote might be part of the current neoliberal rationalities, but they carry the promise of new creative and critical modes of agency.

Therefore, we have here a notion of agency linked to neoliberalism, but this incorporates not only the reproduction of its rationalities, reinforcing liberal thinking and practices, but also the possibilities of rupture, and exploring new modes of power relations and agency that help transform reality in other more communitarian ways. Agency is the force that transforms reality, but it must be enacted and, in that enactment, agency is also transformed. Video games mediate agency and propel it through the social fabric in different directions and under different rationalities. Video games assemblages contain powerful agencies that could transform, and are currently transforming, social reality.

References

Arsenault, Dominic and Perron, Bernard (2009). 'In the Frame of the Magic Circle: The Circle(s) of Gameplay', in Wolf, Mark J. and Perron, Bernard (editors). *The Video Game Theory Reader 2*. London: Routledge, 109–131.

Brookey, Robert Alan and Booth, Paul (2006). 'Restricted Play. Synergy and the Limits of Interactivity in the Lord of the Rings: The Return of the King Video Game', *Games and Culture*, 1 (3): 214–230.

Calleja, Gordon (2011). *In-Game: From Immersion to Incorporation*. Cambridge, MA: MIT Press.

Charles, Alec (2009). 'Playing with One's Self: Notions of Subjectivity and Agency in Digital Games', *Eludamos*, 3 (2): 291–284. [http://www.eludamos.org/index.php/eludamos/article/view/vol3no2-10/140] [Last accessed 07/11/2016].
Crawford, Garry (2012). *Video Gamers*. London: Routledge.
De Marinis, Pablo (2005). '16 comentarios sobre la(s) sociología(s) y la(s) comunidad(es)', *Papeles del CEIC*, (15): 1–39. [http://www.ehu.eus/ojs/index.php/papelesCEIC/article/view/12103/11025] [Last accessed: 19/04/2015].
De Certeau, Michel (1984). *The Practice of Everyday Life*. Berkeley: University of California Press.
Debord, Guy (1995). *The Society of the Spectacle*. New York: Zone Books.
Deleuze, Gilles (1990). 'What is a Dispositif?', in Armstrong, Timothy J. (editor). *Michel Foucault Philosopher*. New York: Routledge, 159–168.
Donzelot, Jacques (2007). *La invención de lo social* [The Promotion of the Social]. Buenos Aires: Nueva Visión.
Dovey, Jon and Kennedy, Helen W. (2006). *Game Cultures. Computer Games as New Media*. Maidenhead: Open University Press.
Egenfeldt-Nielsen, Simon; Smith, Jonas Heide; Pajares Tosca, Susana (2008). *Understanding Video Games: The Essential Introduction*. New York: Routledge.
Foucault, Michel (1990). *The History of Sexuality, Vol. 1: An Introduction*. New York: Vintage Books.
Foucault, Michel (1995). *Discipline and Punish: The Birth of the Prison*. New York: Vintage Books.
Foucault, Michel (2003). 'The Subject and Power' in Rabinow, Paul and Rose, Nikolas (editors). *The Essential Foucault*. New York: The New Press, 126–144.
García Selgas, Fernando J. (2007). *Sobre la fluidez social. Elementos para una cartografía*. Madrid: CIS.
Gere, Charlie (2008). *Digital Culture*. London: Reaktion Books.
Giddings, Seth (2009). 'Events and Collusions. A Glossary for the Microethnography of Video Game Play', *Games and Culture*, 4 (2): 144–157.
Gordon, Colin (1980). *Power/Knowledge. Selected Interviews & Other Writings. 1972–1977. Michel Foucault*. New York: Pantheon Books.
Gordon, Colin (1991). 'Governmental Rationality: An Introduction' in Burchell, Graham; Gordon, Colin; Miller, Peter (editors). *The Foucault Effect. Studies in Governmentality*. Chicago: Chicago University Press, 1–51.
Haraway, Donna (2004). *The Haraway Reader*. New York: Routledge.
Jameson, Frederic (1991). *Postmodernism, Or, The Cultural Logic of Late Capitalism*. Durham, North Carolina: Duke University Press.
Jenkins, Henry (1992). *Textual Poachers*. Routledge: London.
Jenkins, Henry (2006). *Fans, Bloggers, and Gamers. Exploring Participatory Culture*. New York: New York University Press.
Jenkins, Henry; Purushotma, Ravi; Clinton, Katherine; Weigel, Margaret; Robison, Alice J. (2005). *Confronting the Challenges of Participatory Culture: Media Education for the 21st Century*. Chicago: MacArthur Foundation.
Juul, Jesper (2013). *The Art of Failure*. Cambridge, MA: MIT Press.
Kerr, Aphra (2006). *The Business and Culture of Digital Games. Gamework/Gameplay*. London: Sage.
Kirby, Alan (2009). *Digimodernism*. New York: Continuum.
Krzywinska, Tanya (2007). 'Being a Determined Agent in (the) World of Warcraft: Text/Play/Identity', in Atkins, Barry and Krzywinska, Tanya (editors). *Videogame, Player, Text*. Manchester: Manchester University Press, 101–119.

Latour, Bruno (1987). *Science in Action*. Cambridge, MA: Harvard University Press.
Latour, Bruno (1999a). *Pandora's Hope. Essays on the Reality of Science Studies*. Cambridge, MA: Harvard University Press.
Latour, Bruno (1999b). 'On recalling ANT', in Law, John and Hassard, John. *Actor-Network Theory and After*. Oxford: Blackwell, 15–25.
Latour, Bruno (2007). *Reassembling the Social. An Introduction to Actor-Network-Theory*. Oxford: Oxford University Press.
Law, John (2004). *After Method. Mess in Social Science Research*. London: Routledge.
Lyotard, Jean-François (1984). *The Postmodern Condition*. Minneapolis, MN: The University of Minnesota Press.
McGuigan, Jim (2010). *Cultural Analysis*, London: Sage.
Miller, Peter and Rose, Nikolas (2008). *Governing the Present. Administering Economic, Social and Personal Life*. Cambridge: Polity Press.
Millington, Brad (2009). 'Wii has Never been Modern: "Active" Video Games and the "Conduct of Conduct"', *New Media Society*, 11 (4): 621–640.
Monbiot, George (2016). 'Neoliberalism – the Ideology at the Root of All Our Problems', *The Guardian*, [https://www.theguardian.com/books/2016/apr/15/neoliberalism-ideology-problem-george-monbiot] [Last Accessed: 29/07/2017].
Mortensen, Torill Elvira (2016). 'Anger, Fear, and Games: The Long Event of #GamerGate', *Games and Culture*, DOI:10.1177/1555412016640408.
Muriel, Daniel (2016). 'Toward a Sociology of Mediations: Impressionist Mapping and Some (Brief) Rules for a Sociological Method', *REIS*, (153): 111–126.
Navarro-Remesal, Víctor and García-Catalán, Shaila (2015). 'Let's Play Master and Servant: BDSM and Directed Freedom in Game Design', in Wysocki, M. and Lauteria, E. W. (editors). *Rated M for Mature*. London: Bloomsbury, 119–132.
Newman, James (2008). *Playing with Videogames*. London: Routledge.
Oliva, Mercè; Pérez-Latorre, Óliver; Reinald, Besalú (2016). '"Choose, Collect, Manage, Win!": Neoliberalism, Enterprising Culture and Risk Society in Video Game Covers', *Convergence*, DOI:10.1177/1354856516680324.
Planells, Antonio José (2015). 'Video Games and the Crowdfunding Ideology: From the Gamer-Buyer to the Prosumer-investor', *Journal of Consumer Culture*, DOI:https://doi.org/10.1177/1469540515611200.
Poltronieri, Fabrizio (2015). 'Communicology, Apparatus, and Post-history: Vilém Flusser's Concepts Applied to Video Games and Gamification', in Fuchs, Mathias; Fizek, Sonia; Ruffino, Paolo; Schrape, Niklas (editors). *Rethinking Gamification*. Lüneburg: Meson Press.
Rose, Nikolas (1999). *Powers of Freedom. Reframing Political Thought*. Cambridge: Cambridge University Press.
Shaw, Adrienne (2014). *Gaming at the Edge*. Minneapolis, MN: University of Minnesota Press.
Taylor, T. L. (2006). *Play between Worlds: Exploring Online Game Culture*. Cambridge, MA: MIT Press.
Taylor, T. L. (2009). 'The Assemblage of Play', *Games and Culture*, 4 (4): 331–339.
Thornham, Helen (2011). *Ethnographies of the Videogame. Gender, Narrative and Praxis*. Surrey: Ashgate.
Tulloch, Rowan (2014). 'The Construction of Play: Rules, Restrictions, and the Repressive Hypothesis', *Games and Culture*, 9 (5): 335–350.

Ludography

11 bit studios (2014). *This War of Mine*.
Bethesda (1994–to date). *The Elder Scrolls* series.

Bethesda (2011). *The Elder Scrolls V: Skyrim*.
BioWare (2007–to date). *Mass Effect*.
Blizzard Entertainment (2004). *World of Warcraft*.
CCP Games (2003). *Eve Online*.
CD Projekt RED (2007-to date). *The Witcher* series.
Creative Assembly (2014). *Alien: Isolation*.
Dontnod Entertainment (2015). *Life is Strange*.
Frictional Games (2010). *Amnesia*.
FromSoftware (2011–2016). *Dark Souls* series.
Interplay; Black Isle Studios; Bethesda; Obsidian (1997–to date). *Fallout* series.
Quantic Dream (2010). *Heavy Rain*.
Quantic Dream (2013). *Beyond: Two Souls*.
Quantic Dream (2018). *Detroit: Become Human*.
Red Barrel Studios (2013). *Outlast*.
Red Thread Games (2014). *Dreamfall Chapters*.
Rockstar Games (1997–to date). *Grand Theft Auto* series.
Supermassive Games (2015). *Until Dawn*.
Telltale Games (2012–to date). *The Walking Dead* series.
Telltale Games (2013). *The Wolf Among Us*.
Telltale Games (2014). *Game of Thrones*.
Telltale Games (2014). *Tales from the Borderlands*.
Telltale Games (2016). *Batman: The Telltale Series*.
Ubisoft (2007–to date). *Assassin's Creed* series.

4
VIDEO GAMES AS EXPERIENCE

Introduction

When we asked our research participants to define video games, most of them spoke typically about interactivity, entertainment, fun, enjoyment, simulation, or directly alluded to any kind of game that is technologically mediated. However, we also found – partially unexpectedly – that they often defined video games *as* experiences. For example, Marta, a 24-year-old, dedicated video gamer, considers that 'after all, video games are like any other experience', while Albert, a 25-year-old, indie game artist, speaks of them as being 'an enjoyable experience'. After initially conceptualizing video games as a form of media, where there is an interaction between the player and the programme, Carl, a 28-year-old, dedicated, and self-identifying video gamer, concludes that not only are video games a recognized form of art, they are also 'an experience of life'.

The categorization of video games as a form of 'experience' is, to some extent, identified and explored by some game scholars. Katie Salen and Eric Zimmerman's *Rules of Play* is, for instance, mainly about designing experiences for players by 'understanding how a game's formal system transforms into an experiential one' (Salen and Zimmerman, 2004: 316). Experience is a key notion in their definition of video games; which stresses that a games designer does not create technology but rather 'an experience' (Salen and Zimmerman, 2004: 87). Salen and Zimmerman are therefore directly equating video games to experiences; assuming that playing a video game is to have a particular experience.

Furthermore, Ian Bogost (2007: 35) suggests that the representations of reality that video games involve, though not identical to what we could consider as an 'actual experience', are still capable of simulating 'real or imagined physical and cultural processes'. Moreover, the interactivity of video games, he suggests, could locate them towards the very top of a scale of experience 'vividness'. Drawing on the psychologist Charles Hill (2004) and his continuum of vividness, which sets out a scale that ranges from the least vivid information (statistics) to the most vivid one (actual experience), Bogost (2007: 34-35) situates video games right under *actual experience* and above *moving images with sound* (which occupies the second spot in Hill's list). Although, we would suggest, defining *actual experience* is highly problematic, not to mention the very idea of vividness, Bogost seems to reach a plausible conclusion: that video games are a kind of experience similar, but not equal, to what we could call, in the absence of a better expression, a 'real life experience'. Similarly, Grodal (2003: 129) argues that video games 'are simulations of basic modes of real-life experiences'.

Interpreting video games as experiences opens up a vast field of theoretical and practical possibilities, and plays a central role in discerning the different aspects – material, symbolic, political, and social – that constitute video games as culture. When we deem video games to be experiences, we are on the one hand describing part of their fundamental properties and mechanisms of functioning, while on the other, we are connecting it with wider social issues – the construction of social reality as a set of designed experiences, and a series of epistemological concerns drawing on a 'postphenomenological' approach (Ihde, 1993). The concept of 'postphenomenology', and its value in developing our thesis here, will be elaborated further; however, put simply, while phenomenological approaches tend to centre on the individual, postphenomenology extends out and beyond the individual, such as to understand 'how humans, their worlds, and technologies are all necessary and active parts of each other' (Keogh, 2014: 13). As we will see in the following chapters, this has unforeseen, yet interesting, consequences, and most notably, how we can see video games as mediating tools that connect with 'other' (usually distant and unknown) realities (Chapter 5), and the emergence of post-identity, and the changing nature of community (Chapter 6).

Therefore, different actors that belong to video game culture, including academics, video gamers, media professionals, and people working in the industry, express that when they are studying, playing, writing about, and designing video games, they are doing it, mostly, in terms of *experience*. But how can we say that video games are experiences? There are at least six relevant reasons why video games can be associated with the notion of experience, which will be developed in this chapter – as well as how these point to the explanatory possibilities that this concept has for understanding crucial aspects of our societies. First, thanks to a process of 'experience translation', video games help to canalize different experiences in order to connect with other realities that might be (partially) unknown to us. Second, we often find experiences in video games being recounted in a similar fashion to how we would narrate a trip, an anecdote, and any other lived experience. Third, video games often require the player to actively participate in the gaming process – enhancing the sense of this as a lived experience. Fourth, video games are undoubtedly embodied experiences, which in turn, pose numerous questions about our encounters with technology and virtual spaces. Fifth, video games are linked to a wider social tendency that sees reality in terms of a set of experiences.

Hence, finally, video games are also helpful to shed light on our understanding of the notion of experience in a wider social context. The chapter then considers two paradoxes. First, how: on the one hand, the dilemma of the experience that is, at the same time, individual, unique, and contingent, but on the other, also collective, shared, and stable. Second, and partially as a consequence of the first paradox, we are faced with the postphenomenological nature of experience, particularly evident in video games, which situates the idea of experience beyond its traditional phenomenological frame.

Translating experiences

It is a commonly held assumption that video games allow players to access experiences that they would not have otherwise. A lot of our interviewees expressed, in one way or another, that video games give them all sorts of experiences that otherwise would be unattainable. An example of this can be illustrated by how George (male, 42, developer), who was involved in the development of a renowned franchise of racing video games, wanted players to have a good time by letting them experience 'what it would feel like to be driving a Ferrari'. We also have the testimony of Laura, a 26-year-old indie developer, speaking of one of her video games as an 'experience that may change you' to the point of making the player say, 'bloody hell, this game has broken my mind, it's amazing'. In a similar vein, Pawel Miechowski spoke of *This War of Mine* (11 bit studios, 2014) as 'an eye opener'; because feedback from the gaming community who played it told them that it was 'a very emotional experience'. Furthermore, in Pawel's words, there were veterans of war who found the game to be a 'clearing experience, a cathartic one'. This illustrates how video games can work at an experiential level, something that players seem to seek – as Shaw (2014: 87) noted during her research on marginalized gaming cultures: 'For many interviewees, connecting to media characters was about experiences more than anything else'.

Video games push players into the shoes of others, allowing them to experience the world from their perspective. However, players are not exactly experiencing what others feel or what it means to be in a specific situation, after all, video gaming is a mediated experience, not the experience itself; but it lets players at least connect with other realities in different ways. This degree of the connection varies: players might identify or not with the characters and the situation, and they might connect at an emotional or cognitive level (or possibly both); the important thing is that the connection is established and, in doing so, it makes the access to other points of view possible and facilitates an understanding of distant situations. This idea of video games offering the possibility of having a diverse range of experiences, and, in particular, fostering empathetic responses, will be more thoroughly explored in Chapter 5, which will focus on processes that facilitate the connection between a player and a (more or less) distant reality; however, here, in this section, we wish to focus on the process of translating 'real live experiences' into 'video game experiences'.

Video games as experience **87**

FIGURE 4.1 A 'Very long phase' in *Gone Home* (Fulbright, 2013).

According to Salen and Zimmerman (2004: 316), creating great experiences for players 'requires understanding how a game's formal system transforms into an experiential one'. Therefore, once it is possible to establish, at least hypothetically, that video games are able to offer diverse experiences to players, the question arises: How do they do it? How do they channel these various and rich experiences to those who are going to engage with them? The answer to these questions relies on the process of translation that turns specific experiences into gaming experiences.

Focusing on one of the titles we considered more closely, *Gone Home* (Fulbright, 2013), we noted how the games designers use personal interviews as a method to 'get personal experiences' (Karla Zimonja, female, 37, co-founder of Fulbright, and a game artist) in order to employ them as part of the story and as a way to 'make the story authentic'. In particular, they approached other people to gather an array of related life experiences, to ensure they captured appropriately their experiences and were well positioned to *dump* that experience into the game.

This approach can be illustrated with one segment of the game in which the player recovers a part of Sam's diary, your little sister in the game who has a leading role in the story, where she writes about the row she had with her parents when they suspect she is in a lesbian relationship with Lonnie, Sam's new friend. The fragment, which is also read out loud like all diary fragments in the game (see Figure 4.1), enumerates the different forms of denial that the parents are able to articulate in relation to their daughter's sexuality, such as 'you're too young to know what you want', 'you and Lonnie are just good friends', 'you just haven't met the right boy', and 'it's a phase'. Karla Zimonja explained how they used the experience of one of the people they knew when she came out to her parents:

> She had a not-great experience coming out to her parents and a lot of her specific retelling of what her parents said was so instructive. We tried to

88 Video games as experience

>ground what we were writing in that, in those lived experiences. I mean, it's very important to go and do your research when you're depicting something that is not something that you went through yourself.

Even if the experience that the developers are trying to reproduce in a video game is not directly known to them, they attempt to overcome those limitations by feeding on other people's experiences; they are gatherers of experiences, using them as raw material for their own designed gaming experiences. We find another similar example in *This War of Mine*, where, in spite of the fact that none of the developers were ever in a context of war, they constructed the context of the game by using, principally, repositories of war experiences of the siege of Sarajevo as documented in the FAMA Collection.[1] In Pawel Miechowski's words, this archive is like 'a virtual museum, with video interviews with different people from Sarajevo and there are literally thousand video interviews', which they drew heavily on in order to (re)create elements of these experiences in their game.

Similarly, in *Life is Strange* (Dontnod Entertainment, 2015), there is a phase in the game that depicts the situation of a quadriplegic person and her family. In this, we are witnesses to how she lives, her health and mobility problems, her family's emotional impact, and their financial problems, among other everyday circumstances. At some point, you are asked to help her to die. This very intense moment, which revolves around people with severe disabilities and euthanasia, was also an experience that the developers tried to ground in peoples' lived experiences. In an interview, Raoul Barbet, game director of *Life is Strange*, refers to this particular moment in the game, and how they 'put a lot of research into that', in the same way they 'did into all of the themes the game addresses'. He also adds:

>It was important to treat it with respect and show that we're accurate with the subject. We studied specialized home equipment, read blogs by disabled people, and asked them what their setup was at home. One of the designers on the game has had some family issues like we present in the game, at that moment, but we have to be careful as developers and creators to not make the subject too game-y. That could be seen as not respectful, and we really want to talk about the subject and sometimes put the player in a really difficult position, and have them think about this.
>
>*(Barbet as cited in Diver, 2016)*

Video games consist of a transposition of experiences that are transformed, mediated, and adapted to a different medium with the aim of creating new experiences. For this reason, Robert, the 47-year-old head of a video game museum, believes that encouraging a wider range of voices, than those typically seen, with 'different life experiences' would enrich and diversify the gaming culture, becoming 'more representative of the world'. It is about capturing a more diverse pool of experiences, because this will result in new mediated experiences. Video games are, in this sense, experiences of experiences.

Narrating experiences

When Víctor Somoza, director of the 2014 documentary on video games *Memorias: Más allá del juego*[2] (which translates into English as *Memories: Beyond the Game*), speaks about how they ended up with the final title for their film, he is clearly situating video games in the field of experiences, and moreover, narrated experiences:

> So, I was talking about it with a few of my colleagues and we decided that 'beyond the game' was a title with hook and, what's more, it was faithful to the idea; the title implied that we were going beyond the act of gaming and what it meant to live and narrate an experience of that video game.

The film is a collection of different individuals, including video gamers, developers, media professionals, academics, and artists, narrating their gaming experiences in relation to particular feelings and specific moments. In particular, the film revolves around fear, anger, rivalry, sadness, and laughter, amongst other emotions, which are to be read like we would interpret any other life experience. For Somoza, it is clear that when it comes to understanding what it is like to evoke video game experiences, these are not equated to those found in other cultural products, but rather regular events that happen in our everyday lives:

> Conversations on films or music are different from those on video games. To remember video games is closer to remembering a trip, a birthday party, or something like that. In both cases there are coincidences because, even though it's through a controller and a screen, you're experiencing it like you experienced that trip or that party.

This seems to be a constant among people who play video games. Someone who appears in the middle of a person relating his or her game play experiences, might have serious difficulties in knowing if that person was talking about a 'real life'[3] experience or a gaming one. Video gamers talk in terms of what *happened* and what they or others *did* or *felt* when they were playing a video game. That includes, often simultaneously, events happening in the game world and story, and what is happening in the space they are actually occupying in that moment. For example, this is explored by Crawford (2006) in his consideration of the players of *Football Manager* (2004–to date, Sports Interactive) and *Championship Manager* (1992–to date, Sports Interactive) games, where conversations about in-game experiences would easily and often blur with discussions of events in the (out-of-game) world of professional association football. As Gary Alan Fine (1983) argues, in his application of Goffman's frame analysis to pen-and-paper role playing games, gamers often occupy at least three frames, or levels of cognition, often simultaneously. First, there is the primary, 'common-sense', understanding of themselves and their situation within a wider social context; second, is their identity and experience as a player of a game, with its own specific rules and patterns of play; and third, as a character in that particular game. Importantly for Fine, as with Goffman (1986), these frames are not mutually exclusive, but are rather best understood as levels of 'lamination', which the gamer often and easily slips between, or simultaneously inhabits. Hence, video gaming is an embedded experience in the phenomenological universe of players and, certainly, in the way that it is typically narrated.

It is not surprising then to observe video game players speaking in the first person when they recall what *they did* or *happened to them* in the game world. We found several cases of this behaviour in Somoza's documentary. For instance, in a section of the film focusing on fear, one of the participants narrated his experience with *Dark Souls* (FromSoftware, 2011) and expressed how terrified he was to die in the game.[4] 'I didn't want to die. I was afraid to die', he said, as though he was the one at risk of dying instead of the character he was controlling. Similarly, one of the interviewees recounts the experience he had while he was playing *Call of Duty 4: Modern Warfare* (Infinity Ward, 2007):

> And you're crawling around and you're thinking "what do I need to do? Do I need to get to the hospital?" Your character doesn't have its guns, and you're just crawling around. Like "What do I do? How do I survive this?" You literally can't, you just crawl around for a bit and then you die and then it moves to another character.
>
> *(Darius, male, 28, indie game designer)*

Here, Darius, is constantly shifting between the second and first person. The former being that impersonal 'you', the vessel of the active subject (be it him or any potential player who would live that experience), and the latter, referring to the mental process he underwent, which is another sign of what it means to narrate an experience. Even when some distance is introduced, mentioning the existence of a character the player controls, it is quickly bridged: 'Your character doesn't have its guns, and you're just crawling around'. In the same sentence, the difference that was established at the beginning is diluted before it ends.

Cogburn and Silcox (2009) in their discussion of video games and philosophy highlight how players will often use the first-person pronoun 'I', when describing the actions of the in-game characters. This, they seek to explain, using Clark and Chalmers' (1998) idea of the 'extended mind'. This thesis suggests that as humans we are adept at utilizing props to extend our body and mind; such as, for example, using a pen and paper to assist with calculations (Crawford, 2012). Hence, external objects become an extension of our thought processes and bodies. This, Cogburn and Silcox suggest, can be used to explain why people frequently refer to video game characters as 'I' or 'me'; because video games fit easily and readily into our patterns of prop utilization and the extension of self. Hence, even though video gaming is a technologically mediated experience – as with many other experiences, the focus is always on the construction of a lived experience, and how we speak about it points to that conclusion.

Enacting experiences

In Chapter 3 we explored how important the notion of interactivity is for the social imaginary of video games, and the sense of agency it provides. It seems that interactivity is associated with video games, more than other cultural products, because they typically require the active participation of those who consume them. While recognizing that video games most typically necessitate interaction, or at least are more profoundly transformed by their users than other types of works, we have been critical of an approach that directly assumes that books, films, television shows, and other media are just reproducing passive schemes of consumption and cultural appropriation. However, we do align with those who support that video games can also be experiences because players have to (most typically) actively participate in the mechanisms that make them work. Players are, indeed, *enactors* of the gaming experience; that is to say, it is the gamers who act out, and bring into being, the gaming experience.

Coming back to Salen and Zimmerman, they present three definitions of experience taken from the American Heritage Dictionary, all of which imply the idea of active involvement:

1. The apprehension of an object, thought, or emotion through the senses or mind;
2. Active participation in events or activities, leading to knowledge or a skill;
3. An event or a series of events participated in or lived through.

They summarize this dictionary entry by stating that 'experience is participation' (Salen and Zimmerman, 2004: 314), which seems to be a fair approximation of this. There would be no experience without the active participation in the events that provide it. That does not mean that the more active we are in any given situation the more vivid or intense that experience will be, but a certain level of involvement in the process is undoubtedly required. This point of view is shared by many of our research participants, like Alfred (male, 26, dedicated, and self-identifying gamer), who defines video games as 'an interactive experience that you play through some sort of console or some sort of interactive medium'. Interactivity is paramount in many of our respondents' definitions of video games as mediated experiences:

> In a way, there is a class of media, screen based experiences, which certainly need interaction and in which that interaction can change and adjust the flow of material that you get from that screen.
>
> *(Edward, male, 54, head of a Masters' on video game development)*

Edward, who is in the business of educating the future generations of video game developers, suggests that video games are technology mediated experiences that are fulfilled through a necessary interaction. Studying the video games *Minecraft* (Mojang, 2011) and *Don't Starve* (Klei Entertainment, 2013), Costello defines video game as a kind of rhythmic experience. According to her, if the player wants to play a game, they 'must open their attention to the rhythms of the game and bend their behaviour to synchronize with the rhythms of action and response that the game requires' (Costello, 2016: 4). In this sense, playing a video game involves an embodied choreography between the game and the player, some of which will 'require precise rhythmic performance', while 'others will allow players room to expressively play with the rhythms' (Costello, 2016: 4). Following the rhythm metaphor, the interactive experience of video gaming could be described thus as a rhythmic groove that the player 'may feel in or out of sync with and in or out of control of' (Costello, 2016: 5).

This understanding of the gaming experience as rhythmic could be related to Mihaly Csikszentmihalyi's (1988) concept of 'flow', or certainly how it has been applied by several authors, such as Steve Conway (2010), to the gaming experience. Csikszentmihalyi defines flow as a deep psychological state participants go into while engaging in a challenging activity, which: requires skill; has clear goals and feedback; a merging of action and awareness; a concentration on the task at hand; a loss of self-consciousness; the paradox of control; the transformation of time; and 'autotelic experience' (Conway, 2010: 45). However, while flow is an internalized psychological state, Costello's construct we find more useful because it situates the experience of play as articulation, embodiment, and a shared construction of rhythm.

Video games are, therefore, experience because they must be enacted; an enactment that involves the player(s), the video game, the screen, other people, the space in which the action is taking place, the controllers, the furniture, the lighting, the sound, the Internet connection, other devices, potential disruptions, past experiences, manuals, guides, conversations, and so forth. Playing a video game is an enacted experience that involves a setting, a script, and a handful of colourful and diverse actors.

Enactment is a powerful notion that has been used by social scientists because it covers a great deal of social interactions and alludes to specific ontological premises that, in the same way to actor–network theory and other post-structuralist traditions, we find useful for our consideration of video games as culture. According to Muriel (2016), the attention of sociology – and other related disciplines – should be directed at the 'mediations' that make the existence of the social possible. These are the mechanisms that sustain and reproduce social realities in an active manner; that is, the social, 'vanishes when it is no longer performed' (Latour, 2007: 37). John Law (2004: 161) adds that mediation is 'the process of enacting relations between entities that are, as a part of that process, given form'. Hence, mediations 'are entities and relations that did not pre-exist, but that are constituted in the moment the process is carried out' (Muriel, 2016: 114), or in other words, when they are enacted. This means that even the most institutionalized social formations would quickly disappear or collapse if the mediations that allow their existence were not constantly reproduced (or substituted by other mediations, which also would change, at least partially, the characteristics of those formations). Video games are no exception; in order to emerge, the gameplay experience must be enacted, creating a complex socio-bio-technological assemblage of different mediations.

In her analysis of *Escape from Woomera* (EFW Collective, 2003), a 'serious game' that depicts the situation of asylum seekers in a detention centre in Australia, Cindy Poremba describes it as an exercise of translating a difficult, often ignored or actively obscured, reality into a video game.

Furthermore, Poremba explains how this type of gaming experience is a participatory and enacted one. Poremba suggests that video games 'construct player subjects' because the player is not 'an objective observer but an embedded participant' (2013: 355). Poremba portrays this participant as an *enactor*. This means that the success of the video game relies less on a process of immersion and more on 'crafting insight into the enacted subjectivity of Woomera refugees, read through the player's embodied gameplay experience' (Poremba, 2013: 356). According to Poremba (2013: 357), *enaction* is a *situated interaction*, and can be seen as 'a different mode of engagement with media', one that enlivens the recreated situation through an embodied experience.

Reality is always an active entity, a work in progress that must be continuously enacted. Realities, after all, 'are not secure but instead they have to be practised' (Law, 2004: 15) and 'enacted' (Law, 2004: 38). Enactment is, then, fundamental to the understanding of how different aspects of our world work and a core notion of any given experience, particularly, to those that imply an embodied and lived experience like video gaming. Video games, understood as experiences, are not entities sitting out there that exist apart from the act of playing them. On the contrary, video games are also actors in a system that create the gameplay experience through enactment, with the active participation of all actors – including players, hardware, software, peripherals, physical and virtual spaces, and many other participants – involved in the process. All this will be of great relevance when we address what video games can tell us about experience in our contemporary society, particularly in relation to a postphenomenological approach, which we will explore later.

Embodied experiences

Closely related to the notion of enactment – in fact, we would suggest, inseparable from it as we have seen in the previous section – we find the embodied nature of video gaming. Video games are necessarily embodied experiences. Even though we find that emphasis is often placed either on the technological systems or the cognitive processes, the materiality of the augmented and hybrid body of the video gamer is always essential to the game experience. The centrality of embodied practices in this case is something visible in Salen and Zimmerman's definition of video gaming as experience; for them, to 'play a game is to experience the game: to see, touch, hear, smell, and taste the game; to move the body during play, to feel emotions about the unfolding outcome' (Salen and Zimmerman, 2004: 314). Video gaming is then a sensorial, corporeal, and emotional experience that points to the fact that the focus should not be exclusively on what is happening on the screen but on the acknowledgement that players have 'a physical and corporal existence', consequently making the act of playing fundamentally 'an embodied experience' (Crawford, 2012: 85).

It seems obvious that, as Westecott (2008: 11) puts it, our 'physical body is always implied in the game', one way or another. Furthermore, we would state that the presence of the body is more explicit than implicit. When Crick (2011: 266), for instance, describes his experience playing a First Person Shooter (FPS) such as *Call of Duty*, he mentions how his 'heartbeat races', his 'body feels rushes of excitement and jolts', and how his 'body intuitively leans toward the direction to which' he requires his avatar to run. That also contributes to why Elisabeth, one of our interviewees who does not identify as a gamer, hates shooters: as she states, they make her 'jump'. There is indeed a continuous 'physical leakage that takes place in front of the screen during gameplay', and our bodies are constantly escaping 'from the fixed focus of the game' (Westecott, 2008: 2). As Lahti (2003: 163) argues:

> This desire is perhaps best exemplified by players' attempts to control the gameworld more fully with their own, empathetic bodily movement. By this I mean that familiar experience of, say, craning forward, trying to peer around corners by leaning left or right, or ducking as you desperately try to save your character – that is, yourself – from being annihilated. […] In this sense, our pleasure is based on blurring the distinction between the player and the character: we jump, fly, shoot, kick, and race when we are actually clicking the mouse or tapping the controller.

In order to give the proper role to embodiment in video games, we need to circumvent two interrelated theoretical obstacles that are strongly embedded in the collective imaginary of Western culture: the Cartesian distinction between body and mind, and the narratives of disembodiment in cyberspace and virtual reality. Despite the numerous works that have challenged those dispositions (for example, see the works of those such as Featherstone and Burrows, 1995; Turner, 2008; Shilling, 2003; Featherstone, Hepworth, and Turner, 1991), there is still a tendency to think in terms of a material body that is radically and substantially different from the symbolic and cognitive processes of the mind, in the same way that the idea of 'virtual' and 'cyber' spaces are often seen as detached from the topologies and sensorial experiences that our bodies inhabit.

García Selgas (1994: 41) claims that the 'modern gaze on the body is the gaze that separates it from the mind', and adds that the 'modern image of the human being par excellence is the Cartesian image of the ghost in the machine'. Modernity and Enlightenment thought were cemented on the proliferation of dichotomies that somehow, and in spite of the best efforts of postmodern theorists, still linger on in today's popular belief. Inside/outside, action/structure, material/symbolic, nature/culture, community/society, subject/object, or tradition/modernity are some of the most prominent dichotomies that articulated the epistemological substratum of modernity and, among them, the body/mind divide. Consequently, García Selgas suggests using the notion of 'embodiment' to overcome this dichotomy.

According to García Selgas, the utilization of a concept like embodiment help us to understand the fundamental, ontological, and methodological role that the body plays in the 'constitution and knowledge of social reality' (García Selgas, 1994: 43), from which important consequences derive, such as 'the breakage of the opposition subject/corporeality and object/world, and the acknowledgement of an osmotic connection between them' (García Selgas, 1994: 82). Thus, embodiment calls into question distinctions between the material and the symbolic, body and mind, and subject and object. An embodied perspective is based on the unification of those dualities, on 'the fact that that mind and body, or representation and object, are not entities that dwell in two different worlds, but are participants in a single coextensive reality' (Dourish, 2001: 177). In sum, the use of embodiment as a theoretical tool urges us to re-think our relationship with the environment and places the body in a central position to revisit the divide between the corporeal and the cognitive. It reminds us that we experience the world through our bodies; even though their sensorial and action capacities are socially mediated.

Thus, bodies are not clearly bounded and limited by the skin that envelops them. To understand that bodies and their agency 'extend beyond the skin in a continuum of social and material processes' (García Selgas, 1994: 82), is to answer the key question that Donna Haraway poses in her *Cyborg Manifesto*: 'Why should our bodies end at the skin, or include at best other beings encapsulated by skin?' (Haraway, 2004: 36). She proposes a reconfiguration of identity through the augmented, prosthetic, and articulated body. Her *Cyborg Manifesto* concludes with a discussion of the central role that the imagery of the body (and its limits) plays in world view and political language. Haraway argues that, on becoming cyborgs, hybrids, chimeras, and mosaics, individuals are able to modify the limits of their biological, political, and social body, and, in doing so, they subvert the dualisms inherited from modernity such as male/female, mind/body, black/white, and culture/nature. In this way, it is possible to reconfigure these dualisms in the framework of a post-humanist (Haraway, 2004: 47; Hayles, 1999), and prosthetic (Preciado, 2002; Preciado, 2013) landscape, as we partially saw in Chapter 3, around the notion of agency. Hence, this cyborgian approach to video games makes 'the virtual and the physical complementary rather than mutually exclusive realms' (Lahti, 2003: 168).

Overcoming the dichotomy that separates the mind from the body, and with it, those that extract the symbolic from the material and the individual from society, has as a consequence the questioning and eventual collapse of the other great obstacle to fully grasp embodiment as a central part of video gaming: the understanding of cyberspace and the virtual as disembodied experiences. This idea comes from (or is at least heavily influenced by) William Gibson's fictional cyberpunk writings, which popularizes the notion of *cyberspace*; a kind of virtual space where individuals were 'jacked into' and projected their 'disembodied consciousness into the consensual hallucination that was the matrix' (Gibson, 2015: 12). It is tempting to visualize video games as virtual reality devices and producers of *cyberspaces*; where we can have disembodied experiences, completely immersed by what is happening on the screen.[5] But, we argue, that as with virtual reality experiences, in video gaming, the 'participation of the physical body is a primary issue' (Ryan, 2001: 52). When players engage with game worlds, they are not leaving their bodies behind; as Lahti suggests, 'we remain flesh as we become machines' (Lahti, 2003: 169).

Following the mixed reality paradigm, Hansen (2006: 5) argues that 'rather than conceiving the virtual as a total technical simulacrum' – what in the sphere of video games would be a 'self-contained fantasy world', that space should be treated 'as simply one more realm among others that can be accessed through embodied perception or enaction'. It is less about the content and more about 'the means of access' to it. Newman's (2004: 133–134) idea of video gameplay as an embodied experience resembles this approach. Rather than identifying with characters, for him, playing video games is about the capabilities – the things players can do – offered by the system. This is an articulated body formed by the assemblage of the player, the controllers, the video game, the character on the screen, and numerous possible other social actors, which is able to do things, such as jump, run, swim, shoot, and hide. Again, it is more about functionality and means of access, and less about substantiality and content.

If we consider that the body is not just a flesh container for the *superior* cognitive processes, then the video game must be understood as an 'embodied pleasure for the player'; a body that is necessarily 'distributed during play across actual and virtual worlds via the videogame hardware' (Keogh, 2014: 4). This means that the video game action is not just happening on the screen, the mind, the senses, or the space in which players are, but it is 'multiple and distributed across physical and simulated space' (Black, 2015: 19). The embodied experience of video gaming is, thus, that of a cyborgian, multiple, and promiscuous relationality (Walkerdine, 2007: 28).

With the notion of embodiment, we want to reintroduce the body of the video gamer in the analysis; its bodily, material, and fleshy presence that makes, in association with other material and semiotic elements, the gaming experience possible. Playing a video game is therefore a 'fully embodied, sensuous, carnal activity' (Crick, 2011: 267); one that does not stop at the skin's frontier, but it is also extended through an augmented, hybrid, and prosthetic corporality. The activity of playing video games takes place throughout the multiple and complex body that gives a new meaning to what an embodied experience is. Alfred put this idea of the extended body into words:

> So it doesn't matter what game you pick up [...] the controllers are an extension of my body, so when I'm controlling something, it almost [...] it doesn't matter what the game is or if I ever played the game. It's second nature to me.

For Alfred, the controllers are a second nature to him. The activity of playing video games implies this articulation of technology and body, and, in this case, he is clearly stating its embodied nature by making the controllers a part of his own body;

naturalizing their relationship. No matter what game Alfred is playing, he establishes a continuity between him and the interface to make the interaction possible. However, there are other ways to see video games as an embodied experience, precisely by de-naturalizing the relationship between the player and the video game, making its prosthetic and articulated nature explicit. This is the case in video games such as *Heavy Rain* (Quantic Dream, 2010), which are full of *quick time events*; that is, segments of the game where the player has to act, with the controller, in a timely manner, following a sequence of prompts on the screen. In this particular title, there is a part of the game where you have to change a baby's diaper (nappy). During the sequence (see Figure 4.2) you are *asked* to perform a series of actions with the controller, which involves pushing buttons and moving the analogue stick in the right order and direction. After every correctly fulfilled instruction, the character on the screen executes a movement that resembles a diaper change. What happens here is that, as a result of the particular choreography we have to perform using the controller, there occurs a disruption between the bodily actions that would imply changing a diaper physically, and those implied in the gaming experience. The player's awareness of the actions they have to perform through the mediation of a controller and a screen, rather than delivering an 'actual experience' of a diaper change, makes the action a *gamey* experience where the articulation of every actor, human and not, is made clear. Consequently, the embodied and prosthetic nature of video gaming is made clearly explicit: in order to carry out the gaming experience, bodies, game systems, interfaces, and controlling devices have to align.

Certainly, video games could be part of what Dourish (2001: 102) theorizes as *embodied interaction*, which is not just a form of interaction that is embodied, but an 'approach to the design and analysis of interaction that takes embodiment to be central to, even constitutive of, the whole phenomenon'. This means that it is not possible to design a video game without taking into account the bodily nature

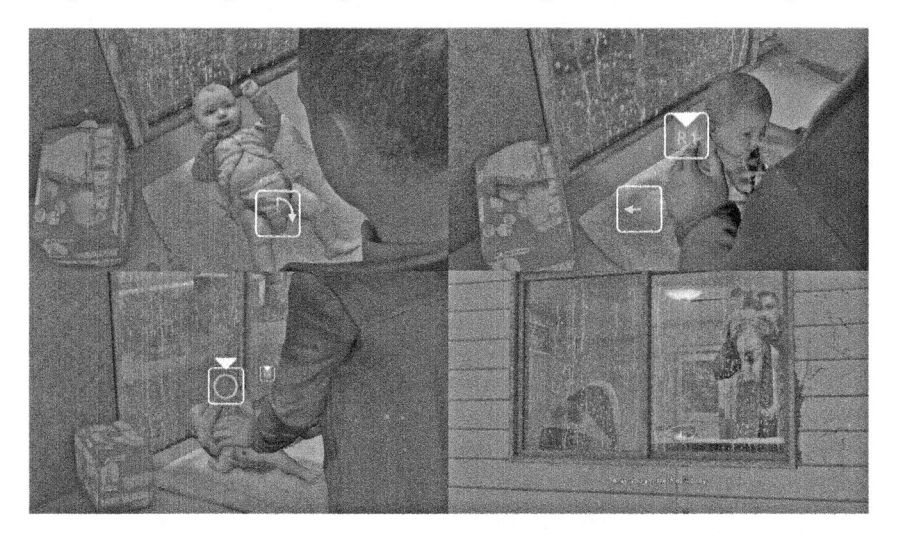

FIGURE 4.2 Changing a diaper in *Heavy Rain* (Quantic Dreams, 2010).

of playing a video game, and how every interaction with the game system has to pass through the filter of the player's body. After all, as Dourish (2001: 189) claims, embodiment is 'a property of interaction' and not just systems, technologies, or artefacts (or even bodies, we should add). Video games can definitely be understood as 'a paradigmatic site for producing, imagining, and testing different kinds of relations between the body and technology in contemporary culture' (Lahti, 2003: 158).

Social reality as a set of designed experiences

Salen and Zimmerman's (2004) *Rules of Play* is primarily a book about designing video games as an experience, something that they acknowledge by stating that the design of experiences is 'a fundamental principle of game design' (Salen and Zimmerman, 2004: 314). Video games are envisaged as experiences and, moreover, constitute the epitome of a trend that is traversing our societies: understanding the social as a set of designed experiences.

We live in an epoch that the production of designed experiences is, at all levels (social, cultural, economic, and political), a constant. The economists Pine and Gilmore (2011) consider that from the end of the twentieth century there was emerging a new kind of economy, one based on the production of experiences. Not only do they think this is an emerging reality, but they also deem it necessary, as the paradigm centred on the production of goods and services is no longer viable in late capitalism. Thus, the aim of their book is to describe and encourage the emergence of a new economy, what the authors call *the experience economy*; which is based on offering staged experiences to customers or (following Alvin Toffler, 1981) *prosumers*, as experiences are co-created, instead of goods (industrial economy), or services (service economy): 'in a world saturated with largely undifferentiated goods and services the greatest opportunity for value creation resides in staging experience' (Pine and Gilmore, 2011: ix). Pine and Gilmore are not necessarily suggesting that experiences are a new genre of economic output, but rather, that they have traditionally been mixed in with the service sector and, for them, experiences need to be decoupled from services in order to open up the possibilities for economic expansion (Pine and Gilmore, 2011: xxiv).

Pine and Gilmore believe that the proliferation of staged experiences is the only way to overcome the limitations of the current economic offerings (commodity, good, or service) and create new added value. The value here, relies on the lived experience in itself; because even though the experience perishes with the end of the performance, its value lingers 'in the memory of any individual who was engaged by the event' (Pine and Gilmore, 2011: 18). In their words, whereas 'commodities are fungible, goods tangible, and services intangible, experiences are memorable' (Pine and Gilmore, 2011: 17). Producing memorable and engaging experiences to be sold and enjoyed seem to be a trend that has always been there, especially in entertainment offerings such as plays, concerts, and cinema; but over the past few decades 'the number of entertainment options has exploded to encompass many, many, new experiences' (Pine and Gilmore, 2011: 3).

According to the authors, the beginnings of this evolution can be traced back to Walt Disney's Disneyland, and the many theme parks that have come since. However, the fast development of new technologies has encouraged 'whole new genres of experience, such as video games, online games, motion-based attractions, 3-D movies, virtual worlds, and augmented reality' (Pine and Gilmore, 2011: 4); and we would suggest, that video games, and similar biotechnological assemblages, appear to be the pinnacle of this new codification of social reality as designed experiences. Andrew Grove (one of the founders of Intel and considered to be an early prominent guru of Silicon Valley) anticipated the explosion of technology-enabled offerings in the mid-1990s at the COMDEX computer show (one of the largest computer expos in the world between the late 1970s and the early 2000s): 'We need to look at our business as more than simply the building and selling of personal computers [that is, goods]. Our business is the delivery of information [that is, services] and lifelike interactive experiences' (cited in Pine and Gilmore, 2011: 4). It is not surprising then to see how traditional service industries are also becoming more experiential.

But this tendency goes beyond mere entertainment. Companies 'stage an experience whenever they engage customers, connecting with them in a personal, memorable way' (Pine and Gilmore, 2011: 5). For instance, many 'dining experiences have less to do with the entertainment motif than with the merging of dining with comedy, art, history, or nature' (Pine and Gilmore, 2011: 5). There are more examples they mentioned: British Airways is not about transporting people from point A to point B, but providing an experience; or The Geek Squad turned mundane services (computer-related services) into striking encounters. However, beyond these examples, it is not particularly difficult to find many other fields that are being articulated, to a lesser or greater degree, in terms of experience. Tourism and cultural heritage, for instance, are areas that have been particularly permeated by experience staging and packages.

One of the fundamental ways in which heritage is represented is through processes that recreate and transmit the knowledge about its reality, including its feelings and experiences. The way we see performers re-enacting daily life scenes of different periods next to the archaeological sites, buildings, or monuments. Those who perform, and the ones who observe, are involved in a cultural performance that implies meaning construction (Smith, 2006: 68) through the experience they create. There are also heritage sites that simulate the experience of those social universes now extinct or in ruins. For example, this is the case of a territory museum that revolves around the iron industry in the Basque Country (Muriel, 2017: 41–43), where some of the most relevant social spaces of the 1950s – a working class bedroom, a classroom, a chapel – are reproduced based upon research into their history. Thus, some of most important referents of that time – labour, education, and religion – are invoked. All of it is staged where everything took place, recreating their social existence and including their buildings, aesthetics, languages, practices, and objects. This social universe is even unified through a route: *'One day in the 50s. The route of the workers'*, which offers the chance of travelling in time and experiencing the universe of working class families in the 1950s.[6] In this manner, heritage, is to be experienced or, moreover, it is the experience in itself (Smith, 2006: 47). Hence, cultural heritage is, like most video games, a designed and staged experience of situations we have not had the opportunity to live or are not possible to experience anymore. We have found similar settings in relation to video game culture, like those described by the director of a museum on video games:

> We have built an environment of a typical arcade from the 1980s around them, and you have the feeling that you are entering inside an arcade. We have also implemented this design in other rooms where we show environments of private rooms, living rooms of the '70s, a hobby room of the '80s, and a living room of the '90s, which represent also important milestones in gaming culture. And so the people can go into these rooms and then they can use a play original consoles and computers there.
>
> *(Emmet, male, 48)*

Hence, even the act of playing video games as they were played in the past has become an experience; the rising popularity and importance of *retrogaming* is further proof of this tendency (Heineman, 2014).

In a similar vein, we have been inundated by tourist products that sell us experiences in packages for the thrill seeker, the gourmet, the sommelier, the athlete, the connoisseur, and the hedonist (for example, see Bagnall *et al.*, 2015). Moreover, this current trend is also reaching other aspects of social reality, such as social relationships (where social interactions are translated into an accumulation, exhibition, and production of experiences in social networks and dating apps), politics (citizens involved in experiences of participative democracy through online voting processes and document discussions, neighbourhood assemblies, and social network activism), and work (using gamification methods as we saw in Chapter 2, with, not surprisingly, the working environments of Google, Facebook, or Apple being paradigmatic examples).

But we would argue, that we see the ultimate expression of this in video games. In particular, Crawford (2015) argues that video games are 'themed' environments. Crawford suggests that video games are like theme parks, in that they are 'non-places' (Augé, 1995). Non-places are spaces, which in themselves, lack a history and identity, such as airports, motorway service stations, and supermarkets. It is these kinds of sites that are then often themed. As Crawford (2015) writes 'a theme, identity or brand, is imposed upon a bland canvas to create an exciting and spectacular customer *experience*' (emphasis added). That is to say, just as a theme park without a theme, is merely a park, video games are at their most basic level made of code and game engines, often borrowed from other games, which are then given their (perceived) 'uniqueness' by the themes applied on top of this. As Aarseth (2007: 163) argues, 'computer games are both representations of space (a formal system of relations) and representational spaces (symbolic imagery with a primarily aesthetic purpose)'. To be exact, video games are both formal systems based upon rules and code, but they also are representational environments, which are there for the gamer to explore and experience. This, Crawford (2015) suggests, can notably be seen in sports(-themed) video games, which offer the gamer the opportunity to visit and play at key sporting locations. As Leonard (2006: 396) writes 'the attractiveness of these games lies in the ability to play at Pebble Beach or battle at Wimbledon. The tourist or colonization aspect of virtual reality are at the centre of this genre of sports game' (2006: 396).

Of course, the idea of a themed experience could also be applied to negative experiences as well, like collection agencies that use shaming techniques to collect debts as if everything were a whole, Kafkaesque, experience. In Spain there is a company, *El Cobrador del Frac* (The Debt Collector in a Tailcoat), which sends men dressed 'like extras from a 1930s Fred Astaire movie to humiliate debtors into paying up' (Webb, 2008). And we would argue, that the playing of certain games, such as, for example, *This War of Mine* (11 bit studios, 2014), cannot always be conceived wholly as a 'pleasurable' experience. And certainly, Joanna Cuttell (2017) explores how certain games, or gaming elements, such as the death of the main protagonist's daughter during the open sequences of *The Last of Us* (Naughty Dog, 2013), revolve around trauma; both in-game and for the players who experience this.

Hence, all sorts of practices are being turned into staged experiences. Staging then plays a central role in the creation of experiences. In the early 1970s, MacCannell coined the concept *staged authenticity* to allude to a type of experience that is 'produced through the use of a new kind of social space that is opening up everywhere in our society' (MacCannell, 1973: 596). That social space is a staged back region that offers visitors the sense they are 'permitted to view details of the inner operation of a commercial, domestic, industrial, or public institution' (MacCannell, 1973: 596). These settings create an experience of authenticity that, somehow, subvert Goffman's (1956) *front–back* dichotomy by letting participants move around spaces that are staged to look like back regions or directly allowing them to peek into the back regions of those social situations (MacCannell, 1973: 598). Staging thus makes the creation of experiences possible.

Three decades later, MacCannell revisits the *staged authenticity* concept and comes to the conclusion that those cultural forms devised for tourists – as we saw above, tourism is one of the first areas to sell experiences on a large scale – are spreading 'out of tourism into every other part of society', adding that the staged tourist experience 'is the beta test version of emerging world culture' (MacCannell, 2011: 13). The fact that he uses a simile (of the 'beta test') grounded in software development, particularly popular in video games, is important here: all designed experiences must be tested prior to their launch and, what is more, it is perhaps hinting (possibly unintentionally), that video game culture is the actual beta test version of this currently emerging culture.

In this regard, it comes as no surprise that Pine and Gilmore consider that the videogame themed film, *The Game* (Fincher, 1997), depicts the ideal, ultimate, 'intricate experience orchestration – staging rich, compelling, integrated, engaging, and memorable events' (Pine and Gilmore, 2011: 65). Other films like *ExistenZ*

(Cronenberg, 1999), *Thirteenth Floor* (Rusnak, 1999), or the *Matrix* trilogy (Wachowski and Wachowski, 1999–2003), along with some recent works on television like *Westworld* (Nolan and Joy, 2016) or *Black Mirror* (Brooker, 2011–to date), delve deeper into this idea that the ultimate designed experience is a video game, or at least very video game-like. Video games have become the prototype of social reality as a set of designed experiences in the twenty-first century.

Hence, we would suggest video games are at the vanguard of this trend, which is pointing towards a society that was anticipated by postmodern theorists; such as most notably in Jean Baudrillard's (1994: 1–42) essay 'The Precession of Simulacra'. Here, Baudrillard explores the notion of the hyperreal, which involves the substitution of the real by models of the real; and similarly, video games can be seen to envisage a social reality with no referents, origin, or substance, but their own designed experience. Although Baudrillard's approach was highly critical of these trends, we do not imply that video games are 'mere' substitutes of *real life experiences*. Video games are full experiences with transforming capacities; they are sensory, and emotional, and draw on the idea of living situations that we would not be able to experience otherwise – a point we explore more fully in the following chapter, where we deal with issues relating to empathy and identification.

Certainly, it can be argued that many video games present key examples of staged authenticity. For example, we have already seen above how the developers of games such as *Gone Home* (Fulbright, 2013), *This War of Mine* (11 bit studios, 2014), and *Life is Strange* (Dontnod Entertainment, 2015), draw on real-life experiences to try and create (stage) an 'as-authentic-as-possible' gaming experience. As Julian Stallabrass (1996: 102) writes, 'many [video]games take the form of staged, tourist exploration]…] [but] as with the exploitation of "heritage" themes […] they are collected, combined and packaged as entertainment, inevitably with a strong flavour of pastiche'. This is an important point made here by Stallabrass, and one that returns to the ideas of Baudrillard (1994) on hyperreality. Though at one level video games may seek to stage an authentic experience, they blur this with the unreal. In that, they introduce more 'game-like' elements, such as the HUD[7] indictors that appear next to a character's images in *This War of Mine*, which indicate their levels of health, hunger, fatigue and other factors, and also the unrealness that the gamer is experiencing in these environments, not first hand, but in a mediated video game. Hence, Crawford (2015), drawing on the work of Feifer (1985), suggests that possibly the video game player is best conceived as a 'post-tourist'; where the post-tourist accepts elements of staged inauthenticity next to the 'real'. As Julier (2014: 167) writes:

> Designing for the post-tourist must therefore involve a strong measure of self-conscious artifice. Situations, events or places may be simulated. At the same time, however, this trickery is deliberately incomplete. There is little point in pretending that the real thing is being delivered.

Hence, we would suggest that this turn towards a society understood as a set of designed experiences is most clearly evident in video games. Pine and Gilmore remind their readers that 'staging experiences is not about entertaining customers; it's about engaging them' (Pine and Gilmore, 2011: 45). It is not uncommon to read in game design manuals that a video game designer should know how to translate 'the formal intricacies of the rules into an engaging experience of play' (Salen and Zimmerman, 2004: 330). This is then what video games are supposed to be: designed, engaging experiences that are necessarily enacted. It is in the articulation of these experiences in which we all participate, humans and non-humans, where, issues related to agency, power, freedom, identity and community formation, culture, and everyday life are assembled.

Video games and the postphenomenological approach to experience

Our argument is that, being cultural artefacts that actively participate in the process of re-imaging social reality as a set of staged experiences, video games can cast important light upon the very notion of experience in contemporary society. Two main axes, in the shape of interrelated paradoxes, sustain the theoretical substrate of experiences: first, experiences as both personal and collective, and second, experiences as postphenomenological realities.

Experience as both unique and shared

In the introduction of his book *Frame Analysis: An Organization of Experience*, and drawing on a tradition of phenomenologist philosophers, Erving Goffman states that his aim is to understand 'the structure of experience individuals have at any moment of their social lives' (Goffman, 1986: 13). This implies that, even though experiences might be deemed as individual, they are in fact, socially structured. In Goffman's theory, frames are the basic elements that mediate and define a situation that 'are built up in accordance with principles of organization which govern events – at least social ones – and our subjective involvement in them' (Goffman, 1986: 11–12). Frames constitute, then, the social utensils – norms, rules, roles, expectations – that 'are available to the actors to make sense of any given situation or encounter' (Crawford, 2012: 27). Regardless of its limitations, the notion of frame can be a very useful starting point to understand the two-faced articulation of experiences, which are individual and personal, but also socially mediated.

Additionally, we would suggest that the work of the French sociologist François Dubet, 2010) on the sociology of experience is also of value here. In particular, Dubet (2010: 86) seeks to define 'experience as a combination of action rationalities', and in doing so, deal with the action–structure dilemma that has haunted sociology from its origins. Before developing his proposal, Dubet offers a definition of the ordinary notion of experience, invoking two contradictory phenomena.

First, he depicts experience as something the individual feels; as a way to incorporate the world. This results in social actors being 'invaded by an emotional state intense enough to make them feel, while they discover their own personal subjectivity, they are not in control of themselves' (Dubet, 2010: 86). On the one hand, experience is introduced as 'truly individual' and, on the other, as 'the superposition of society and individual conscience' (Dubet, 2010: 86). Consequently, this process of absorbing the world through the senses is both personal and social. What we experience is part of our phenomenological understanding of reality, but this understanding is also socially mediated by other actors that have participated – either close or distant in time or space – in the emergence of that experience.

Second, there is at least one consequence that follows from this first phenomenon; not only is social experience a way to incorporate reality through feelings and emotions, but it is also 'a mode of construing the world' (Dubet, 2010: 86). Experience is, therefore, something that you also pour into the social, a tool to define reality. In both cases, the tension is palpable. Experiences are unique, personal, and exceptional, but, at the same time, they are shared, collective, and common.

The tension that we find in the idea of experience as both individual and collective is obvious in Dubet's theory. Similar to the notion of frames, experience is not the expression of a pure subject – whether we understand it as the process of assimilating what surrounds us or the emotional flow that is born in the individual and projected to the world – since it is socially constructed and is able to identify situations by rummaging 'in the cultural stock that is available' (Dubet, 2010: 93). Even if experience is often purely individual, it only exists when it is recognized, shared, and confirmed by others.

This is something explored in the documentary *Memories: Beyond the Game* directed by Somoza. The testimonies and the editing encourage the formation of shared experiences, seeking to evoke in the spectator the same emotions that are being narrated on the screen, and triggering their memories of playing that game or similar ones:

> I want people to identify with not only saying 'Look, I've had that exact experience', but with living a similar moment either in the same game or in a similar game.

Experiences are shared, collectively compared, contrasted, and connected with other experiences. In one of the documentary chapters, focusing on *scares*, at least five different participants noted a particular frightful experience in the original *Resident Evil* (Capcom, 1996) video game where two dogs come through windows in a narrow corridor and (most commonly) startle the player. By doing this, these players are collectively shaping the experience they had individually. This then becomes *the resident evil dogs' moment*, which transforms their own experience and that of those who watch the film, in the same way it might mediate the experiences of those who will play the video game in the future. Experience is not just a phenomenological unique event; it is in continuous transformation.

Journey (Thatgamecompany, 2012) is a video game that perfectly encapsulates this paradox. Described as a 'unique' and 'very personal experience' by some of our interviewees, *Journey* can also be seen as a powerful shared experience. The game is based on a very simple idea: the player has to reach a mountain in the distance traveling through a desert. It is the story of, unsurprisingly, a journey. The journey can be done alone, but if played online, the player might come across players with whom to go over the rest of the route or just part of it. Players can help each other during the journey, but there is no direct communication between them, neither vocal nor text; they are only able to emit a sound. This creates this particular experience of being a very personal journey but, at the same time, is widely transformed by the experience of other players:

> I think there was a large part of engagement in the game, because when you play the game, you play the game online, and you might come across people that are playing the game as well, because you're all in one world. I came across this person, and he actually went through half the journey with me until near the end, and then he had to log off, and as soon as he log off, I did feel a bit saddened "oh, he's gone". (Zelda, female, 25, a dedicated and self-identifying gamer)

Even when we play video games that are designed to be a profoundly intimate experience, they can easily transform into a shared experience. This is an example of what Dubet, as we saw above, understands for experience: the paradoxical combination of the most inner and individual processes, along with the wider structural aspects of collective action. In this sense, participatory culture, which we analyzed in Chapter 3, provides us with a good way of understanding this constitutive contradiction of experience. For example, the gaming community often produces wikis of specific video games. They are the product of a collective collaboration between actors that are scattered all over the world. One of the main characteristics of these wikis is that potentially anyone can participate in their elaboration; it is a group, horizontal, and collaborative work. In order to illustrate this point, let us have a look in more detail at one of the wikis of *Bloodborne* (FromSoftware, 2015).[8]

FromSoftware is a Japanese company that has been part of the video game industry for the last 20 years. Lately, it has been best known for the acclaimed *Dark Souls* series, praised for its uncommon and creative narrative, universe, and mechanic design. As part of that design, the *Dark Souls* series is also famous for its challenging difficulty. *Bloodborne* (see Figure 4.4) is a standalone game also by FromSoftware, which is not part of the *Dark Souls* universe, and introduces its own mechanic and aesthetic innovations, but shares with the *Dark Souls* series many of the features that have made this so celebrated, among them, its daunting difficulty and environmental (and quite cryptic sometimes) storytelling.

Playing *Bloodborne* can be a rather frustrating endeavour since the game is not very explicit when it comes to unfolding its narrative and what is commonly known as the lore of the universe. The player has to be very attentive to every conversation, object, description, and detail of the environment. Even if they are, the player will probably miss an important part of the story and the richness of

106 Video games as experience

the world they have before them. To partially alleviate that deficit, *Bloodborne* wikis (Figure 4.3) offer a detailed account on the different characters, enemies, places, weapons, objects, history, and lore that inhabit the universe, which can help the player to piece together all the narrative elements that are being told discursively and by other means to them. In this case, the player's experience of *Bloodborne*'s universe, always partial and unique in principle, is being modified collectively by the action of the community that plays it.

In a similar way, in order to have a better opportunity to progress in the game, it is of the utmost importance to adequately level up your character by knowing

FIGURE 4.3 A *Bloodborne* (FromSoftware, 2015) wiki (FANDOM Games Community).

FIGURE 4.4 Screenshot from *Bloodborne* (FromSoftware, 2015).

in which stats the player should invest their *blood echoes* (a currency of sorts in *Bloodborne*, which can only be acquired by defeating enemies).[9] Again, the game is deliberately abstruse in this matter, leaving the player wondering which build would work better for them. Wikis are therefore useful as they contain builds (different combinations of stats that favour specific classes and styles of game) based on diverse people's experiences and what worked for them. In this way, the player can modify their stats following this advice and, in doing so, merge both experiences (the individual and the communal). Bosses (big, dreadfully difficult, enemies) also fall into this logic, and again wikis are useful to suggest a list of weaknesses, different strategies to defeat them, and even links to videos where other players show how they succeeded. Hence, there is an overlap of experiences that mediate these encounters with bosses. Some of our interviewees mentioned similar dynamics:

> I think any game can bring people together, as long as there is enough people are playing it. For single player games that might be hard, but you can still talk about your shared experiences. People can still theorize about what's happening or maybe like, for example, with Legend of Zelda, that's a largely single player experience, but people still share strategies and guides on it and people talk about the story of the game and how it interlinks with the other games, how it creates a timeline about how each game appears.
>
> *(Carl, 28, male, self-identifying gamer)*

Therefore, when players *dump* their experiences in a wiki (or a forum, a social network, a comments section, a YouTube video, a website, a review, a face-to-face conversation, and so forth), they are turning their particular experiences into global ones; in a similar sense, when players *retrieve* the collectively accumulated experiences of other players, they are moulding their specific experiences in accordance with that multi-layered set of different occurrences. This is where it is possible to see the socially structured nature of experience that Goffman describes in his works. Experiences are therefore points of encounter rather than individual events.

Experience as a postphenomenological reality

On a cloudy evening, one of the authors of this book was playing *Call of Cthulhu: Dark Corners of the Earth* (Headfirst Productions, 2005) on his PC. At some point, the game started to feel as if it was having problems with its frame rate. Everything felt clumsy and it took him a lot of effort to use the mouse in order to control the game camera. Even his partner, who was sat behind him on the couch and started getting upset by the erratic movements he was doing with the mouse, shouted at him: 'what the hell are you doing?'. At first it was bearable but eventually it started getting on his nerves: 'it is impossible to play!'. His mind frantically went through different possibilities and none of them were looking promising: 'Do I have to quit and restart it? Is it another bug of this dammed game? Do I have to downgrade the settings again in order to keep it working properly?' In the end, he realized it was not the game's problem, the rechargeable batteries in his wireless mouse were out of charge. That was the reason he could not play the video game properly; a disruptive mediation (uncharged batteries) that broke the alignment of mediations (non-responding mouse, controlling difficulties, bodily movements not matching player's intentions, the game's camera moving uncontrollably, external factors weighing in the game's experience, and so forth) that altered the gaming experience.

Here, in this example then, the player was perceiving the gameplay through his senses. Nevertheless, the experience was also embodied through a particular performance, magnified when he had to move the mouse up and down – instead of sliding it over the surface – hitting it repeatedly off the table. This made other elements involved in the experience surface, making them explicit. There was a system of inputs and outputs, such as the controllers (mouse, keyboard), hardware (the computer, the screen, the graphics card, the wireless connection device, batteries) and software (the video game, the operative system, drivers). Moreover, everything was happening inside a determined space, a social one, where the experience could be altered at any moment (according to how they were behaving in relation to the player's activity), such as the player's partner, the television on in the background, the sound of the refrigerator, the noisy neighbours, and the lights coming from the street through the windows. Past experiences were also invoked, previous problems with the game, which had required him to search for help on the Internet in order to solve the issues raised. Hence, this simple event revealed the complexities behind the articulation of a gaming experience; making explicit the socially and physically embedded reality that it is.

When we explored above how video games are enacted and embodied experiences, we identified a series of actors (human and not) that were part of the enactment. That joint social choreography reminds us that what we experience at any given moment is mediated by factors that occupy the same space and time where the experience is taking place (other players or people in the room, the space layout, in-game tutorial, the story, the mechanics, the inputs and the outputs of the game, the controllers, the environment, sounds, objects, or animals that might interfere) along with others that can be acting at a distance (expectations, previous games, other people playing online, what we saw, heard, or read about the game – reviews, comments off and online, video gameplays on YouTube or Twitch, ads, guides, tutorials, and so on). This is also what the paradox of experience as unique and shared implies. We are therefore entering into a *postphenomenological* social setting.

Every phenomenological approach, from the humanities to social sciences, has *experience* at the centre of its analysis. However, the most classical traditions of phenomenology are often fitted within a subjectivist and humanist focus, where the human being is the experiencer of the world. This usually includes a sense of embodiment as an important factor in the experiential activity, as well as a certain organic interrelation with the environment, but the phenomenon (etymologically 'that which appears or is seen') always seems to principally lie in the individual who interprets reality through their senses or makes representations of it.

*Post*phenomenology takes experience to a new ontological level; it brings experience to the twenty-first century.

According to Don Ihde (2009: 23), postphenomenology is 'a modified, hybrid phenomenology'. This hybrid is sustained by key aspects of three philosophical developments: pragmatism, phenomenology, and philosophy of technology. Moreover, these are seen by the author as three key steps toward postphenomenology. From pragmatism, it takes the 'way to avoid the problems and misunderstandings of phenomenology as a subjectivist philosophy'. Then, phenomenology provides a 'rigorous style of analysis', including the use of embodiment and the notion of lifeworld (Ihde, 2009: 11–19). Finally, the emergence of a philosophy of technology shows an 'empirical turn' (Ihde, 2009: 20–23), which understands technologies as multidimensional material cultures within a lifeworld, what in contemporary science and technology studies is known as *technoscience* (Haraway, 2004: 240–246).

This creates a theoretical framework that sees experience as a complex process that entails an epistemological rupture (the aforementioned implosion of dichotomous distinctions such as subject/object, body/mind, external/internal), an interrelational ontology (the human experiencer and the world are interrelated in a way that 'both are transformed within this relationality' [Ihde, 2009: 23]), and the dispersion of the phenomenon (the articulation of body, technology, perception, and other varied elements). Hence, postphenomenology helps decentre human agency as the fundamental (or unique) force that experiences and transforms the world, and resituates our understanding of experience as the articulation of the different elements that have a role in its construction. In sum, what we experience does not solely rely on what we feel, see, and interpret, but it is mediated by multiple external and internal factors.

A gaming experience is then an event in which human subjects, a set of technologies, and a media-cultural practice come together; an event that 'emphasizes the dynamic between the elements *in play*: entities coming together, material and aesthetic chains of cause and effect or feedback' (Giddings, 2009: 149). As we saw with the problematic experience with *Dark Corners of the Earth* and the lack of charged batteries, the idea of video games as experience can only 'be adequately addressed through acknowledgement of its bringing together of heterogeneous part(icipant)s' (Giddings, 2009: 150). In this sense, postphenomenology offers a framework to understand 'not how human subjects change their world through technology, but how humans, their worlds, and technologies are all necessary and active parts of each other' (Keogh, 2014: 13). The notion of social reality as the articulation of heterogeneous elements continuously reverberates in this postphenomenological approach:

> If, for Durkheim, as found in his Rules of Sociological Method, 'the first and most basic rule is to consider social facts as things' (1986: 53), here the social is not a substance, but is considered as the product, always contingent and in continual reproduction, of the articulation of distinct ingredients: actors, associations, processes, practices, etc. Attention is focused on movements,

displacements and transformations through which the social is made and unmade, which permits us to explain and observe the emergence of formations, structures, institutions, relations and social agents.

(Muriel, 2016: 124)

Seldom will the reader find a cultural product, a social reality, or a phenomenon like video games and its culture that can be such an open window to so many social aspects of contemporary society. Video games clearly help us to understand how experience is (co-)constructed in our present social settings.

Conclusions

In this chapter, we have explored the idea of video games as experience, and more specifically, an embodied and collective experience. This notion is central to understanding other aspects that will be analyzed in the following chapters, such as, empathy, identification, identity, and community. In particular, the introduction of the experience into the field of video games informs and determines these concepts in a fundamental way. On balance, if we wanted to identify the crucial element in any given definition of video games, even in the most elemental ones, it would be the idea of video games as *designed experiences* mediated by some sort of interactive digital technology. This leads us to recognize (at least) six ways in which video games can be associated with experience, and how this helps us to assess the nuances of experience in contemporary society.

To begin with, video games can be seen as translations of experiences (real or imagined ones). Developers often make efforts to research particular topics in order to translate others' personal or social experiences into a game experience. Video games are, in this sense, technologically mediated experiences of other(s') experiences. Second, we visualize video games as experiences because, frequently, social actors narrate their encounters with video games as they would do other experiences such as a trip, an anecdote, a party, a problem at home or work, a walk, and so forth. They are part of the *experience pool* of everyday life. Third, the interactive nature of video games makes them qualify as experiences, since they must be enacted in order to exist. This enactment requires the participation of different actors into play, who are demanded to perform a social choreography that brings the experience to life. Fourth, video games are, as with any other experience, embodied experiences. However, what video games help to make visible in an explicit manner is how embodiment is in our contemporary societies a mixed, articulated, prosthetic, and cyborgian, experiential body. Fifth, video games connect with, but also lead, a wider social trend: understanding social reality as a set of designed experiences. The real, in sociological terms at least, is progressively becoming a repository of technologically mediated experiences, and the logic of video games, is anticipating this process. Hence, lastly, video games help us to analyze the contemporary nature of experience, by unfolding its main constitutive paradoxes: experiences as unique, personal, contingent and, at the same time, as shared, collective, and structural; experiences not as a group of phenomena, but as the heterogeneous elements that make the phenomena emerge. In sum, video games are embodied, enacted, and postphenomenological experiences, which are at the vanguard, if not helping drive, profound, ongoing changes in our societies.

Notes

1 http://famacollection.org/eng/fama-collection/fama-original-projects/10/
2 It can be watched here: https://www.youtube.com/playlist?list=PL6th9XqkD_C19K_eSPbcVvV4VL9fTa-TH
3 This distinction here is more analytical than empirical, since video gaming is of course part of 'real' everyday life.
4 The *Dark Souls* series is renowned for being a very punishing game that greatly penalizes players' deaths.
5 In Chapter 5, we also challenge the idea of the video game as a radical 'other' space in which players can lose themselves or escape to.
6 http://lenbur.com/es/rutas/ruta-obrera/
7 HUD, or Head-Up Display, is a visual display of information often on a transparent screen in front of the eyes, first seen in aviation, but is now regularly represented in many video games, particularly First Person Shooters.
8 http://bloodborne.wikia.com/wiki/Bloodborne_Wiki
9 We must add that they are very precious because, if at some point the player's character is defeated by an enemy, they will lose all their blood echoes, only having one opportunity to recover them at the same spot they died.

References

Aarseth, Espen (2007). 'Allegories of Space: The Question of Spatiality in Computer Games', in F. von Borries, S.P. Walz; M. Böttger (editors), *Space Time Play: Computer Games, Architecture and Urbanism: The Next Level*. Berlin: BirkHäuser, 44–47.
Augé, Marc (1995). *Non-Places: Introduction to an Anthropology of Supermodernity* (Translated by John Howe). Verso: London.
Bagnall, Gaynor; Crawford, Garry; Petrie, Matthew; Schutt, Becky (2015). '*Monetising Cultural Experiences: Research and Development Report*', Digital R&D Fund for The Arts, London, Nesta, [http://webarchive.nationalarchives.gov.uk/20161104002922uo_/http://artsdigitalrnd.org.uk/wp-content/uploads/2013/07/Monetising-Cultural-Experiences-Final.pdf] [Last accessed: 14/08/2017].
Baudrillard, Jean (1994). *Simulacra and Simulation*. Ann Arbor: The University of Michigan Press.
Black, Daniel (2015). 'Why Can I See My Avatar? Embodied Visual Engagement in the Third-Person Video Game', *Games and Culture*, DOI:10.1177/1555412015589175.
Bogost, Ian (2007). *Persuasive Games*. Cambridge, MA: MIT Press
Clark, Andy and Chalmers, David J. (1998). 'The Extended Mind', *Analysis*, (58): 10–23.
Cogburn, Jon and Silcox, Mark (2009). *Philosophy through Video Games*. London: Routledge.
Conway, Steven (2010). "It's in the Game and Above the Game", *Convergence*, 16 (3): 334–354.
Costello, Brigid Mary (2016). 'The Rhythm of Game Interactions: Player Experience and Rhythm in Minecraft and Don't Starve', *Games and Culture*, DOI:10.1177/1555412016646668.
Crawford, Garry (2006). 'The Cult of Champ Man: The Culture and Pleasures of Championship Manager/Football Manager Gamers', *Information, Communication and Society*, 9 (4): 496–514.

Crawford, Garry (2012). *Video Gamers*. London: Routledge.
Crawford, Garry (2015). 'Is it in the Game? Reconsidering Play Spaces, Game Definitions, Theming and Sports Videogames', *Games & Culture*, 10 (6): 571–592.
Crick, Timothy (2011). 'The Game Body: Toward a Phenomenology of Contemporary Video Gaming', *Games and Culture*, 6 (3): 259–269.
Csikszentmihalyi Mihaly (1988). *Optimal Experience: Psychological Studies of Flow in Consciousness*. Cambridge: Cambridge University Press.
Cuttell, J. (2017). 'Traumatic Prologues and Ethical Responses', paper presented to *DiGRA UK Conference*, University of Salford, Salford, 5 May 2017.
Dourish, Paul (2001). *Where the Action Is. The Foundations of Embodied Interaction*. Cambridge, MA: MIT Press.
Dubet, François (2010). *Sociología de la experiencia* [Sociology of Experience]. Madrid: CIS.
Featherstone, Mike and Burrows, Roger (editors) (1995). *Cyberspace, Cyberbodies, Cyberpunk. Cultures of Technological Embodiment*. London: Sage.
Featherstone, Mike; Hepworth, Mike; Turner, Bryan (editors) (1991). *The Body*. London: Sage.
Feifer, Maxine (1985). *Going Places: The Ways of the Tourist from Imperial Rome to the Present Day*. London: Macmillan.
Fine, Gary Alan (1983). *Shared Fantasy: Role Playing Games as Social Worlds*. Chicago: Chicago University Press.
García Selgas, Fernando (1994). 'El cuerpo como base del sentido de la acción', *REIS*, (68): 41–83.
Gibson, William (2015) [1984]. *Neuromancer*. London: HarperCollins.
Giddings, Seth (2009). 'Events and Collusions. A Glossary for the Microethnography of Video Game Play', *Games and Culture*, 4 (2): 144–157.
Goffman, Erving (1956). *The Presentation of Self in Everyday Life*. Edinburgh: University of Edinburgh.
Goffman, Erving (1986). *Frame Analysis. An Organization of Experience*. Boston: Northeastern University Press.
Grodal, Torben (2003). 'Stories for Eye, Ear, and Muscles: Video Games, Media, and Embodied Experiences', in Wolf, Mark J. P. and Perron, Bernard. *The Video Game Theory Reader*. London: Routledge, 129–155.
Hansen, Mark Victor (2006). *Bodies in Code: Interfaces with Digital Media*. London: Routledge.
Haraway, Donna (2004). *The Haraway Reader*. New York: Routledge.
Hayles, Katherine (1999). *How We Became Posthuman. Virtual Bodies in Cybernetics, Literature, and Informatics*. Chicago: University of Chicago Press.
Heineman, David S. (2014). 'Public Memory and Gamer Identity: Retrogaming as Nostalgia', *Journal of Games Criticism*, 1 (1): 1–24.
Hill, Charles (2004). 'The Psychology of Rhetorical Images', in Marguerite Helmers and Charles A. Hill (editors). *Defining Visual Rhetorics*. Mahwah, NJ: Lawrence Erlbaum Associates, 25–40.
Ihde, Don (1993). *Philosophy of Technology: An Introduction*. New York: Paragon Press.
Ihde, Don (2009). *Postphenomenology and Technoscience*. Albany, New York: State University of New York.
Julier, Guy (2014). *The Culture of Design* (3rd edition.). London: Sage.
Keogh, Brendan (2014). 'Across Worlds and Bodies: Criticism in the Age of Video Games', *Journal of Games Criticism*, 1 (1): 1–26.
Lahti, Martii (2003). 'As We Become Machines: Corporealized Pleasures in Video Games', in Wolf, Mark J.P. and Perron, Bernard (editors). *The Video Game Theory Reader*. London: Routledge.

Latour, Bruno (2007). *Reassembling the Social. An Introduction to Actor-Network Theory*. Oxford: Oxford University Press.
Law, John (2004). *After Method. Mess in Social Science Research*. New York: Routledge.
Leonard, D. (2006). 'An Untapped Field: Exploring the World of Virtual Sports', in A.A. Raney and J. Bryant (editors), *Handbook of Sports and Media*. London: Lawrence Erlbaum, 393–407.
MacCannell, Dean (1973). 'Staged Authenticity: Arrangements of Social Space in Tourist Settings', *American Journal of Sociology*, 73 (3): 589–603.
MacCannell, Dean (2011). *The Ethics of Sightseeing*. Berkley: University of California Press.
Muriel, Daniel (2016). 'Toward a Sociology of Mediations: Impressionist Mapping and Some (Brief) Rules for a Sociological Method', *REIS*, (153): 111–126.
Muriel, Daniel (2017). 'The Network of Experts and the Construction of Cultural Heritage: Identity Formation in Contemporaneity', *Tecnoscienza*, 8 (1): 23–50.
Newman, James (2004). *Videogames*. London: Routledge.
Pine, Joseph and Gilmore, James H. (2011). *The Experience Economy*. Boston: Harvard Business Review Press.
Poremba, Cindy (2013). 'Performative Inquiry and the Sublime in Escape from Woomera', *Games and Culture*, 8 (5): 354–367.
Preciado, Paul B. (2002). *Manifiesto Contra-Sexual*. Madrid: Opera Prima.
Preciado, Paul B. (2013). *Testo Junkie. Sex, Drugs, and Biopolitics in the Pharmacopornographic Era*. New York: The Feminist Press.
Ryan, Marie-Laure (2001). *Narrative as Virtual Reality*. Baltimore: The Johns Hopkins University Press.
Salen, Katie and Zimmerman, Eric (2004). *Rules of Play: Game Design Fundamentals*. Cambridge, MA: MIT Press.
Shaw, Adrienne (2014). *Gaming at the Edge. Sexuality and Gender at the Margins of Gamer Culture*. Minneapolis, MN: University of Minnesota Press.
Shilling, Chris (2003). *The Body and Social Theory*. London: Sage.
Smith, Laurajane (2006). *Uses of Heritage*. London: Routledge.
Stallabrass, Julian. (1996). *Gargantua: Manufactured Mass Culture*. London: Verso.
Toffler, Alvin (1981). *The Third Wave: The Classic Study of Tomorrow*. Bantam: New York.
Turner, Bryan S. (2008). *The Body and Society*. London: Sage.
Walkerdine, Valerie (2007). *Children, Gender, Video Games. Towards a Relational Approach to Multimedia*. New York: Palgrave Macmillan.
Webb, Jason (2008). 'In Top Hat and Tails, Spanish Debt Agents Prosper', *Reuters*, [http://uk.reuters.com/article/us-spain-debtors-idUKLJ55251720080821] [Last accessed: 08/11/2016].
Westecott, Emma (2008). 'Bringing the Body Back into Play', *The Player Conference Proceedings*, Copenhagen.

Ludography

11 bit studios (2014). *This War of Mine*.
Capcom (1996). *Resident Evil*.
Deconstructeam (2014). *Gods Will Be Watching*.
Dontnod Entertainment (2015). *Life is Strange*.
EFW Collective (2003). *Escape from Woomera*.
FromSoftware (2011). *Dark Souls*.
FromSoftware (2015). *Bloodborne*.

Fullbright (2013). *Gone Home*.
Headfirst Productions (2005). *Call of Cthulhu: Dark Corners of the Earth*.
Infinity Ward (2007). *Call of Duty 4: Modern Warfare*.
Klei Entertainment (2013). *Don't Starve*.
Mojang (2011). *Minecraft*.
Naughty Dog (2013). *The Last of Us*.
Quantic Dream (2010). *Heavy Rain*.
Sports Interactive (1992–to date). *Championship Manager* series.
Sports Interactive (2004-to date). *Football Manager* series.
Thatgamecompany (2012). *Journey*.

Films and television

Brooker, Charlie (2011–to date). *Black Mirror*.
Cronenberg, David (1999). *Existenz*.
Fincher, David (1997). *The Game*.
Nolan, Jonathan and Joy, Lisa (2016). *Westworld*.
Rusnak, Josef (1999). *The Thirteenth Floor*.
Wachowski, Lana and Wachowski, Lilly (1999–2003). *The Matrix* (series).

5
VIDEO GAMES BEYOND ESCAPISM
Empathy and identification

Introduction

We frequently associate the act of video gaming with escapism. That we play video games in order to escape the ordinariness of our everyday lives is a widely accepted idea. It is often suggested that video games provide opportunities to build an alternative or parallel reality in which players are able to live an immersive experience far from the ones they are having in their regular lives. In this sense, video games are helping create a new range of social and personal experiences, but by doing so, they are not only fostering escapism, but they are also enabling connections with other aspects of social reality.

Escapism is indeed an important part of why people play video games, but it is not the only cause or consequence of video gaming. We would suggest that, far from escaping from reality, video games can also connect us with (other aspects of) reality in surprising and unexpected ways. For instance, video games can help us put ourselves in the shoes of others and provide new experiences. Video games work then as mediation devices between players and reality, which could potentially encourage players to empathize with different, even extreme, situations – such as, civilians in a context of war in *This War of Mine* (11 bit studios, 2014), parents of a boy with cancer in *That Dragon, Cancer* (Numinous Games, 2016), migrants trying to pass through a border post in *Papers, Please* (Pope, 2013), or groups living through a scenario of social catastrophe in *The Walking Dead* (Telltale Games, 2012). Chapter 4 has set out our case for understanding video games as experience, and hence here, this chapter will seek to further explore some of the forms of those experiences.

In particular, in this chapter, we explore how video games can create different experiences of play, focusing especially on those that promote social empathy and processes of identification. Thus, we first challenge the primacy of video games as an exclusive escapist activity. In doing so, we acknowledge the importance of escapism as part of the act and appeal of playing video games, but we show that this is only one aspect, which ignores other ways of understanding video games; and in particular, how they can open doors to different aspects of reality. We do this by challenging two concepts that create a strong divide between the video game experience and our everyday lives: *virtual reality* and the *magic circle*.

After this, we delve into two important mechanisms through which video games can help us to connect with social reality in multiple ways: empathy and identification. The key to understanding these interrelated notions rests on the idea that video game experiences do not necessarily substitute the experiences they are based on, but rather, mediate between them and the players, creating brand new experiences. However, we also discuss some of the limitations that video games have in their ability to foster empathetic responses and identification processes.

Escapism and video games

According to Yi-Fu Tuan (1998), escapism is inherent in human culture. It is a notion that, ironically, human beings cannot escape from, and can be found in times, places, and practices as distant as the prehistoric era, Disneyland, shopping malls, religion, the contemporary city, imagination, and cooking. Escapism implies 'going from somewhere we don't want to be to be somewhere we do' (Evans, 2001: 55), and this place we seem to desperately want to escape from always points to the notion of *reality*. This outlines then a canonical definition of escapism as the process through which we (temporally) escape from some aspects of our current reality, such as boredom, work, routine, or stress, for example. However, having defined escapism as about *getting away* from 'reality' (even though we acknowledge that 'reality' is a concept that is particularly difficult to define and filled with multiple nuances), we are still left with an unanswered question: where are individuals escaping to?

This idea then, seems to suggest that people seek relief and shelter in *places* in which their current socio-material conditions of existence – what we know as reality – are suspended or altered in a way that, typically, makes them, for example, more pleasant, safer, under control, or more exciting and thrilling. In this sense, *virtual* versions of reality – imagined (Tuan, 1998), simulated (Evans, 2001), or staged (MacCannell, 1973; Pine and Gilmore, 2011) – appear to be preferred destinations. In particular, taking into account the argument that we live in a digital age, as we saw in Chapter 2, video games could be seen as one of the most typical contemporary forms of escapism. Moreover, according to Gordon Calleja (2010: 336), it is possible to assert without exaggeration that 'digital games are considered the epitome of contemporary escapism'.

This is the case for many of our interviewees, who stated that one of the main reasons they play video games is to *escape* from their daily life problems and routines:

> I also play because of that, because it helps me to break away […] it's my time to chill out.
>
> *(Iker, male, 43, regular player but not self-identifying gamer)*

For many of our research participants, video games are, at least partly, about escapism, and they expressed their wish to be transported to a different world where they would be able to live diametrically opposed realities from those they experience normally. Thus, video games involve an idea of escapism realized through the *realistic fiction* of entering in an *alternate-reality*: 'Sometimes I wish I could be transported to this world and just live that part' (Carl, male, 28, self-identifying gamer). Hence, our participants identify a movement across a boundary line between reality and the video game, and then, articulate this boundary-crossing as an escape from the vicissitudes of the real world to the pleasures of the video game universe. As we find in the following definition of video games:

> I guess it's an interactive experience, yes, for temporary escapism, for different reasons. A medium to tell stories, like a place to escape to, something safe and fun.
>
> *(Albert, male, 25, indie developer, game artist)*

Playing video games is, for this interviewee and many others, a place to visit, a location to escape to, a space to inhabit; it is also (typically) a pleasant experience: enjoyable, safe, and fun. The experience of video gaming is defined by the elaboration of an alternative reality, detached from the one players normally live in; a reality that is construed as a better version of its mundane counterpart, which is usually riddled with routine and boredom.

Thus, this is why the direct association of video games with escapism often seems taken for granted. It is commonly assumed that individuals play video games to escape from the mundanity and limited possibilities of our reality, in order to enter into an alternative world where we can do and experience things that would not usually be available to us. Video games are seen as digital artefacts shrouded in this halo of unreality, and even attempts to create a 'realistic' depiction of the world are still escapist in their lack of significant consequences. Calleja (2010: 336) argues that, in fact, video games suffer from a double – problematic – binary of unreality in their virtuality and gameness. This translates into a radical separation between the reality we inhabit and the reality of the game world: the delineation of a virtual frontier and the construction of an alternate space called *the magic circle* (Huizinga, 1949) – an idea and concept we will explore more fully later in this chapter.

Virtual reality

Previously, when we explored the notion of embodiment in Chapter 4, we challenged the modernist distinction between the material and the symbolic, which included other dichotomies such as body/mind or real/virtual. In relation to the latter, popular culture in the 1980s and 1990s was populated with versions of the virtual as radically alternate, clearly differentiated, and substantially new spaces, such as in films like *The Lawnmower Man* (Leonard, 1992), or the cyberpunk literature of writers like William Gibson. This 'application of the frontier metaphor to cyberspace'

(Calleja, 2010: 337) still has strong resonances in today's representation of escapism, where the 'binary division places virtual environments (of which digital games are a subset) on the other side of a boundary whose crossing implies escapism' (Calleja, 2010: 337–338).

In particular, scientific and social representations of the virtual, and this includes video games, tend to spatialize it; to understand virtuality as a totally distant autonomous space and see it as something ethereal, volatile, and radically different from the real, which is considered solid, grounded, and durable. This creates and accentuates a division between these two perceived spheres, which become incommensurable. It is like, after turning on a games console, computer, or virtual headset, and launching a video game, the material foundations of the act of video gaming are transubstantialized (denying completely the corporeal biological materiality that it implies) and turned into an intangible and abstract activity. The logic follows that if you are in cyberspace or absorbed playing a video game, you cannot be in 'reality' at the same time; for example, such as how players of MMOGs like *World of Warcraft* (Blizzard Entertainment, 2004) or residents in online worlds like *Second Life* (Linden Lab, 2003) frequently refer to the out-of-game as 'irl' ('in real life').

When we seek to establish a boundary that demarcates and differentiates two different realms (the real and the virtual), then 'crossing that boundary becomes a form of escape' (Calleja, 2010: 339). This means that video games' virtuality is reduced to a software generated universe; ignoring the fundamental role and presence of material supports, for example, hardware. Calleja, drawing on the work of authors such as Lévy, Serres, and Deleuze, reaches the conclusion that the usefulness of applying the notion of the virtual to video games 'lies in emphasizing their creative potential for actualizing a theoretically infinite range of possible experiences' and, more importantly, that the 'ontological value of these experiences are very much of the order of the real, not its opposite' (Calleja, 2010: 340).

Hence, Calleja argues that we need to break from this idea of two spheres, completely separated by an ontological frontier, and instead make the continuities that define both visible. In doing so, this reveals that everything belongs to the domain of the real. For example, the player's corporality pushing buttons in front of a screen is simultaneous to the events unfolding on it. Everything is a continuum of symbolic materiality and human and non-human hybridity. Cyberspace as an autonomous territory is only possible in science fiction. Thus, rather than a clearly demarcated virtual space, we are faced with emerging relationships defined and constructed via heterogeneous elements and actors. For example, as we explored in Chapter 4, video gaming implies the assembly of a bio- (bodies), techno- (hardware, network connections, software, interfaces), and socio- (real time conversations, interactions, information exchange) artefact that blurs any essentialist frontier. Hence, agreeing with Calleja, we consider that obliterating the 'boundary between the virtual and the real is a first step toward exorcising the commonly held, but erroneous assumption that digital games, as forms of virtual environments, are fundamentally escapist in nature' (Calleja, 2010: 340).

The magic circle

The other theoretical development that has commonly contributed to seeing video gameplay as something separated from reality, is another sort of frontier (in this case, a normative one): the magic circle. It is well known that the notion was firstly used, at least in a ludic context, by Johan Huizinga in his *Homo Ludens*. In this, the magic circle is given as an instance of a playground; alongside other examples, such as the card table, the temple, the stage, the arena, the screen, and the tennis court. For Huizinga (1949: 10) these are imagined as 'temporary worlds within the ordinary world, dedicated to the performance of an act apart'. This concept has then been applied by numerous scholars working in the field of game studies, and in turn, its use has been widely challenged by many others; resulting in one of the most heated debates in the relatively short history of video game studies. In particular, the application of the magic circle to games research was, most notably, popularized by Salen and Zimmerman (2004). Here, they define the magic circle as follows:

> The term is used here as shorthand for the idea of a special place in time and space created by a game. […] As a closed circle, the space it circumscribes is enclosed and separate from the real world. As a marker of time, the magic circle is like a clock: it simultaneously represents a path with a beginning and end, but one without beginning and end. The magic circle inscribes a space that is repeatable, a space both limited and limitless. In short, a finite space with infinite possibility.
>
> *(Salen and Zimmerman, 2004: 95)*

In an ideal, theoretical, and abstract way, the magic circle can be summarized as alluding to four major features. First, the act of play sets boundaries to every game; this means that the experience of playing a video game is bounded, and perfectly framed. Second, the game has its own clearly delimited space-time. The magic circle is where the game takes place; you are in the game or not. Third, the reality of the game is self-contained and bound by rules; rules that only apply to that particular game and make sense inside the magic circle (or at least they have a particular meaning that is not necessarily shared when they are invoked outside). Fourth, although the experience of play is not completely detached from the social context in which it takes place, the magic circle works as if it were an exception or interruption to the general norms and rules that govern the regular social relationships.

As Crawford (2012: 23) notes, one of the 'key criticisms levelled at the magic circle hypothesis concerns the divide between play and the wider social world'. Certainly, in theoretical terms then, the magic circle appears to foster a radical distinction between the game experience and the world experience; a premise that has been challenged by many other game scholars. Marinka Copier (2007: 133), for instance, suggests that the magic circle 'creates a dichotomy between the real and the imaginary which hides the ambiguity, variability, and complexity of actual games and play', making the 'boundary between "game" and "non-game" even stronger', while Pargman and Jakobsson (2008: 227) suggest that the magic circle represents 'a strong boundary between games and ordinary life' that does not correspond with the complexities of the game experience. TL Taylor (2007: 113) criticizes the rhetoric of the magic circle that 'often evokes a sense that the player steps through a kind of looking glass and enters a pure game space', without taking into account how players push 'against these boundaries'. Hence, Calleja (2010: 342) suggests that any 'attempt to create a clean demarcation between the game experience and the experience of the world', something that the magic circle does in various degrees, is going to run into the issue that the 'lived experience of the players invariably informs […] the experience of the game and vice versa'.

Even when theorists that advocate the use of the magic circle try to diminish the strength of its boundaries, such as suggesting these are 'negotiable' (Juul, 2008: 62), 'fuzzy and permeable' (Salen and Zimmerman, 2004: 94), or asserting that the '(almost) magic circle' is surrounded by a 'porous membrane' (Castronova, 2005: 146), the (even softened) magic circle still promotes the idea of video games as an escape from reality:

> any departure from reality across the boundary that defines its many binaries is an act of escapism. As escapist activities removed from reality, they become imbued with triviality and other, usually negative, connotations of escapism.
> *(Calleja, 2010: 343)*

As Alfred, a 26-year-old, dedicated video gamer, argues, 'escapism is just a part of the experience'. For him, playing video games is 'half and half', adding that there is 'definitely an element of escapism', but that it is also about keeping 'in touch with people'. Alfred also narrates how he often has conversations with friends and family about out of the game matters while he is playing, and will shift in and out of focusing on the game, depending on the level of attention needed at a particular point. Hence here, Alfred is describing a continuous process that does not make clear distinctions between the game world and everyday life. Gamers articulate both the (perceived) distinctions and continuities between the two (or more) *realities*. They speak in terms of *ins* and *outs*, *ons* and *offs*, entering and exiting, but also make connections and recognize overlaps between both universes. In the end, according to Pawel Miechowski, the developer at 11 bit studios (creators for *This War of Mine*), escapism is undoubtedly part of the appeal of video games, as gamers often 'want to run into power fantasy', but escapism 'is not everything' because the 'world isn't such'. For a game to be enjoyable, often they have to retain, at least some sense of believability; the fantasy has to connect to some sense of (alternative) *reality*. And therefore, we would suggest, that video games might also lead the player toward not just escapism, but also empathy, identification, and connection to other roads.

Connecting with other realities

As we write this book in mid-2017, we are sadly witnessing an endless amount of news, images, and discourses on the ongoing Syrian refugee crisis.[1] But this is not a new phenomenon. It is merely the latest version of a story told many times, which narrates the tale of those human beings who are seeking something very simple but, apparently, very difficult to achieve: a better life (or simply just a life; since it is often for many, a matter of life or death). They escape from war, famine, misery, all kinds of persecutions. It does not matter what awaits them on the other side of the multiple frontiers they have to cross, they are ready to risk their lives to escape the horrors that make up their current situation. Border after border, these people only yearn for one thing: to reach their destination.

The frontier – that liminal space – is a place between two places; it is a universe with its own rules and meanings, which are different from those we find on both sides of the border. The frontier is a transit area but it is also a detention zone, where the authorities decide who enters and who stays out. It is in that paranormal borderline sphere where *Papers, Please* (see Figure 5.1) takes place. In this game, we put ourselves in the shoes of an immigration officer at a border checkpoint, dealing with the people piled up on the other side of the border who want to enter our territory, the (fictional land of) *glorious Arstotzka*. The player spends most of the time checking documents such as passports, work permits, IDs, visas, and vaccination records, with the task of deciding on who enters into the country, and who does not.

It is widely accepted that Lucas Pope's game, *Papers, Please*, recreates a frontier that reminds us of a former Soviet republic. It is almost impossible not to notice that the game features all those things that we would typically associate with what happened on the East side of the Iron Curtain: from the fictitious names of the

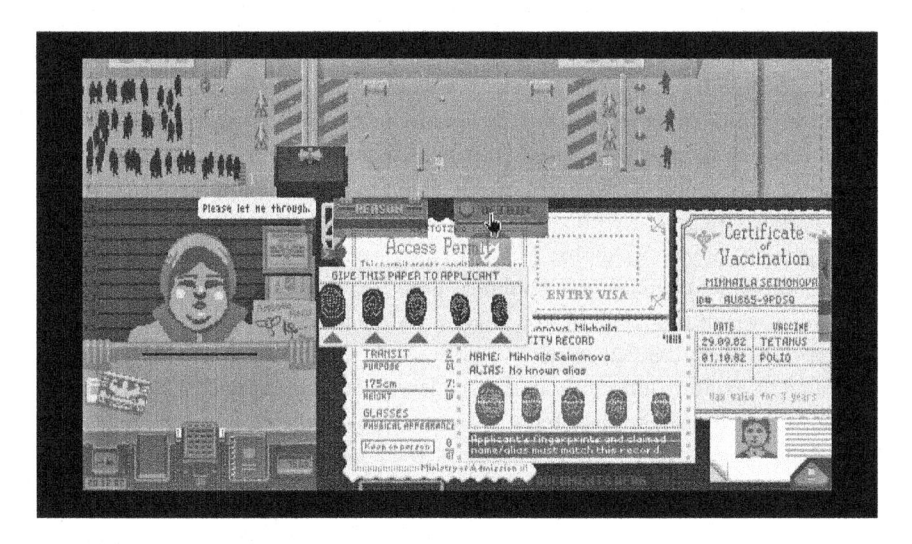

FIGURE 5.1 Screenshot from *Papers, Please* (Pope, 2013).

countries to the dull aesthetic that impregnates its whole design, characteristic of the Soviet bloc. However, the more time we spend as Arstotzka's frontier inspector, the more it reminds us of the present. Passports, ID cards, work passes, forms, entry visas, frisks, augmented security measures due to terrorist threats, full body scans, inquisitorial interrogations, deportations, detentions, use of deadly force, and so on. Is all of this just the realm of extinct Soviet republics? Or is this closer to how the frontiers of *advanced* Western democracies work; especially in these moments of global distress, where millions are being forcibly displaced worldwide?

The player has to make a tremendous effort in order to survive and provide for their family because everything depends, to a great extent, on how efficient they are in managing that crossing point we call the frontier. That means we are forced to leave several human beings behind, maybe abandon them to a terrible fate; people who wish to be reunited with their family, who might be victims of abuse, exploitation, and persecution. But if the player helps them, they will be punished and have consequences later, affecting the in-game player's own family welfare. The player will be forced to face the consequences of their actions, like not being able to provide their own family with food, medicine, and heat, or having to choose which of their family members receive those vital elements.

Fortunately, *Papers, Please* gives the player some leeway to, from time to time, make decisions that are against the rules and regulations: smuggling products, accepting bribes, letting people in danger cross without the proper papers, stopping dangerous individuals that are trafficking people, collaborating with a resistance group that, later on, will plan terrorist attacks, and so forth. There is the possibility to poke holes in the system, giving opportunities to those who have none, and trying to help yourself and your family. The player might be creating a greater evil or damaging their own interests, but at least they are able to negotiate beyond the limits of this frontier. *Papers, Please* is about embodying the bureaucrat; assuming the role of the dull civil servant. However, it also allows the player the opportunity of becoming the saviour and the ally of pariahs; the anarchist working from the heart of the iron cage.

But our question is: is this a *reality* we would like to escape to? Does a video game like *Papers, Please* offer an attractive universe that invites players to get lost in it as a break from their daily lives? Is this video game avoiding reality or, actually, chasing it? Although *Papers, Please* puts the player in a frontier inspector's shoes, it is in fact connecting them with wider social issues; it is giving players an experience of migration processes, global security, modern politics, abuse, responsibility, abandonment, and similar socio-political processes and consequences. The game puts the player in thousands, if not millions, of people's shoes. And the popularity of *Papers, Please*, and similar games, would seem to suggest there is a desire (at least for some) to explore other realities that are less fantasy but more closely tied to the world we live in: 'I'm more interested in emotionally profound experiences […] something which pushes those boundaries' (Edward, male, 54, head of a Masters' on video game development).

In this sense, Jordan Erica Webber (2017a: online), co-author of the book *Ten Things Video Games Can Teach Us* (Webber and Griliopoulos, 2017), argues that video games are potentially 'a compelling medium through which to engage in philosophical thought'. This implies that video games are, unlike philosophical thought experiments that only occur as imagined scenarios, 'counterfactual narratives that test the player' in an interactive scenario. Video games offer opportunities to engage in the most varied situations and approach different questions such as perception, personal identity, free will, and ethics. Video games then help connect us with multiple realities and experiences.

However, how does this connection with other realities work? We will explore now two similar and interrelated mechanisms through which video games are mediating in processes that *connect* players with other realities rather than helping them *escape*: empathy and identification.

Empathy

Video games have often been perceived, especially by clinical psychologists but also by other media scholars and social scientists (Appelbaum *et al.*, 2015), as a medium that can have a negative impact on their players, particularly in triggering or even promoting violent behaviours. It is not unusual for the media to report on studies that supposedly highlight causal links between increased levels of aggression (particularly among children and adolescents) with the habit of playing video games. In the same way, it is not uncommon to be told that perpetrators of acts of great violence, such as mass shootings, are avid gamers (Scutti, 2016). The assumption that is often made, either implicit or explicitly, is that playing video games supresses any hint of empathy in those who play them; inducing in these video game players a state of personal, emotional, ideological, and social numbness (Dean, 2004).

However, what we found during our research is the existence of numerous cases in which the participants reflect explicitly on the relationship between empathy and video games. There is even a label called *empathy games* to refer to a certain genre of video games like the aforementioned *Papers, Please*; a categorization that could similarly be applied to other titles such as *Gone Home* (Fullbright, 2013), *Firewatch* (Campo Santo, 2016), *Valiant Hearts* (Ubisoft, 2014), *That Dragon Cancer* (Numinous Games, 2016), *Cart Life* (Hofmeier, 2011), *To the Moon* (Freebird Games, 2011), *Spec Ops: The Line* (Yager Development, 2012), *Dys4ia* (Anthropy, 2012), *Depression Quest* (Quinn, 2013), *Brothers: a Tale of two Sons* (Starbreeze Studios, 2013), *Inside* (Playdead, 2016), and *This War of Mine* (11 bit studios, 2014). In fact, the last title, according to one user on a comments section of the website *GiantBomb*, was 'this year's *Papers, Please* in terms of empathy simulator' (Luck702 in Oestreicher, 2014). Moreover, this was even something that was recognized by the developers of *This War of Mine*: '*Papers, Please* was a great a game that inspired us to move on with our project, to make an empathy game' (Pawel Miechowski, male, 40, senior writer). It seems that video games have also embraced a global trend where empathy is, at least in theory, on the rise. This is what authors like Jeremy Rifkin (2010) and Frans de Waal (2009) call *The Empathic Civilization* and *The Age of Empathy* respectively, to describe the current transformations in the role played by empathy in the fields of psychology, biology, law, education, politics, communication, social relationships, and economics, to the point of suggesting that empathy 'is the very means by which we create social life and advance civilization' (Rifkin, 2010: 10).

According to Carolyn Dean (2004: 6), the noun *empathy* derives from the German word *eifühlung* (*feeling-in* or *feeling into*), which was used by Robert Vischer at the end of the nineteenth century to describe the process of contemplating art objects as a projection of our own feelings. Later on, the also German philosopher, Theodor Lipps proposed *empatheia* as its Greek equivalent, alluding to the idea of feeling strong emotions even if it is through a second-hand experience, moving the focus from an aesthetic experience to a social one: we watch apprehensively a high-wire artist 'because we vicariously enter his body and thus share his experience' (De Waal, 2009: 65). It was the American psychologist Edward Titchener (1909) who coined the English term *empathy* (Davis, 1996: 5) as a translation of *eifühlung*, as understood by Lipps, in his book *Lectures on the Experimental Psychology of the Thought-processes*. Empathy becomes then 'the willingness of an observer to become part of another's experience, to share the feeling of that experience' (Rifkin, 2010: 12).

Empathy is a very difficult notion to define because the academic literature, and its popular representations, allude to both mind and body, cognitive and emotional processes, and ontological and phenomenological problems. In some accounts, it could be understood as 'the mental process by which one person enters into another's being and comes to know how they feel and think' (Rifkin, 2010: 12). In this basic definition, empathy encompasses both the emotional and the rational aspects of an embodied, yet imagined, experience. The problem with this definition, is that it is mainly based on a cognitive model; what we can process through our imagination and thinking, as if the emotional experience that empathy implies is, somehow, knowable.

Opposing this strong cognitive-driven notion of empathy, the primatologist Frans De Waal considers that empathy is, above all, an 'automated response over which we have limited control' (De Waal, 2009: 43); diminishing the importance of imagination as one of the core elements that determines empathy. Instead of the predominantly cognitive approach in psychology, he opts for emotional and embodied engagement as the key elements in the construction of empathy:

> Seeing another's emotions arouses our own emotions, and from there we go on constructing a more advanced understanding of the other's situation. Bodily connections come first – understanding follows.
>
> *(De Waal, 2009: 72)*

Empathy builds on the emotions that arise after watching other people expressing their feelings through their bodily presence. This corporeal connection precedes the cognitive process that follows in the shape of empathetic understanding. Moreover, De Waal argues that, of all bodily connections, facial expression is the most important. The face is depicted as the emotion highway because it 'offers the quickest connection to the other' (De Waal, 2009: 82).

It is not surprising then to see certain video games using faces to put the player in this empathy highway. In *This War of Mine* every character controlled by the player is identified by a close-up picture of a real person's face. In fact, its developers photographed themselves, including their friends and family, because they wanted to confront the player with 'regular people, looking like people you may meet on the street' (Pawel Miechowski). *Gone Home* uses drawn – realistic – portraits and pictures of characters – mainly your family – to help the player empathize with them, by putting a face on those whose story you are trying to figure out. Even the

FIGURE 5.2 Different face representations in *Papers, Please* (Pope, 2013), *This War of Mine* (11 bit studios, 2014), and *Gone Home* (Fulbright, 2013).

simple pixelated graphics used to portray faces in *Papers, Please* are fundamental in establishing a connection with the situations and individuals depicted in the game. Those quasi-faces parading through the border crossing point remind players that they are dealing at the same time with nobody in particular and potentially anyone, triggering an uncanny sense of empathy towards a problem that might have affected them and their relatives in a more or less distant past, or might happen to them in the future, but, surely, it is afflicting thousands of people around the world as we write/read this.

The importance of faces and their gestures is something that Team Bondi, developers of *L.A. Noire* (2011), fully understood. Taking on the role of a detective, the player has to solve a number of cases by collecting evidence and, as the key aspect of the game, interrogating suspects and witnesses. Players must decide whether the characters are lying based on their facial expressions. Team Bondi used *MotionScan*, a motion capture technology developed by their sister company, Depth Analysis, which focuses on capturing facial expressions (Alexander, 2011). Though Telltale have not developed a dedicated technology for facial expressions, they soon realized faces were of the utmost importance in order to elicit emotions among players. The Lead Writer of *The Walking Dead*'s first season video game, Sean Vanaman, stated that after 'writing the first episode we start to make lists of the type of things characters are going to feel in the story and then start to generate isolated facial animations to convey those moods and emotions' (Madigan, 2012). As Smethurst and Craps (2015: 284) suggest, this is how the game represents traumatic events: 'by showing us its impact on the faces of characters who are suffering through the shock of losing loved ones in harrowing situations'. This means that video games, using the proper technology, can translate emotions expressed by human models into animated facial expressions that will be scrutinized by players, affecting their choices and capacity to create connection channels with others.

Thus, video games are powerful mediators that are able to develop empathic responses in those who play them, mediating between realities and connecting them: the ones inhabited by players in their regular lives and those materialized in the universe of the game. In this way, Rifkin stresses the importance of play in the development of empathic potential:

> What makes play such a powerful socializing tool, then, is that it is the means by which imagination is unleashed. We create alternative realities and delve into them for suspended amounts of time. We become explorers of the vast other – all of the infinite possible realms of existence that could be. Through play, we incorporate parts of these other imagined realities into our being. We become connected. The imagination process allows us to bring together embodied experience, emotions, and abstract thoughts into a single ensemble, the empathic mind. In this sense, the human imagination is both emotional and cognitive.
>
> *(Rifkin, 2010: 95)*

Although Rifkin is speaking about play in general, this is something that can be easily applied to video games. As we saw in Chapter 3, objects, animals, and other non-humans can be considered as social actors as well. This means that players can obviously engage with other players, but also with the complex bio-technological entity that emerges from the interaction between those heterogeneous actors. We connect with the universe, the characters, the story, the problems represented in the game, and by doing so, we explore that *vast other* (those realities that might surround us but are not within reach) and incorporate, through particular mediations, parts of it. Video games promote, in a mediated way, the emotional and cognitive connections that are made by players with other realities. Not only is this an imagined connection, it is also an embodied and sensitive experience.

This fundamental idea is summarized by Karla Zimonja, artist developer and co-founder of Fullbright, when she was speaking about *Gone Home* and its potential to show the intricacies and tribulations of an adolescent girl's life (realizing she is gay, coming out to her parents, her first relationship), but also other mundane stories about parenting, abuse, professional and personal frustration, friendship, infidelity, loneliness, marriage, and so forth:

> That's the thing about video games, they can give you experiences that you can't have in real life, that you haven't had, so it can be, hopefully, an experience that can add to someone's conception of how people are in the world.

Video games, therefore, are able to provide new experiences to players, but ones that are rooted in (someone else's) lived reality. They facilitate the possibility to 'step into someone else's shoes' and 'experience the world from someone else's perspective' (Harris *et al*., 2015: 58). It is an open window to other people's lives, problems, and situations; an open window video games invite us to step through. An invitation that has the potential 'to foster greater empathy, tolerance, and understanding for others' (Simkins and Steinkuehler, 2008: 352).

This is the case of the video game *The Tearoom* (Yang, 2017), which is described as 'a (free) historical public bathroom simulator about anxiety, police surveillance, and sucking off another dude's gun' (see Figure 5.3), and is heavily inspired by Laud Humphreys' (1970) classic sociological study of men who have anonymous sex with other men in public toilets ('cottages' in the UK, and 'tearooms' in the US) (Yang, 2017). In this, its creator Robert Yang, seeks to simulate a public bathroom in Mansfield (Ohio) in 1962, where the player can have sex with other men. According to its developer, Robert Yang, *The Tearoom* is based on a historical fact; in 1962, the Mansfield Ohio police department hid a surveillance camera behind a two-way mirror in a public bathroom in order to film men having sex with other men. Later, the police department used this footage to arrest and imprison these men under Ohio's sodomy laws. Thus, in this game, Yang tries to raise awareness of several key social issues. At its most obvious level, *The Tearoom* allows gamers to experience aspects of the lives of homosexual men in a time and place where they

128 Video games, empathy, and identification

FIGURE 5.3 Licking other guy's guns in *The Tearoom* (Yang, 2017).

were being particularly targeted and persecuted. As Webber (2017b: online) wrote about the game in *The Guardian*:

> In the game, large icons clearly indicate when it is or isn't appropriate to look towards the man at the other urinal. It's like a subversion of the stealth genre, as this time you want to be seen (though not by the cops). Yang wrote on his blog[2] that this mechanic was difficult to design because – as he puts it – "decades of male heterosexual hegemony have trained gamers into thinking of 'looking' as a 'free' action, with few consequences or results". Players who are used to works that pander to the straight male gaze may struggle to empathise with someone for whom a glance may be punished.

However, in placing the contemporary gamer in this historical setting and role, it also raises questions and emotions about the continued marginalization and persecution of gay men (and women) today. In particular, Yang states that he wanted to 'make players feel anxious about what they've got to lose' (Webber 2017b: online). Also, significantly, in the game penises are replaced by guns. This is a direct response to *Twitch* banning the streaming of Yang's previous games, but more generally, it also highlights the absurdity that a video game industry, and society more widely, which is happier to accept the depiction of a deadly weapon in a video game, than it is male genitalia. This game then, seeks to make important political points, and raise awareness of historical and contemporary social issues, by placing the gamer in a specific social setting and role; in the shoes of a gay man in 1960s Ohio.

Proof of video games' effectiveness as mediated experiences of other perspectives can be found in testimonies of people who have been able to better understand a person's situation thanks to playing them. According to Miechowski, the developer of *This War of Mine*, that would be the case of a woman who is the daughter of a war refugee. After playing the game, she declared that it helped her to understand her mother 'and the horrors she went through during the war'. Although spatial, cultural, and emotional proximity can help in the process of empathizing with others, sometimes additional mediations are needed, and video games are able to provide them. This hypothesis seems to be corroborated by the experimental study of Bachen *et al.* (2012) carried out in three Northern California high schools with 301 students, examining the effects of playing the video game *Real Lives* (Educational Simulations, 2010) – defined as an 'interactive life simulation game that enables you to live one of billions of lives in any country in the world'[3] – on empathy. The study concluded that, even when there was geographical and cultural distance involved, those who played the video game experienced an increase in their 'sense of global empathy' and boosted 'their interest in learning more about the countries in which their characters live' (Bachen *et al.*, 2012: 452). These kinds of video games allow players, Bogost (2007: 135) suggests, to 'engage in political actions that many will never have previously experienced', which, in the end, will probably 'deepen their understanding of the multiple causal forces that affect any given, always unique, set of historical circumstances'.

These mediations can be so powerful that they are capable of unleashing strong emotional responses in players. Laura, a 26-year-old indie developer, narrates how specific individuals empathized with the characters in one of her video games, which is replete with difficult decisions to make, usually involving survival and violent scenarios, and the high probability of hurting other characters. Some players identify with the characters as human beings, 'bloody hell, it's a person!' (Laura); this would explain some of the reactions to playing the video game, like a girl who was streaming her gameplay – in a playable section that depicts a long and explicit process of torture that your character and one of his companions have to endure – and started to cry:

> And she got to the point in which she started to cry. It was like, 'I can't take more of this', she was crying and very upset.
>
> *(Laura)*

This is not an isolated example. For instance, Miechowski enumerates a list of intense emotional responses that were triggered by *This War of Mine*:

> I know people depressed because they saw suffering in the game. I saw people excited, because they survived. I saw people having a sort of catharsis feeling when they survived, and I saw people being embarrassed or even had feelings of remorse, because of the evil deeds they had made in the virtual world.

Excitement, depression, embarrassment, remorse, and relief were some of the usual reactions amongst players of *This War of Mine*. This is linked to the developers' decision to place a morale system into the game with different states: content, sad, depressed, and broken. This affects the characters' performance and can be crucial to their survival. The morale status is affected by the decisions made, either negatively – by stealing from vulnerable individuals, hurting and killing other people, not helping your neighbours or people in need, being ill, wounded or hungry – or positively – by helping vulnerable people in distress, listening to music, sleeping comfortably, speaking to other survivors. This means that players' actions have a direct impact on the characters they are controlling; which enhances the emotional and empathic reactions to the extent that there are some players who wish they could control a character with a lack of empathy:

> The game is tough! I wish some of my characters were sociopaths/psychopaths. I mean fuck! Steal some food from an old couple causing them to starve to death, or kill someone who isn't an armed thug, and they go into a huge depression and just become worthless!
>
> (John, 1912 in Oestreicher, 2015)

There is no doubt that video games connect players to other realities in a mediated way by using and provoking a sense of empathy. However, as shown by this comment, the notion of identification – in this case with characters – also plays an important, and interrelated, role in understanding the different ways in which video games connect us to other situations.

Identification

Empathy and identification are, to a certain extent, interdependent concepts. There could hardly be empathy without a process of, at least partial, identification with the reality that is being shown to us; on the other hand, identifying with someone or something requires a sense of empathy, the possibility to recognize oneself in the other – human or not – and their tribulations. In accord with De Waal (2009: 80), it is reasonably safe to affirm that if 'identification with others opens the door for empathy, the absence of identification closes that door'. In fact, when it comes to video games, the player has more chance to develop their empathy when this 'not only takes the perspective of another, but also begins to identify with the character represented' (Bachen et al., 2012: 440). These notions are difficult to disentangle, but offer important nuances that contribute to advancing our understanding of how video games help players to connect with new realities.

Beyond the similarities or interdependencies between identification and empathy, it is noticeable that the former has several implications when it comes to dealing with ideas of identity formation, a sense of belonging, group attachment, and subjectivity. We will explore these implications further in Chapter 6; however, here it is more specifically our intention to focus on identification as a mechanism of sharing experiences with someone, or something, which is separate from us. Moreover, the possibility of identification lies in, that what we identify with must be seen as a different entity; in sum, everything relies on the difference that identification precisely tries to overcome. According to Judith Butler (2006: 145), the 'one with whom I identify is not me, and that "not being me" is the condition of the identification'. An argument that is also endorsed by Stuart Hall (1996: 3), who asserts that identification is 'a process of articulation, a suturing, an overdetermination not a subsumption'. When we identify with someone or something, we are not subsuming us into the other, on the contrary, we articulate our *selves* with others and their situations, as separate – yet connected – assemblages. In the end, since identification is a process that operates around difference, it inevitably has frontier effects and requires 'what is left outside, its constitutive outside' (Hall, 1996: 3). This is directly related to the fundamental distinction between *identify with* and *identify as*.

In her research on the relationship between identity, identification, and media representation among people who play video games and are members of marginalized groups, Adrianne Shaw (2014) draws a clear distinction between *identifying with* a video game character and *identifying as* a member of a group. This means that not everyone that shares a specific identifier such as gender, sexuality, race, and nationality with other individuals will automatically identify with a character or a situation that supposedly resembles or *represents* them. In fact, it is possible, and not uncommon, to hear individuals state that they identify with characters that are not necessarily like them. For instance, Shaw suggested that, even though the interviewees gave her different definitions of identification, the tying thread among them was 'finding a connection with a character' (Shaw, 2014: 69). This connection could range from a strong identification with the character, with whom they may share several social and personal characteristics and experiences, to recognizing some aspects of themselves in the character without clearly identifying with them; it could also take the shape of empathy or sympathy, including different shades of intellectual or emotional connections. Therefore, identification might be defined as 'a process by which we come to feel an affective connection with a character on the basis of seeing that character as separate and yet a part of us in some way' (Shaw, 2014: 94).

Hence, identification between a player and a video game character or text (and the realities it enacts) can be then understood in multiple ways. Having this in mind, we would like to suggest three ideal types (in the Weberian sense) of identification:

First, it can be seen as a mimetic relationship, in which the gaming experience would temporarily 'induce players to change their self-concept toward the properties of the character they steer or the action role they enter during game play' (Klimmt et al., 2009: 358). This is a trend that, mainly in the field of social psychology, utilizes 'the metaphor of identification as the perceived "merger" of player and game character' (Klimmt et al., 2009: 357); suggesting the player becomes the character by adopting its perceived characteristics. The player then becomes the character or is at least fully immersed in the reality depicted by the game, and – though limited by the technology of the medium and selectivity of the identification process – they adopt the character's attributes to their temporary self-perception. This approach relies on a definition of identification that seeks a synthesis between *oneself* and *the other*; 'making oneself the same as someone or something' (Klimmt et al., 2009: 359).

Second, there is a notion of identification mostly driven by homophily. Homophily is a well-known principle in the social sciences (McPherson *et al.*, 2001; Centola *et al.*, 2007; Kossinets and Watts, 2009) that describes the tendency of people with similar features (including cultural, physical, attitudinal, behavioural, socioeconomical, and educational characteristics) to interact and engage in all sorts of relationships (professional, personal, social) at a higher rate than those with dissimilar attributes. In this respect, players could identify with those characters and situations that reflect, somehow, one or more aspects of their lives, comprising their lifestyle, gender, sexuality, ethnicity, political perspectives, class, level of education, taste, personality, and so on. This is sometimes the case, which could be particularly relevant for those groups who do not normally find their social profiles represented in the media. For instance, LGBTQ gamers may be able to find characters and circumstances in a game like *Gone Home* that might resemble their own lives, to the point of feeling validated; as Karla Zimonja expressed when she was asked about what the main emotions people conveyed to them were: 'queer people were often like: "We're validated by this!"'.

However, the mere introduction of characters or aspects in a game that might resemble someone's particular social situation, is not automatically followed by a process of *identification as* that character. As Shaw shows in her research, most of her interviewees did not give too much importance to being represented in the games they played, since 'it is not game play that stands to benefit from, or even be dramatically transformed by, more diverse representations but rather culture more broadly' (Shaw, 2014: 143). Of course, video games can be validating, and help those who occupy marginalized positions to realize they are also important to the medium and culture, but they are probably more useful to show the existence of other life experiences to the general public. In Chapter 3, when we discuss how video games – in consonance with neoliberal rationalities – held players responsible for representing diversity through avatar customization, the flimsiness of the approach was evident; hence, we agree with Shaw (2014: 143) that the goal in 'increasing representation in games is not expanding customization options but rather making more games that reflect more modes of being in the world' (Shaw, 2014: 143). It is about normalizing those on the margins. Hence, the important thing is to establish connections between different experiences; making access to a wide range of realities possible for a wider audience.

Third, we find a more promising – though more loosely defined – notion of identification in understanding it as a multifaceted connection between a player and a video game character or situation, which can entail different grades of involvement, empathy, and (self)recognition. It implies that, as we saw above, there is always a difference between the one who identifies with someone or something, and those that are the recipient of that identification process. The connections that are established between players and video games are diverse and promiscuous, and they are not necessarily based on previously shared identifiers of characteristics. After all, identification is conceptualized 'as contextual, fluid, and imaginative' (Shaw, 2014: 64); an open notion that invites researchers to 'embrace the diversity of those experiences' (Shaw, 2014: 70). In this case, identification is a sort of connection, a process by which it is possible to relate to other people, stories, situations, and realities. The key to this connection is not necessarily similarity (no matter how big or small), but rather, relatability:

> Giving people other perspectives is good. I think that it is valuable by itself. Empathy, I think, will come if you try to make the characters relatable.
>
> *(Karla Zimonja)*

In this case, making the characters of *Gone Home* relatable does not make them inevitably equal or similar to someone in a specific social category or group. Resemblance, or likeness, is not the prerequisite for the connection (although it might be important in certain cases as we show above) to take place. Relatability alludes to the possibility (and easiness) of understanding someone or something, and by doing so, it facilitates the emergence of connections with those situations, even if these are completely alien to them. This opens the opportunity to give people other perspectives, without forcing them, even temporarily, to occupy those positions without question, resistance, or critical distance. Shaw summarizes this approach to perfection:

> Identification, then, is not about a static, linear, measurable connection to a character. Rather, it is about seeing ourselves reflected in the world and relating to images of others.
>
> *(Shaw, 2014: 70–71)*

In these processes of identification, an exclusive one-to-one connection with a character is rare and mainly not relevant. That would be like establishing a connection only based on a single correlation between a player and a character, as if the authors of this book could imagine they are Guybrush Threepwood while ignoring the remaining characters and the rich universe of situations, places, and adventures drawn in *The Secret of Monkey Island* (LucasArts, 1990). Dealing with the contrast between identification and disidentification (Muñoz, 1999; Staiger, 2005) processes, Shaw learnt from her research participants' experiences that 'we can enjoy texts that are in no way about us, just as we can feel excluded from texts that presume to be about us but fail to ring true to our experiences' (Shaw, 2014: 78). In this regard, and after analyzing online comments relating to the game *Gone Home*, we are able to reach similar conclusions and highlight the intricacies of empathy and identification in video games. For instance, there are those – even amongst gay and lesbian players – who think *Gone Home* is a stereotyped, bland, and stigmatizing title, which only works for the self-indulgence of those who consider themselves trendy, progressive, and liberal:

> As someone who the story should relate to (supposedly), it's a rather poor portrayal. [...] If the idea was to portray (stigmatise) the overly dramatic people

in our community who like to stick together, lavishing over their personal sappy stories as to how things were terrible for them and they have made it now (most of them stay stuck into that state), then mission accomplished. If it was to make some people feel better about themselves and comfort their own open-mindedness and liberalism by praising the subject, then mission accomplished there as well.

(Muskatnuss in Polygon, 2013)

In contrast, there are others, both those who identify as gay or not, who consider *Gone Home* an appealing and laudable game. However, as the following comments highlight, simply having 'queer' elements (whatever they maybe) in a game is not necessarily going to make it more relatable or appealing:

Just to make a point, as a gay gamer myself, while I definitely did experience *Gone Home* and would recommended it, I don't pick games just because they do or do not have gay content. I play games that appeal to me in general. If *Gone Home* had been a crappy game, then it'd still be a crappy game whether or not it had queer content in it. Just adding a gay element doesn't automatically make it appeal to me.

(oxHanoverxo cited in Allen, 2014)

The process of identifying with a game, its characters, story, and universe is not automatic and does not necessarily rest on specific shared identifiers, since it is more of an emergence. As outlined in Chapter 4, video games are experiences, and experiences are there to be lived, felt, enjoyed, and suffered.

Therefore, the mediation that video games operate when connecting players to different circumstances has more to do with resonances of a set of experiences than the exact reproduction of particular vivid experiences. Experiences of others' experiences that, as we saw in previous chapters, are reflective, enacted, and embodied:

The enactments that supported insight are vivified through embodied encounters – not scenarios where we play pretend, but scenarios in which we maintain a reflective encounter that allows our experience to inform our understanding of another.

(Poremba, 2013: 361)

In the end, we identify with not just one aspect of a video game, but rather with its complexities, and what is articulated in and around it: the story, the characters, the universe, the events, the actions, the mechanics, reviews, other players' experiences (accessed on offline and online accounts), and so forth.

It is also important to bear in mind, that a video game is also rarely a set and self-contained text. Not only do video games change as we interact with them, but they are frequently updated or patched by games developers. Moreover, our understanding and opinions of a game, and our identification with (elements of) it (or not), will be influenced by a whole range of para-textual elements, such as advertising, game reviews, others' opinions and interpretations, and much more beyond. How we identify with a game, and what we identify with, is far from straightforward.

Thus, identification sometimes works better on an imprecise evocative level, rather than on a specific and perfectly measurable dimension. This is the case of the documentary on video gamers' memories, *Memorias: más allá del juego* ('Memories: Beyond the Game'), directed by the 27-year-old filmmaker Víctor Somoza, which sought to make the audience connect with the testimonies and feelings of other players:

> First, it is about making people feel what is being said on the screen, make them feel something and evoke that memory. Secondly, it is about people identifying with that.

This connection is, at the same time, literal and metaphorical, concrete and abstract, and, like empathy, identification is a process that is sparked off by video games, helping – intentionally or not – people who play them connect with other realities rather than necessarily escape from them. Video games are therefore seen, according to Poremba (2013: 357), as a 'rich and multilayered experience', where the idea of a player really becoming a character or really experiencing a virtual space is just a 'misrepresentation of the complexity of the game-player relationship'. This complex relationship is something that the developers of *Life is Strange* (Dontnod, 2015) took seriously when they tried to address a particularly difficult situation, that of bullying (and its potential terrible consequences). Mikel Koch, one of its co-directors, talked in an interview about the particular storyline where they approach the problems of a girl, who is being bullied and harassed, including cyber-bullying, by her schoolmates, and how they had to be 'careful as designers and writers to be sure that the player is connected to the characters', so they felt obliged to 'develop the right relationship between Max [the character controlled by the player], the player and her [the bullied woman]' (Skrebels, 2016).

We see that empathy and identification processes are mainly describing experiences that are through video games, connecting us to the reality that surrounds us. Instead of the immersive, absorbing experiences of those who play video games as a form of escapism, we see how video games are also capable of other kinds of mediations: they transform our everyday life experiences in ways that multiply, instead of severing, our links to society.

The limits of video games as mediators of experience

Despite being powerful devices that make unexpected associations with the most varied agents, video games show also significant limitations when it comes to fostering processes of empathy and identification. In fact, the idea of video games as a medium for developing empathic responses, including the aforementioned label of *empathy games*, has drawn fierce criticism from some individuals. This is the case of

Anna Anthropy, a game developer that, among many other works, created the video game *Dys4ia* (Anthropy, 2012), in which she tried to convey part of her experience as a trans woman and the process of undergoing a hormone replacement therapy. The game was widely praised, still is, as a video game that can help people to put themselves in the shoes of transgender people. However, this conceptualization of the game was sharply contested by Anthropy (2015) in a post on her website, where she strongly criticizes the notion of empathy games:

> Empathy Game is about the farce of using a game as a substitute for education, as a way to claim allyship. You could spend hours pacing in a pair of beaten-up size thirteen heels to gain a point or two – a few people did![4] – and still know nothing about the experience of being a trans woman, about how to be an ally to them. Being an ally takes work, it requires you to examine your own behavior, it is an ongoing process with no end point. That people are eager to use games as a shortcut to that, and way to feel like they've done the work and excuse themselves from further educating themselves, angers and disgusts me. You don't know what it's like to be me.

She considers that video games are capable of 'communicating meaningful information and experiences' (Anthropy, 2015), but they cannot ever fully replicate the complexities and nuances of other people's experiences, especially of those who occupy a marginalized position. She particularly despises how the *empathy game* label has been mostly used and nurtured by 'the ones with the most privilege and the least amount of willingness to improve themselves' (Anthropy, 2015). The luring appeal of 'playing as the other' (Shaw, 2014: 176) implies the risk of cultural and political appropriation (Nakamura, 2002) that is far from a trigger for empathetic behaviours. In particular, parallels can be drawn here to the critique of sports video games made by David J. Leonard (2004). Here, Leonard argues, though sports video games, such as those in the EA Sports' hugely popular *NBA Live* (1994–2009; 2013–to date) and *Madden NFL* (EA Sports, 1988–to date) series, frequently allow (predominantly) white gamers to play the role of black sports stars, this does nothing to 'unsettle dominant notions' or 'break down barriers', but rather they reinforce dominant stereotypes of Black athleticism, and allows the (white) gamer to put on 'Blackface'.

Hence, there even could be cases in which video games go beyond empathetic inefficacy or appropriations from dominant and privileged sectors of society, and have other unforeseen negative consequences. In an article at *The Guardian*, Simon Parkin (2016) points to the example of *Spent*[5] (McKinney, 2011), a free online video game on surviving poverty and homelessness in the context of the United States. The game aims to make players understand the people who live in poverty in order to generate a current of empathy towards those in need. Nevertheless, *Psychology Today* (Roussos, 2015) carried out a study that suggested that many individuals who played the game were not affected by it and, furthermore, there were some participants on whom it had a negative effect (including some players who were sympathetic to the poor beforehand). It seems that the problem rests with 'game's mechanics, which leave players with the impression that people living in poverty are able to change their circumstances simply by changing their choices' (Parkin, 2016). Certainly, parallels could be drawn here to the arguments we set out in Chapter 3, which highlight video games as an exemplar of neoliberal culture *par excellence*. Video games have a tendency to quantify the unquantifiable and turn complex social situations into simple rational choices. For example, buying alcohol instead of food may not appear to be the most rational of choices for someone living in poverty, but for that individual it may be an addiction, or a way to dull the pain of their situation, or even the only pleasure they get in their limited lives. What it really feels like to live on the breadline can never be communicated in a video game, and to turn this into simple rational choices massively oversimplifies complex and multifaceted situations. Parkin therefore reaches the conclusion that although games can 'create empathy and deepen our understanding of social systems', they also 'enforce problematic values in profound ways'. In a similar vein, Gorry (2009: 11) is worried about how digital culture 'exposes us to the pain and suffering of so many others, it might also numb our emotions, distance us from our fellow humans, and attenuate our empathetic responses to their misfortunes' and he adds that in 'our life on the screen, we might know more and more about others and care less and less about them'. This could be described as a dissonant empathy process by which video games, far from connecting us with other realities, are estranging us from them even more.

Similarly, other cases point to the difficulties, if not impossibility, of transmitting an experience. This is perfectly visible in one of the campaigns that UNICEF launched in 2014 to raise awareness of the situation of children in South Sudan.[6] They sent an actor to simulate a pitch for a new video game in front of an audience of video gamers, developers, and video game journalists that thought the pitch was real at the Video Gamers United convention in Washington, DC.[7] The game is entitled *Elika's Escape* and players control a seven-year-old girl – Elika – in extreme war time situations. The aim is to make her and her little brother survive in those particular life-threatening conditions. *Elika's Escape* supposedly starts with Elika's mother dying of cholera, her big brother being killed for defending her from attackers, and she fleeing home with her baby brother. At that point, the *pitchman* enthusiastically shouts 'we are taking the level of horror in this game even to infants! Are you guys with me?' The reaction of spectators is that of notable discomfort, nothing is left of the initial enthusiasm before they knew what the video game was about. The presenter continues relating Elika's story: now the player reaches a refugee camp without food and the most elemental sanitary conditions. In order to survive and save her baby brother, Elika, the player, must decide whether to submit to prostitution to get the money they need. That is when several attendees walk out of the room, disgusted with what they are witnessing. After this, the pitchman passes the microphone to Mari Malek, a South Sudanese refugee, on whose life *Elika's Escape* is based: 'This is not a game. Elika's story is true, she is me and she is so many of the South Sudanese children that are going through this experience at this moment'. In UNICEF's promotional video, they assert that 'What is too much for a video game is happening daily to children in South Sudan'. This shows the *untranslatability* of certain experiences, evincing the limits and great difficulties of the medium when it comes to communicating and expressing those extreme realities in order to create game experiences grounded on them.

All of this demonstrates that the relationship that players can have with video games, their rich universes, and reality is complex and, even if they have the potential to foster empathic responses, it is not a connection that is established easily. No matter how close or far we are from the circumstances depicted in those video games, how complex or simple the situations reproduced in the video game are, or even if there are aspects of the experience that are, by definition, irrepresentable, we will experience different grades of connection with them (or none) depending on the processes that facilitate or impede the (dis)associations.

Haraway offers a solution or a way to circumvent this issue: it is not about constructing a universal device in order to convey any experience to anyone, but a way to translate experiences between different people and cultures: we need an 'earth-wide network of connections, including the ability partially to translate knowledges among very different – and power-differentiated – communities' (Haraway, 1991: 187). Therefore, it is not about having the same experience that others have, but a way to connect, and partially understand their situation. Identification and empathy are not absolute experiences, but rather, mediated ones. Video games, as any technology (biological or otherwise), are active and producing new meaning, adding layers (hiding others) to the experience. That is why we prefer to speak about connecting with different aspects of any given situation, rather than completely empathizing or identifying with *the other*.

Conclusions

In this chapter, we have seen how video games are not just about 'escapism', rather, we have been able to demonstrate that video games are also mediation devices that allow us to experience situations that we have never had or would not have otherwise. This presents the opportunity of encouraging empathy and identification processes amongst players, and as a way to connect with circumstances and people whether they are familiar or alien to us. Video games not only work as sophisticated instruments for escapism, but can also open multiple paths towards other aspects of reality that can help us to (re)connect with it in unforeseen ways.

Nevertheless, it is important to keep in mind these are *game* experiences that may convey some aspects of those experiences that they are recreating, representing, simulating, or re-enacting, and they are not the experience themselves. As we showed in Chapter 4, enactment is a key notion in understanding not only video games as experience, but also how reality works. When John Law reflects on the relationship between the methods of studying reality and the reality studied, he suggests that methods 'participate in the enactment of those realities' and they are not 'just a more or less complicated set of procedures or rules, but rather a bundled hinterland' (Law, 2004: 45). In the same way, video games as experiences are not just a way to discover or depict a reality, they are actively participating in the enactment of those realities that are translated into a game experience. The relationship with the player and those realities expressed in a video game is therefore not defined in terms of correspondence but of connection, emergence, or enactment. Video games are a bundled hinterland of experiences.

Notes

1 http://edition.cnn.com/specials/middleeast/syrian-refugees/
2 http://www.blog.radiator.debacle.us/2017/06/the-tearoom-as-record-of-risky-business.html
3 Definition extracted from Educational Simulations website: http://www.educationalsimulations.com/
4 She is making reference to the interactive art exhibit at *Babycastles* (http://babycastles.com/event/babycastles_presents_anna_anthropy_presents_the_road_to_empathy) that featured a pair of old used boots that belonged to Anthropy, a pedometer, and a chalkboard. Visitors were encouraged to walk along in her shoes, measure the distance walked with the pedometer, and then register their score on the chalkboard (one point per mile). The installation was the product of the ironic response she gave to someone who asked her permission to exhibit *dys4ria* as a way to show how video games could 'make us empathize with others by letting us walk a mile in their shoes' (Anthropy, 2015).
5 http://playspent.org/html/
6 https://www.unicef.org/infobycountry/southsudan_78090.html
7 The pitch was recorded to register the audience reactions and to use the video for their campaign. The video can be accessed here: https://www.youtube.com/watch?v=iN6Wc-9r3l4

References

Alexander, Leigh (2011). 'Interview: Making Faces with Team Bondi's McNamara, *L.A. Noire*', *Gamasutra*, [http://www.gamasutra.com/view/news/123427/Interview_Making_Faces_With_Team_Bondis_McNamara_LA_Noire.php] [Last accessed: 11/01/2017].
Allen, Samantha (2014). 'Closing the Gap Between Queer and Mainstream Games', *Polygon*, [http://www.polygon.com/2014/4/2/5549878/closing-the-gap-between-queer-and-mainstream-games] [Last accessed: 07/01/2017].
Anthropy, Anna (2015). 'Empathy Game', *Auntiepixelante*, [http://auntiepixelante.com/empathygame/] [Last accessed: 04/01/2017].
Appelbaum, Mark; Calvert, Sandra; Dodge, Kenneth; Graham, Sandra; Hall, Gordon N.; Hamby, Sherry; Hedges, Lawrence (2015). '*Technical Report on the Review of the Violent Video Game Literature*', Washington: APA Task Force on Violent Media, [http://www.apa.org/pi/families/review-video-games.pdf] [Last accessed: 31/01/2017].
Bachen, Christine M.; Hernández-Ramos, Pedro F.; Raphael, Chad (2012). 'Simulating REAL LIVES: Promoting Global Empathy and Interest in Learning Through Simulation Games', *Simulation & Gaming*, 43 (4): 437–460.
Bogost, Ian (2007). *Persuasive Games*. Cambridge, MA: MIT Press.
Butler, Judith (2006). *Precarious Life: The Power of Mourning and Violence*. London: Verso.
Calleja, Gordon (2010). 'Digital Games and Escapism', *Games and Culture*, 5 (4): 335–353.

Castronova, Edward (2005). *Synthetic Worlds: The Business & Culture of Online Games*. Chicago: University of Chicago Press.

Centola, Damon; González-Avella, Juan Carlos; Eguíluz, Víctor M.; San Miguel, Maxi (2007). 'Homophily, Cultural Drift, and the Co-Evolution of Cultural Groups', *Journal of Conflict Resolution*, 51 (6): 905–929.

Copier, Marinka (2007). '*Beyond the Magic Circle: A Network Perspective on Role-play Online Games*', PhD dissertation, Utrecht University.

Crawford, Garry (2012). *Video Gamers*. London: Routledge.

Davis, Mark H. (1996). *Empathy: A Social Psychological Approach*. New York: Avalon Publishing.

De Waal, Frans (2009). *The Age of Empathy: Nature's Lessons for a Kinder Society*. Toronto: McClelland & Stewart.

Dean, Carolyn (2004). *The Fragility of Empathy After the Holocaust*. Ithaca, New York: Cornell University Press.

Evans, Andrew (2001). *This Virtual Life: Escapism in the Media*. London: Vision.

Gorry, Anthony (2009). 'Empathy in the Virtual World', *Chronicle of Higher Education*, (56): 10–12.

Hall, Stuart (1996). 'Who Needs Identity?', in Hall, Stuart and Du Gay, Paul, *Questions of Cultural Identity*. London: Sage, 1–17.

Haraway, Donna (1991). *Simians, Cyborgs, and Women: The Reinvention of Nature*. New York: Routledge.

Harris, Barbara; Shattell, Mona; Rusch, Doris C.; Zefeldt, Mary J. (2015). 'Barriers to Learning about Mental Illness through Empathy Games – Results of a User Study on Perfection', *Well Playerd*, 4 (2): 56–75.

Huizinga, Johan (1949). *Homo Ludens. A Study of the Play-Element in Culture*. London: Taylor & Francis.

Humphreys, Laud (1970). *The Tearoom Trade: Interpersonal Sex in Public Places*. London: Duckworth Overlook.

Juul, Jesper (2008). 'The Magic Circle and the Puzzle Piece', *Philosophy of Computers Games*, Conference Proceedings, [https://publishup.uni-potsdam.de/opus4-ubp/frontdoor/index/index/docId/2554] [Last accessed: 26/04/2017].

Klimmt, Christoph; Hefner, Dorothée; Vorderer, Peter (2009). 'The Video Game Experience as "True" Identification: A Theory of Enjoyable Alterations of Players' Self-Perception', *Communication Theory*, (19): 351–373.

Kossinets, Gueorgi and Watts, Duncan J. (2009). 'Origins of Homophily in an Evolving Social Network', *American Journal of Sociology*, 115 (2): 405–450.

Leonard, D. (2004). 'High Tech Blackface – Race, Sports Video Games and Becoming the Other', *Intelligent Agent*, 4 (2): Online at: [http://www.intelligentagent.com/archive/Vol4_No4_gaming_leonard.htm] [Last accessed: 04/02/2107].

MacCannell, Dean (1973). 'Staged Authenticity: Arrangements of Social Space in Tourist Settings', *American Journal of Sociology*, 73 (3): 589–603.

McPherson, Miller; Smith-Lovin, Lynn; Cook, James M. (2001). 'Birds of a Feather: Homophily in Social Networks', *Annual Review of Sociology*, (27): 415–444.

Madigan, Jamie (2012). 'The Walking Dead, Mirror Neurons, and Empathy', *The Psychology of Video Games*, 7 November, retrieved at [http://www.psychologyofgames.com/2012/11/the-walking-dead-mirror-neurons-and-empathy/] [Last accessed: 08/09/2016].

Muñoz, José Esteban (1999). *Disidentifications: Queers of Color and the Performance of Politics*. Minneapolis, MN: University of Minnesota Press.

Nakamura, Lisa (2002). *Cybertypes: Race, Ethnicity, and Identity on the Internet*. New York: Routledge.

Oestreicher, Jason (2014). 'Quick Look: This War of Mine', *GiantBomb*, [http://www.giantbomb.com/videos/quick-look-this-war-of-mine/2300-9724/] [Last accessed: 11/01/2017]

Pargman, Daniel and Jakobsson, Peter (2008). 'Do you Believe in Magic? Computer games in Everyday Life', *European Journal of Cultural Studies*, 11 (2): 225–244.

Parkin, Simon (2016). 'Video Games are a Powerful Tool which Must be Wielded with Care', *The Guardian*, [https://www.theguardian.com/technology/2016/apr/03/games-social-issues-who-cares-wins] [Last accessed: 04/01/2017]

Pine, Joseph B. and Gilmore, James H. (2011). *The Experience Economy*. Updated Edition. Boston: Harvard University Press.

Polygon (2013). 'Looking back: Gone Home', *Polygon*, [http://www.polygon.com/features/2013/12/25/5241552/looking-back-gone-home] [Last accessed: 07/01/2017]

Poremba, Cindy (2013). 'Performative Inquiry and the Sublime in Escape from Woomera', *Games and Culture*, 8 (5): 354–367.

Rifkin, Jeremy (2010). *The Empathic Civilization: The Race to Global Consciousness in a World in Crisis*. Cambridge: Polity Press.

Roussos, Gina (2015). 'When Good Intentions Go Awry. The Counterintuitive Effects of a Prosocial Online Game', *Psychology Today*, [https://www.psychologytoday.com/blog/sound-science-sound-policy/201512/when-good-intentions-go-awry] [Last accessed: 04/01/2017].

Salen, Katie and Zimmerman, Eric (2004). *Rules of Play: Game Design Fundamentals*. Cambridge, MA: MIT Press.

Scutti, Susan (2016). 'Do Video Games Lead to Violence?', *CNN*, [http://edition.cnn.com/2016/07/25/health/video-games-and-violence/] [Last accessed: 11/01/2017]

Shaw, Adrienne (2014). *Gaming at the Edge. Sexuality and Gender at the Margins of Gamer Culture*. Minneapolis, MN: University of Minnesota Press.

Simkins, David W. and Steinkuehler, Constance (2008). 'Critical Ethical Reasoning and Role-play', *Games and Culture*, 3 (3–4): 333–355.

Skrebels, Joe (2016). 'Directors Commentary - Revisiting Life is Strange with its Creators', *Gamesradar+*, [http://www.gamesradar.com/life-is-strange-interview-directors/] [Last accessed: 03/01/2017].

Smethurst, Toby and Craps, Stef (2015). 'Playing with Trauma: Interreactivity, Empathy, and Complicity in The Walking Dead Video Game', *Games and Culture*, 10 (3): 269–290.

Staiger, Janet (2005). *Media Reception Studies*. New York: New York University Press.

Taylor, T. L. (2007). 'Pushing the Borders: Player Participation and Game Culture', in Karaganis, Joe. (editor). *Structures of Participation in Digital Culture*. Ann Arbor, MI: University of Michigan Press, 112–132.

Titchener, Edward (1909). *Lectures on the Experimental Psychology of the Thought-processes*. London: Macmillan.

Tuan, Yi-Fu (1998). *Escapism*. Baltimore: Johns Hopkins University Press.

Webber, Jordan Erica (2017a). 'Learning Morality through Gaming', *The Guardian*, [https://www.theguardian.com/lifeandstyle/2017/aug/13/learning-morality-through-gaming] [Last accessed: 18/08/2017].

Webber, Jordan Erica (2017b). 'The Tearoom: The Gay Cruising Game Challenging Industry Norms'. *The Guardian*, [https://www.theguardian.com/technology/2017/jul/11/the-tearoom-game-gay-cruising-1960s-industry-norms-robert-yang] [Last accessed: 18/08/2017].

Webber, Jordan Erica and Griliopoulos, Daniel (2017). *Ten Things Video Games Can Teach Us*. London: Robinson.

Yang, Robert (2017). 'The Tearoom as Risky Business', *Radiator Design Blog*, [http://www.blog.radiator.debacle.us/2017/06/the-tearoom-as-record-of-risky-business.html] [Last accessed 16/08/2017].

Ludography

11 bit studios (2014). *This War of Mine*.
Anthropy (2012). *Dys4ia*.
Blizzard Entertainment (2004). *World of Warcraft*.
Campo Santo (2016). *Firewatch*.
Dontnod Entertainment (2015). *Life is Strange*.
EA Sports (1988–to date). *Madden NFL series*.
EA Sports (1994–2009; 2013–to date). *NBA Live series*.
Educational Simulations (2010). *Real Lives*.
Freebird Games (2011). *To the Moon*.
Fullbright (2013). *Gone Home*.
Hofmeier (2011). *Cart Life*.
Linden Lab (2003). *Second Life*.
LucasArts (1990). *The Secret of Monkey Island*.
McKinney (2011). *Spent*.
Numinous Games (2016). *That Dragon, Cancer*.
Playdead (2016). *Inside*.
Pope, Lucas (2013). *Papers, Please*.
Quinn, Zoe (2013). *Depression Quest*.
Starbreeze Studios (2013). *Brothers: A Tale of two Sons*.
Team Bondi (2011). *L.A. Noire*.
Telltale Games (2012). *The Walking Dead*.
Ubisoft (2014). *Valiant Hearts*.
Yager Development (2012). *Spec Ops: The Line*.
Yang, Robert (2017). *The Tearoom*.

Film

Leonard, Brett (1992). *Lawnmower Man*.

6
VIDEO GAMERS AND (POST-)IDENTITY

Introduction

Identity is a difficult notion to approach. Those who study identity often try to tackle it without mentioning it. Paradoxically, in order to understand identity, we need to flee from it. Stuart Hall (1996: 2) considers identity as a notion that operates 'under erasure', that is, 'an idea which cannot be thought in the old way, but without which certain key questions cannot be thought at all'. His point here is that the concept of identity is no longer useful or applicable, but we seem to have no suitable alternative to replace it.

Quite generally, we can see identity as the ways in which we define ourselves, both individually and collectively, and as the processes by which we *identify with* and *differentiate from* others. Identity takes different shapes, ranging from its more essentialist conceptualizations that build on ideas of *being*, and therefore see this as fairly solid, and those based on acts of *doing*, and therefore tend to see identity as more fluid. The former idea of identity as set is usually associated with pre- and modern societies, while the latter way of seeing identity as more fluid is often linked with the postmodern or advanced modernity. Hence, it is often argued that we live in times where identities become more flexible and even elusive, but where residual configurations of identity have not disappeared either.

In this chapter, we will explore the contemporary nature of identity in relation to video gamers and the video gamer community. In particular, we suggest that video games provide a useful vantage point to observe one of the most complex, debated, and elusive processes: identity formation. Therefore, the chapter begins with a brief review of some of the theoretical discussions on identity; or, more precisely, the related crisis that has taken place in the social sciences in recent years. After that, and primarily drawing on our interviews, we look at the different conceptualizations of the video gamer and the communities that emerge around video games. This will help us connect these more discursive conceptualizations of identity with previous theoretical discussions, which we hope will shed new light on contemporary processes of identity and community formation. Finally, we envisage the rise of post-identity; in which the processes of identity formation change radically and the very notion of identity is put in jeopardy. In particular, we argue that video game culture anticipates and helps us to understand new modes of meaning and processes of identity construction.

The question of identity in contemporary society

It seems inevitable that any sociological reflection on identity starts with a digression, but we will try not to stay too long in a territory that might be the realm of ghosts, or as Beck may see it, 'zombie categories' (see Beck and Beck-Gernsheim, 2001).

We should start by admitting that the term *identity* has become a *sociological buoy*, that is, it is a concept sociologists cling to, which allows us to think in sociological terms about certain aspects of social reality; however, outside of sociological conversations, discussions of identity are often absent, if not strange, or even obscene. Nevertheless, we, like so many others, will cling to this sociological buoy, at least for now, as this does still provide a useful analytical tool for understanding the contemporary nature of video gamers and their community.

Initially, we wish to start by highlighting how we do not want to approach identity; that is, as a substantial entity, as total unity, or as something that remains immutable in time. In other words, we do not see identity as that 'bit of the self which remains always-already the same' (Hall, 1996: 3). From here, there are several options. But before moving our discussion forward it is useful to start with a basic and functional definition of identity, such as that offered by Richard Jenkins (2008: 18):

> Identity is our understanding of who we are and who other people are, and, reciprocally, other people's understanding of themselves and of others (which includes us). It is a very practical matter, synthesising relationships of similarity and difference.

This definition of identity encompasses the fundamental aspects of this concept: in that it defines identity as a way to represent ourselves and others, which is constructed around the tension between what makes us similar and different. Once we have set out the fundamental aspects of how this term is most often employed, where we then go from here is more open.

In particular, identity can be seen as either strong, solid, and permanent, or as flexible, fragmented, and temporary. In other words, identity can be seen as essentialist, that is to say, what someone is, or rather as a disposition, and hence, part of a process of identification. We will explore these ideas, and more, throughout the chapter; however, the existing social science literature on identity is so vast, it is not possible to cover all of this, even in a superficial way. Thus, for an introduction to the main debates in this area we would recommend the works of Jenkins (2014), Lawler (2014), Hall and Du Gay (1996), and Burke and Stets (2009); while, here, in this chapter we are specifically going to focus on how identity intersects with the contemporary nature of video games. Nonetheless, before we do so, it is necessary to reflect, at least a little, on the contemporary nature of identity, and how we got where we currently are.

Identity in crisis

In this section, we will focus on identity as a notion in crisis. There has been a widespread diagnosis amongst contemporary social theorists that suggests that some of the fundamental institutions of modernity are in crisis or in decline; an idea encapsulated neatly in Ulrich Beck's (2002) idea of 'zombie categories'. That is to say, ideas that are kept alive, most commonly by social scientists, to describe social phenomena that no longer exist, or certainly not in the way that they were initially theorized. Among other writings, this diagnosis materializes in a *Runaway World* (Giddens, 2002), *The Postmodern Condition* (Lyotard, 1984), *Liquid Modernity* (Bauman, 2000), *Risk Society* (Beck, 1992), *The Decline of Institution* (Dubet, 2006), or *The Coming Community* (Agamben, 1993). The Enlightenment project of modernity then shows signs of exhaustion, and a period of uncertainty rises, which numerous academics have attempted to characterize and name in different ways. Several headings of 'the post-' are deployed: post-modernity (Lyotard, 1984; Lyon, 1999; Jameson, 1990), post-industrial society (Touraine, 1971; Bell, 1976), post-capitalist society (Drucker, 1994), or even the post-postmodern (Kirby, 2006); along with others that try to catch the 'essence' of our current society, such as network society or the information age (Castells, 2010), liquid modernity (Bauman, 2000), reflexive modernity (Beck, Giddens, and Lash, 1994), cybersociety (Jones, 1998), or knowledge society (Stehr, 1994). Regardless of the term used, all of them agree in their assessment that 'the social' has become more fluid, unstable, risky, aimless, fragmented, or even meaningless.

This implies that modern models for social meaning and identity construction have changed dramatically. Taking these diagnoses into account, it is possible to conclude that modern identities have at least been decentred, if not disappeared altogether. We are witnessing then, the emergence of new kinds of identities, and new ways of constructing social universes of meaning. The way we have understood social reality for almost a century has radically changed, and this transformation may have only just begun.

In these analyses of contemporary society, we find certain analogies with what can be considered as part of the foundational mythology of sociology as a discipline. Sociology is often seen as emerging in a period of traumatic and fundamental social change, with the birth of modernity in the eighteenth and nineteenth centuries. In other words, what Durkheim (2013) described as the historical change from societies governed by a 'mechanical solidarity' towards those governed by 'organic solidarity', or what Weber (1968) depicted as the process of rationalization in

Western societies that led to a growing bureaucratization and individualization of society. In short, the now classic distinction between community and society, which Tönnies (2001) defined in his distinction between *Gemeinschaft* and *Gesellschaft*.

Similarly, it has been suggested by many social commentators that we are now witnessing another period of great social upheaval and change, and just as with the birth of modernity, we can highlight two main aspects of these times: the existence of an unstable reality, and a crisis in the meaning and forms of identity. Moreover, in our contemporary society, the origins of the current crisis can be traced back precisely to the development of the Enlightenment, and seen as this project taken to the extreme.

With the birth of modernity, a (probably idealized) pre-modern version of reality in which the meaning of social life was *taken for granted* is seen to shift to a form where social meaning is problematized, planned, and has to be constructed (Berger and Luckmann, 1997: 80). Once the self-regulatory mechanisms of pre-modern communities were removed, the question of social control became much more central in modernity. This propelled the birth of what we know, in Foucauldian terms, as the question of 'governmentality' (Foucault, 1991). This encompasses the ideas of sovereign power, discipline, biopolitics, and technologies of the self, and can be defined as 'the common ground of all our modern forms of political rationality, insofar as they construe the tasks of rulers in terms of a calculated supervision and maximization of the forces of society' (Rose, 1999a: 5).

Society emerges then as a planned reality. The social is explicitly designed (Bauman, 1989: 54), deploying a myriad of elements, techniques, and processes in order to govern it (Rose, 1999b: 51–55). It is then with the dawn of modernity and rise of the modern State, when, as Zygmunt Bauman suggests (2004: 20), identity as a problem and, moreover, as a task, is born. In pre-modern societies (the realm of *community* in Tönnies's theory), it was not possible to think in terms of identity; because to ask 'who you are' only makes sense if 'you believe that you can be someone other than you are' (Bauman, 2004: 19). In the pre-modern world, identity was determined by birth and there were very few occasions when this could ever change. Identities were solid and unquestioned because they were *taken for granted*; hence, identity as a notion did not make sense in a pre-modern world, and paradoxically as we will see, possibly the same could be said now in contemporary society.

Therefore, it is modernity where identity acquires its full meaning and became 'tasks which individuals had to perform' through their 'biographies' (Bauman, 2004: 49). It is, according to Giddens (1990: 121), the 'quest of self-identity', or 'construction of the self as a reflexive project', where individuals must find their 'identity amid the strategies and options provided by abstract systems' (Giddens, 1990: 124).

Identity as a project or a quest, in comparison to the pre-modern ascription of identity at birth, is often seen as an act of liberation; where the individuals seek to fulfil their full potential and become their 'true' selves. However, although these are identities that individuals needed to choose and pursue, as Bauman (2004: 49) suggests their trajectories were 'unambiguously laid out' and each class had their 'career tracks' that were 'punctuated with milestones'. Hence, though identity becomes a project, it is a project one has to pursue, to set ends; it is about becoming who we were meant to be.

However, as Bauman argues (2004: 53), the idea of a 'cohesive, firmly riveted and solidly constructed identity' progressively became a limitation on 'the freedom to choose', and hence, identities began to liquefy. Modernity was meant to remove ambivalence, but it resulted in its exponential growth: 'In this environment arises most of the ambivalence and insecurity, and thus most of the perceived dangers' (Bauman, 1993: 214).

Transforming the construction of identity into an individualized project, liquid modernity erodes collective forms of identity and association. Hence, the certitudes of social life and the foundations of modern identity such as social class, occupation, family, and location start to not only erode, but become obstacles. In an increasingly shifting and liquid world, set identities become redundant, worse still, impediments to survival in an ever-changing world.

In this regard, identities are reinvented in strange, fragmented, and multiple ways. According to Bauman (2000: 82), the 'search for identity' is a 'struggle to arrest or slow down the flow, to solidify the fluid, to give form to the formless'. As with notions of community, identity constitutes a sense of security, a sense of stability, of knowing who we are and where we are. Accordingly, Bauman (2000: 82) writes:

> Whenever we speak of identity, there is at the back of our minds a faint image of harmony, logic, consistency: all those things which the flow of our experience seems – to our perpetual despair – so grossly and abominably to lack.

But unlike in modernity, there is no longer a set trajectory, no longer a 'real' self which we are moving towards. Instead, identities become the product of consumer choices. Bauman (2005: 23) suggests that 'ours is a consumer society'. Of course, all societies are consumer societies, to a lesser or greater extent, but Bauman (2005: 24) suggests, there is something 'profound and fundamental' about the nature of contemporary consumer society that makes it distinct from all other societies.

Most significantly, Bauman argues that all prior societies have primarily been producer societies. Before an individual could fully participate in society they had to be part of the production process, and an individual's position within the social order was based upon their location within this process. However, in 'our' consumer society an individual 'needs to be a consumer first, before one can think of becoming anything in particular' (Bauman, 2005: 26). According to Bauman, it is consumption that defines who we are and who we can be. Therefore, our identities become fluid, flexible, and based increasingly on individualized consumer choices, which can easily be changed to meet the needs of our liquid world.

In this new consumer society, Hayward (2012: 214) argues, consumer capitalism aims at 'undermining and eroding established stages of the life cycle in the search for corporate profit'. The well-established stages of age progression, from childhood, to youth, to adulthood, have (as with those of identity formation) been eroded, as they no longer serve the purposes of an advanced capitalist neoliberal society. This consumer society sells the idea that we can choose to be who we want to be (reflecting political rationalities associated with neoliberalism that we saw in Chapter 3); be that a young person wanting to be older, or an adult trying to hold onto their youth. Insecurity becomes not only a given then, but desirable. It significates a lack of (adult) responsibilities; of not staying still, of not settling down. Consumer culture then becomes infantilized, particularly for men (Smith, 2014). It sells (particularly older men) a 'leisure life' (Blackshaw, 2003); free from responsibility, where life becomes a series of inconsequential lifestyle and playful choices.

For example, the video gamer identity and sense of community are enacted through certain activities and consumer choices that reproduce it and give it a temporary, though unstable, consistency: reading game reviews, participating in online forums and social networks, purchasing video game-related merchandise and memorabilia, attending events, using game guides, and speaking about video games with others. The materiality of the gamer identity is then sustained and expressed by means of the diverse elements that, according to Zelda (female, 25, mild self-identifying gamer, highly involved in gaming culture), keep the game 'going on for as long as possible': figurines, posters, signings, t-shirts, and photographs. In this way, Zelda suggests that belonging to the community of gamers is an act that can be performed through consumption: 'Sometimes I like to purchase things that show that I'm a gamer'. This practice describes, according to Miller and Rose (2008: 101), a process of 'affiliation to communities of lifestyle through the practices of consumption' that 'displaces older devices of habit formation that enjoined obligations upon citizens as part of their social responsibilities'.

Hence, in our contemporary, late-modern, liquid society, identities become both irrelevant and a central concern for us all. As with ideas of community (see Bauman, 2001), identity becomes fluid, even elusive, which (ironically) makes it even more important and even more desirable. The things we cannot quite grasp are often those we try the hardest to hold onto. We will empirically explore some of these concerns around the notion of identity through the video gamer category, which embodies the main characteristics that define the contemporary nature of identity, and what is more, shows us what lies ahead for the notion.

The gamer conundrum

When we asked Alfred, a 26-year-old, dedicated video gamer, if he considered himself a gamer, his answer came loud and clear: 'Would I define myself as a gamer? Yeah!' He then elaborated on this, stating that this was clear to everybody: 'this is me,' and video gaming is 'at the very core of what I do'. This enthusiastic adhesion to a video gamer identity contrasts with Elisabeth's (female, 25, not self-identifying gamer) response to the same question: 'No. Definitely a thousand times I would say no, no!' Alfred and Elisabeth are at opposite ends of a gamer (self-)identification spectrum. One clearly identifies himself with a gamer identity, the other denies and severs any connection to the category. The 'gamer' identity is powerful because it takes, to a greater or lesser degree, the forms of political, cultural, and social articulations. It is both solid and volatile, and fosters loyalties in the same way it enables identity promiscuity; it is sometimes a casual label that becomes broadly inclusive, while, on other occasions, it is so restrictive that it comes to be very excluding. The identity of the video gamer is, in many ways, a boundary construct, to the point of exceeding the very notion of identity. The 'video gamer' is a category that causes discomfort and, as such, is a useful way to explore how identity is formed, and also, dissolved in today's society.

In order to understand how identities around video games work, it is useful to begin by considering to what extent the interviewees identify themselves as gamers, and how important this is to them. The notion of *identification* is, as we saw in Chapter 5, central to these discussions. According to Hall (1996: 2–3), identification is a 'construction, a process never completed', and, most importantly, also a process that ties individuals to other people without completely merging with them. In this sense, the process of identification implies that identity is, above all, a strategic and positional concept, and not what signals 'that stable core of the self' (Hall, 1996: 3). Identities are, in the end, 'constituted within, not outside representation' (Hall, 1996: 4). This means that individuals' own representations of who they are – along with the representations that others hold of them – are crucial to their identity formation. Building on Althusser's (1971) theory, Hall (1996: 5–6) argues that identity is 'the meeting point' between 'the discourses and practices which attempt to interpellate'[1] us and the processes that 'construct us as subjects which can be spoken'. Identity is, then, the result of the intersection between where we want to be and what others want us to be.

For their part, there are those who are highly involved in gamer culture and consider that being a video gamer is a big part of their identity. Alfred is, obviously, one of them. He brings up the topic several times during the interview: 'I don't know if you hear this a lot, but I think computer games have always been a big part of my life'. He is not alone in this strong association with a gamer identity. Carl (male, 28), another enthusiastic video gamer, expressed similar sentiments:

> I think it's a big part of my identity. I mean, there's multiple things that make up who I am […] but video games is a big part of my life.

Hence, though Carl acknowledges that video games are just one of many things that define his identity, he is very clear that video games play an important role in who he is, in his identity. For both Carl and Alfred, video gaming is a big part of their lives. Moreover, it is suggested that this strong identification, based on a type of cultural consumption, is particularly associated with video game culture. For example, Klimmt *et al.* (2009: 363) argue that 'models of interactive video game experiences can claim the utility of "identification" with an especially strong legitimization', while Gee (2003: 58) characterizes the identification of video game players with game characters as 'quite powerful', transcending the identification processes that take place 'in novels or movies'. Similarly, King and Krzywinska

(2006: 168–169) argue that, due to the 'active nature of play', players seem to be more 'directly implicated than traditional media consumers'. These authors consider that games are 'potent sources of interpellation' and players are 'more literally interpellated' (King and Krzywinska, 2006: 197), which leads to a form of interpellation that configures the video game player *as player* or *as gamer*. This promotes a generalized and strong awareness of the gamer as a subject position that is occupied for those who play video games.

The strong affiliation and identification that some gamers have is sometimes used to criticize video gaming and gamers, such as the negative stereotypes of 'gamers' as addicted, obsessed geeks, violent, or intolerant people. However, in our opinion, this makes gaming identity and affiliations particularly interesting, at least from a sociological point of view. What do video games and their identity constructs have to turn them into powerful social artifacts? We believe the answer should not be ignoring the label 'gamer'; on the contrary, we need to deal with it, dissect it, and understand how it is formed. As sociologists, we are here to understand the processes that result in determined definitions of reality, including – to the extent it is possible – every actor that is involved in the construction of this definition.

When it comes to defining what a gamer is, Carl, Alfred, and Elisabeth represent different articulations of the category, on a semantic arc that goes from the more restrictive, purist, and elitist definitions of gamer, to the more open, vague, and inclusive ones; including those who explicitly do not identify themselves as gamers. It is on this spectrum of identity, and its constitutive outside (Butler, 1993), where the gamer as a subject position is imagined and realized. For this reason, we will explore five non-excluding categories – understood as representational tools (ideal types) rather than fixed identities – that help us understand the video gamer identity as a fluid, flexible, and unstable construct: 'hardcore-subcultural gamer', 'casual gamer', 'gamer as a foodie-connoisseur', 'cultural-intellectual', and 'everyone is a gamer'.

Hardcore-subcultural gamer

The 'hardcore gamer' is a restrictive and excluding classification of a gamer. This could also be referred to as the classic or canonical version of 'the gamer', the one that was born in the 'historical anomaly of the 1980s and 1990s when video games were played by only a small part of the population' (Juul, 2010: 20). In this sense, the hardcore gamer is inseparable from the formation of gaming as a subculture that was produced in the 1980s. Graeme Kirkpatrick (2015) has shown how specialized gaming magazines fundamentally contributed to the creation, in the 1980s, of a gaming subculture clearly distinguishable from other circulating artefacts of wider computer culture. Particularly important to this, is the emergence and popularization of the notion of 'gameplay' in the second half of the 1980s, which marked a tendency 'to assess games in terms of their feel' (Kirkpatrick, 2015: 64). That is to say, games began to be understood as experiences (see Chapter 4). Gameplay, Kirkpatrick (2015: 66–67) argues, becomes central to 'gaming's bid for autonomy as a cultural practice' and 'signifies the tastes and preferences of the authentic gamer'. According to Kirkpatrick (2015: 68), it is in the 'discovery of gameplay' that 'the player gets incorporated into the game and it marks the point at which gaming is established as a field, as a cultural institution with an established group of participants'. Therefore, gameplay serves to 'affirm and to regulate gamer identity' (Kirkpatrick, 2015: 69), which outlines the shape of the 'real gamer' as the experienced and knowledgeable individual whose performance with games places them in a superior plane in relation to the novice gamer or non-gamer. These 'true gamers' are then associated with 'male adolescents' (Kirkpatrick, 2015: 80) as the preferred target audience for both the media and the industry. This is how the traditional image of the gamer was born in the light of an emerging gaming culture during the 1980s.

This subcultural type is probably the most problematic definition of gamer, the one that rouses irate debates around the category, but it is central to understanding the contradictory nature of the gamer identity. For instance, Frans Mäyrä (2008: 25) depicts gamers within a subcultural framework by stating that they seem to share the same language (for example, adopting specific terminologies for the games they play), rituals (such as gathering together to play, and collecting artefacts like gaming devices, books, and posters), and space (such as on websites or discussion boards). Mäyrä (2008: 26) argues, that of course, this category does not account for all individuals who play video games, but rather applies more specifically to so-called hardcore gamers. According to our interviewees, there are three main characteristics that most typically define this kind of hardcore gamer: dedication/passion, immaturity, and tribalism.

This subcultural type of gamer, often referred to as the hardcore gamer, is principally defined by their dedication and passion to video games, but, above all, this version of the gamer is identified by their intensive and consistent schedule of game playing. Precisely, King and Krzywinska (2006: 220) suggest that those 'who invest a great deal of time, money and energy in playing games are more inclined to identify themselves as part of a distinct category of "gamers"'. Hence, gamers are seen as spending great amounts of time playing video games:

> A gamer as such, I think [...] you should be someone who [...] invests an important part of your life playing.
> *(Iker, male, 43, not self-identifying gamer but regular player)*

> To be a gamer you need to be passionate about playing them and be a consistent player. So, someone who says 'yes, I can say that I play a certain amount of hours a week'. That to me is a gamer, not someone like me, who maybe plays games for one or two days, and then doesn't use it again for three months.
> *(Elisabeth)*

The time spent playing video games seems to be crucial to determine whether someone is a gamer in this case. The people who introduced us to Iker – relatives of him, who are not particularly interested in video game culture – told us that he was a 'hardcore gamer' who played video games 'all the time'. However, Iker does not identify as a gamer in those particular terms, because he does not think he spends the amount of time required to qualify as a hardcore gamer, even though others close to him see him as someone highly devoted to gaming.

Therefore, there is certainly a perceived dedication and passion in this definition of gamer. However, unlike the expert or connoisseur approach of the foodie type, as we shall see below, our interviewees depict the subcultural gamer as someone who does not address their efforts to exploring the culture as a whole, but 'dedicates to one game or one specific type of games only and plays it very intensely' (Zelda, female, 25, mild self-identifying gamer, highly involved in gaming culture). This follows, Juul (2010: 29) suggests, a *hardcore* ethic: 'spend as much time as possible, play as difficult games as possible, play games at the expense of everything else'. The hardcore gamer focuses on specific games and plays them thoroughly, rather than approaching video games as a medium and culture. This is seconded by the only interviewee who clearly defined himself as a hardcore gamer, Alfred; although he did so in the following terms: 'I probably would say I'm a hardcore gamer, but at the light end of the scale'. As we saw above, Alfred believes that anyone that considers themselves a gamer, is one. However, in order to be a hardcore gamer, Alfred considers that it is necessary to 'play a lot' and do it 'on hard mode'. This is an approach that certain behavioural studies (such as Kapalo *et al.*, 2015) have used to distinguish between a hardcore gamer and a casual gamer. For these psychologists, a hardcore gamer is not defined by their expertise, but by the time and money they invest in gaming. Hardcore gaming is then not about expertise but mastery.

The second key categorization of the hardcore-subcultural gamer is the association of this type of gamer with youth, or even more typically, immaturity. For example, Elisabeth, as we saw above, a young woman who sporadically plays certain video games, especially games on online social networking sites and on mobile devices, views gamer culture and dedicated players in quite negative terms. In spite of recognizing that playing video games is a widely extended and accepted activity in our society, her representation of the typical gamer is that of a solitary, young male with scarce social skills. In sum, the gamer as what Bergstrom *et al.* (2016: 234) call 'That Guy', a stereotypical perception, fixed in popular culture, of the archetypal video game player as a white, 'male teen, likely overweight and socially awkward or isolated'. Kowert *et al.* (2012: 473) sustain a similar portrayal of gamers as 'socially anxious and incompetent, mentally stunted and withdrawn, and physically unhealthy (e.g., over-weight, pale)'. Elisabeth offers an almost cartoonish account of this kind of gamer:

> The typical gamer that I think of are guys between the ages of 12 and 30 in tracksuit bottoms, with half a pizza next to them. This is how I imagine them, sat like this, with the hood halfway up, with like a silver chain. […] I see people who are gamers in this way, that they have nothing better to do

with their lives, that they're a bit stupid and they can switch off and play all day and they sit in their own filth and they don't wash, that's what I imagine.

The gamer figure is often associated, both literally and metaphorically, with adolescence and immaturity. This narrow representation of adolescence here shows the adolescent as a problematic, foolish, and lazy individual who does not 'care about personal hygiene' (Zelda). The hardcore-subcultural type of gamer is then linked to the video game as an object of consumption and, moreover, to particularly aggressive consumption practices. Hence, the hardcore gamer is often linked to immature and impulsive behaviours. As Edward (male, 54, head of a Masters' on video games) states:

> You go to any game convention and it really is like going to a porn convention – not that I got experiences of the latter [laughter], but it's full of adolescent boys, still, with problematic complexions. It's not real and not diverse. You could say that most gamers are adolescent boys of all ages and all sexes. In other words, they could be a 45-year-old woman, but still has that mentality of an adolescent boy.

Gamers as 'porn convention goers' is a powerful, though disturbing, simile. Not only is this a category imagined as mainly formed by a group of male adolescents, but also it is suggesting a mental state, a mode of conduct, and a way of representing the world. Edward alludes to a particular mentality that is typically associated with, but not necessarily limited to, adolescent boys. The oxymoron he uses, which includes *adolescents of all ages and boys of all sexes*, points to a central assumption: that gamer culture is still that of adolescents, regardless of the specific sociodemographic characteristics of its members, and despite its growth and consolidation in recent years.

This representation of the subcultural gamer as a homogenous body of dedicated individuals leads us to the third characteristic that is usually associated with them: their tribalism. Darius is a 28-year-old, male, indie game designer who is critical of certain aspects of the game industry, the media, and the community of gamers, and in particular, the hardcore-subcultural type. Darius speaks of gamers as a tribal group that appears to feel like they are losing their cultural and social space as a consequence of a growing, and in the process of consolidation, game culture:

> It's tribalism as well. There is this massive thing that geeks are growing up, they believe in [...] you identify like [...] 'video games were our thing and now they're becoming embedded in the wider culture and we resent it'; and depending on who we talk to, 'girls are ruining the games industry'. There is all this animosity, all this tribalism. It's the line where we draw them, we're looking at it [...] not 'we', but that sort of Doritos, *Halo* playing crowd.

The derogatory tone of his discourse downgrades this group from community to crowd, a particular mass that is identified with *Doritos* tortilla chips (a brand that, along with *Mountain Dew*, is typically associated pejoratively with this kind of gamer) and *Halo*, a AAA game that, in the same vein as *Call of Duty*, *FIFA*, and *Grand Theft Auto*, is considered to be part of a 'hardcore' series of titles. We find again a representation of this type of gamer that directly links them to careless, unhealthy, and impulsive patterns of consumption. But, moreover, Darius suggests a situation in which this group sees themselves as a community under attack and in peril. These hardcore gamers, Darius argues, feel threatened by a wider culture, which they see as trying to steal their place and the culture they have built. As with other interviewees, Darius describes the social demographic of these gamers: 'It's white, straight, male'. As harsh as Darius' comments on gamers seem to be, they do not reach the heights of Edward's opinion, the head of a master on video games, who compares gamers with jihadists:

> They are used to being in an environment where, with the flick of a thumb, they can wreak virtual havoc and destruction with no consequence. By typing a few keys on a keyboard in Twitter, they can tell someone who is threatening their view of the world that they will die at their hands. It's the same as Jihadism, seems to me. Very, very similar.

Edward here is describing what he sees as an extremely territorial group of individuals who antagonize anyone who might be threatening their *status quo*. Conversely, Alfred does not share this adolescent and tribal vision of the gamer, and believes that the individuals who behave in that fashion are only a minority and cannot be deemed as gamers under any circumstance:

> I don't think they're proper gamers, I think they're despicable. The vast majority of people that would actually call themselves a gamer, or consider themselves to be a gamer, are very supportive people, and I think it's a really, really good culture that it breeds.

Alfred insists on the idea that gamers, far from being that 'idiot, a 13-year-old', are 'such a supportive community' that 'always helps each other out'. As an example of the empathetic conduct of gamers, he also adds that when 'it comes to things like charity […] it'll be second nature to help each other, to support each other'. According to Alfred, gamers are not a group of selfish adolescents, but a diverse group of people who support each other. In this vision then, gamers are not part of a tribe, but rather a community.

Therefore, it is important to recognize that 'gamer' has always been a rather ill defined, fluid, and inclusive, as well as at times, exclusive term. It has always, and probably even more so today, been used to describe a wide range of people, and has also sometimes been (re-)appropriated by others typically excluded from this identity, such as 'grrrl gamers' (Bryce and Rutter, 2005) and 'gaymers' (Pulos, 2013). The gamer label then works as a screen where others can project the discursive elements they use to build (or negate) their own definitions of the gamer. For some, the gamer can extend to include categories, such as casuals, connoisseurs, and intellectuals – as we shall see below. However, most typically we find the gamer is associated with a particular negative stereotype of immature, obsessed, and tribal young men. It is then, against this stereotype, that most of our interviewees sought to distinguish themselves; as not this 'typical' (hardcore) gamer – a point we will discuss further below. This is also probably why then we only found one person, amongst the research participants, willing to define themselves as a 'hardcore gamer', and then only partially. However, this subcultural type still appears to be the dominant representation of the gamer and, despite its mainly stereotypical characteristics, is also clearly embodied by certain individuals.

Casual gamers

Traditionally, often both many gamers and academics draw a distinction between 'hardcore' and 'casual' games (such as Juul, 2010; Aarsand, 2012; Kapalo *et al.*, 2015). For example, playing certain types of video games that require 'shorter commitments' (Juul, 2010: 9) is often directly associated with the idea of being a casual gamer or even, a *non-gamer*, by individuals who strongly associate with gaming culture. This was very evident when, back at the end of 2014, a *Reddit* user shared in the subreddit *r/Games* thread two pieces of media that discussed the possibility that half of all video gamers were women. The first one was an article from *The Guardian* newspaper echoing a study published by the Internet Advertising Bureau, which suggested that 52% of the gaming audience was made up of women (Jayanth, 2014). The second piece was a YouTube video entitled 'Are 50% of Gamers Women?',[2] which was part of the PBS Digital Studios' *Game/Show*, and where its conductor, Jamin Warren, spoke about the generalized skepticisms regarding the statistic that claims that half of gamers are women. A typical response to these posts from members of this discussion thread was to seek to clearly differentiate the activity from the category:

> Is everyone that eats, a foodie? Is everyone that watches films, a movie buff? Is everyone that reads, a book worm? Is everyone that plays a game, a gamer? No, no, no and no. Half of all people that play games might be women, but half of all gamers are clearly not women.
>
> *(Azradesh, reddit user)*

> I think a gamer is someone who is more likely to be exploring new experiences, looking for new games to play. A non-gamer who plays games is going to depend far more on word-of-mouth from their peers to tell them what games to play next. They'll have their small number of games that they like, and they're far more likely to stick to those.
>
> *(Reliant, reddit user)*

Here we are faced with the idea that, in order to achieve the category of gamer, an individual needs a certain level of commitment and expertise, and moreover, for the majority of those on this discussion thread, it seems they felt that there are particular demographics for whom this label does not apply: 'My parents and sisters play *Angry Birds*, *Words with Friends*, and *Bejeweled*. Do I see them as gamers? Not really. I see them as casual players' (joester049, reddit user). In these accounts, older people and women are usually depicted as casual players and rarely as gamers. The final conclusion for these individuals is clear: women cannot represent 50% of the gamer population, because they are not playing games, but rather 'inane, pointless shit like *Flappy Bird*' (deleted account of a reddit user). Of course, these comments cannot be separated from the fact that Reddit has largely a young white male user group, who it seems, often seek to justify the lack of diversity in their community, as Massanari (2015: 4) argues, 'under a banner of choice – that the reason more women or people of color do not participate is because they do not want to – rather than a recognition of the structural barriers that might make participation difficult or unappealing'. This is something that we clearly see exacerbated with discussions relating to what constitutes a gamer.

In many respects, this description matches what Jesper Juul (2010: 8) describes as the stereotype of a 'casual gamer'; who has 'a preference for positive and pleasant fictions, has played few games, is willing to commit little time and few resources toward playing video games, and dislikes difficult games'. There is thus, at least with some of our interviewees, an explicit disdain for those who play casual games, particularly video games on mobile devices or social networks that, no matter how many hours players invest in them – and in video games like *Candy Crush Saga* (King, 2012), people can invest as many hours as any hardcore gamer in *Call of Duty* or *FIFA* – are still most commonly depicted as *non-games* for *non-gamers*; both by gamers, but also often by themselves too. As Elisabeth thinks of herself: 'I don't associate being a gamer with someone who plays games on the apps, and stuff like that. So I wouldn't say that I was a casual gamer, I would say that I get addicted to silly games for a while, and then stop'. Similarly, Jack, a 46-year-old programme coordinator who works at a university that specializes in teaching game design, does not believe he is a gamer:

> On my iPhone, I play games. I have a few games on my laptop on work. I play the student's games, but I'm not a gamer. I don't sit in front of the screen for hours.

Even after admitting he often plays at work and on his mobile devices, Jack still does not see himself as a gamer. The reasons why Jack does not identify as such are that he does not play on consoles or high-end computers, which he associates with being a gamer, and because he does not believe he puts in enough hours of gaming. Casual gaming is seen as a superficial and non-dedicated activity and casual gamers 'are deemed to deliberately avoid the corporeal attachment of dedicated console or PC game-play so that they are perpetually ready to resume their temporarily interrupted activities' (Richardson, 2011: 423). Some of our interviewees that identify as casual gamers, like Jill (female, 26, loosely involved in gaming culture), seem to have similar views:

> I think a proper gamer knows when the game's coming out and pre orders them, so he knows when they're coming out and he'll be the first one to try them. […] So, obviously buying the games […] but also as well spending more time playing them.

In this view then, the casual gamer does not necessarily know when a game is going to be released and, in general, does not care for everything that surrounds video game culture. Equally, the casual gamer does not invest too much time playing video games, because for them it is simply a leisure activity. When Jill explains why she does not aspire to be a regular gamer or hardcore gamer, even though she likes playing video games, she concludes: 'I'm just too busy, because I got work full time'. Casual gaming is also the product of the evolution of game culture and of individuals' changing situations: people who started playing video games when they were a child have 'less time on their hands than they used to, but are looking for video game experiences that work for them today' (Juul, 2010: 147).

The casual gamer, then, is a more recent construct that is typically located in opposition to the hardcore gamer. It is also the first sign of a category that is not only being widened (more and more diverse people playing video games in increasingly different ways), but is starting to lose its defining capabilities. As we start to see a shift away from the stereotype of all gamers as isolated young men, and the game 'industry's construction of the hard-core gamer as the ideal market' (Shaw, 2014: 45), casual gaming practices gain traction and, with it, initiate the emptying of 'gamer' as an identity label. The 'everyone is a gamer' idea, then, which we explore below, begins with the generalization of casual gaming and casual gamers.

Gamer as a foodie-connoisseur

Carl is an avid and self-identifying gamer who is highly involved in gaming culture. He attends video game conventions and concerts, follows the news on video games, is interested in game design, and plays *Super Smash Bros* (Nintendo, 1999–to date) competitively. In spite of having a preference for some genres and platforms, Carl likes to explore a wide range of titles. He spends a fair share of his spare time playing, reading about, or listening to the music of video games. His major interest is, undoubtedly, video games. Interestingly, Carl uses another controversial figure, the foodie, as an analogy to define what a video gamer is:

> I think a gamer is someone that explores the medium. For example, there are lots of people that just play nothing but *Call of Duty*, and they say they're a hardcore gamer. […] That's like saying 'oh, I eat at McDonalds, I'm a foodie'. You know? A foodie is someone that explores different foods, like

different cultures of food. [...] They look up other chefs, recipes or whatever. They explore the entire medium or the culture of food. So, you don't just play games. You listen to music, you follow [...] you read about design and you follow the business of it. You don't just play the most marketed games, because you'll be back to McDonalds again.

The analogy between the gamer and the foodie places the gamer identity in a restrictive, elitist, space. The fact that Carl resorts to the 'foodie' category – with its own grey areas – to illustrate the gamer notion, highlights how porous this has become. However, the analogy works; it situates the gamer label in a delimited semantic and sociocultural space, with discriminating capacities. Carl expands more on his analogy:

> I have a friend who considers himself a gamer, and [...] what he does play is the most marketed things. He plays Minecraft and you know, whatever, Pokémon. Sure, by all means, enjoy that game, but I don't really consider you a gamer. You just eat at the McDonalds, the Burger Kings, and the KFC's of the world. That's all you're doing. You are not trying, you know, Japanese soba noodles or whatever, you are not trying all these different things what's out there to you. It's fair enough that you don't like that, but when you say "oh, McDonalds has the best burger" [...] Ironically he also likes McDonalds.

He keeps pushing the analogy by comparing, what he refers to as, the most marketed and popular games such as *Call of Duty* (Activision, Infinity Ward, 2003– to date), *Minecraft* (Mojang, 2011), and *Pokémon* (Nintendo, Bandai Namco, 1996– to date), with fast food restaurants, implying that those who just play these kinds of games cannot be considered gamers in the same way that those who only eat fast food cannot be considered foodies. In this conceptualization of the gamer, the self-identification with the category or the time dedicated to playing video games is not enough or, directly, relevant. And he is not alone in this representation of the gamer. For instance, Javier, a 32-year-old game designer at an indie company, portrays a similar version of the gamer:

> Basically, a gamer is someone who plans to play video games in his spare time. I'll give you an example: my girlfriend. She has *Candy Crush* on her mobile phone and she may play it if she's on the bus or waiting for someone in the street. But rarely she sits down and plays a game. There are people who wait for games to come out. There are people who research, who visit websites looking for news on video games. There are people who download video games' podcasts and listen to them because they're interested in them. To me, that's the people who are part of the community of gamers. Neither my girlfriend, nor my cousins who just play a few games like *Gran Turismo* and *Grand Theft Auto* can be considered gamers.

According to these definitions, a gamer is someone who gets profoundly involved with the medium and explores it as a whole, paying attention to its artistic, cultural, technical, and economic dimensions. In this case, the gamer has to become a videoludic connoisseur and treat the video game with care and respect; for them, it is a medium, an art, a culture.

In this definition, the act of playing video games is not enough; this demands an active and substantial participation in the wider gamer culture. However, it is never clearly defined what level of involvement would qualify in order to turn a casual player into a gamer. There are some indications, though. It seems to these interviewees that a gamer is someone informed and knowledgeable about game culture. Gamers should explicitly dedicate a good amount of their time to playing video games, and more importantly, exploring its wider culture. Hence, for these interviewees, video gaming is a planned, not casual, activity, and it is complemented with other pursuits related to video games. There is no room for casual gaming practices because, according to Javier, that would imply using 'the game as a pastime', and those who engage in such practices, play video games in the same way they might 'pick up stones from the ground and throw them into a river'.

Hence, our foodie-connoisseur gamers seek to distinguish themselves from casual players, but also, what might be described as the subcultural type of gamer; those who Carl (cited above) would see as just playing the 'most marketed', AAA games, like *Call of Duty*. There does seem to be a contempt towards these kinds of players, and foodie-connoisseur gamers often group both casual and hardcore gamers together as individuals who are only interested in gaming as 'mere entertainment'. The gamer as foodie-connoisseur does not see video games primarily as an entertainment industry, but rather as culture, and themselves as being different to both those who only play the most 'marketed games' and also 'casual gamers'.

The cultural–intellectual

Closely related to the notion of gamer as a foodie–connoisseur is what we would like to suggest as the cultural–intellectual approach to video games. This is a category of individuals who, like the foodie–connoisseur, explore the medium, usually (but not necessarily) play different types of games, and approach video games as culture. The main differences between them is that, while the foodie–connoisseur identifies as a gamer, the cultural–intellectual does not necessarily. Furthermore, the cultural-intellectual establishes a distance between them and the video game as a medium; they study, analyze, and approach video games from a critical point of view. On the other hand, the foodie-connoisseur, although they might approach video games critically, they are always in search of new experiences and like to get close to video games and their culture. The cultural-intellectual category is formed by journalists, scholars, researchers, critics, curators, and artists; video games are often part of what they do for a living. They have an intellectual and professional relationship with video games, whereas the foodie–connoisseur has a visceral relationship with video games (it is a hobby, a passion for them). Using the food analogy again, the difference between the intellectual and the connoisseur is similar to the one that exists between the food critic and the foodie: both of them eat a lot of different things and they treat food as culture, but the latter does it as a hobby and as an experience, while the former does it as a job, as part of an intellectual approach to the food and its culture. Of course, both the intellectual–cultural and the foodie-connoisseur can be passionate about video games, but they deal with them differently.

Edward, a director of a Masters' degree in video game development who tries to inculcate a sense of cultural studies in his students, explains that what they are trying to do is 'to create a wider and more culturally enlightening arena for games'. He embodies the cultural–intellectual approach to video games to perfection: 'I'm not interested in the trivial. I'm not that interested in fun […]. I'm more interested in emotionally profound experiences or, and if they are fun, it's more that they are engaging on a cerebral and emotional level'. In the same way, Emmett, a 48-year-old director of a museum dedicated to video games, makes this distinction clear and does not describe himself as a 'hardcore gamer' because his approach to video games is 'a more cultural approach than an entertaining approach'. Within this category, the cultural and artistic aspects of video games prevail over ludic ones. The cultural–intellectual does not primarily pursue video games as mere entertainment, rather they seek a better understanding of video game culture as a whole. For instance, Dante is the director of a specialized video game website, on which he suggests they try to build a cultural and professional space around video games. In this sense, Dante tries to distance himself and his website from the typical view of gamer culture as adolescent:

> We stopped publishing news. We didn't mark games. We decided to address video games as any other cultural product. Emphasize that aspect. In short, we grew in diverse aspects by speaking of video games in serious and professional ways, moving away from the gamer who looks for their eventual gaming fix. In brief, a series of things and details that I think perpetuated the adolescent view on video games.

What Dante implies they are trying to do with their website is to cater more to, what might be seen as, a cultural-intellectual audience; and he openly admits that he does not like the term 'gamer' at all. This open hostility of the cultural–intellectual towards the gamer category is one of their most prominent characteristics. In order to better understand this, it can be of great assistance to briefly discuss the *gamergate* phenomenon that burst onto the gamer scene in the second half of 2014, and is still reverberating in gaming culture today.

In August of 2014, gamergate was born as a movement that allegedly advocated for ethics in games journalism, right after Eron Gjoni posted an online diatribe in which he accused his ex-partner, Zoe Quinn, the indie developer of the game *Depression Quest*, of having sex with a journalist in exchange for favourable reviews of her game (see Massanari, 2015; Shepherd *et al.*, 2015 ; Braithwaite, 2016; Mortensen, 2016; Perreault and Vos, 2016). It is then alleged that the actor Adam

Baldwin coined the Twitter hashtag #gamergate to identify online posts relating to the debate surrounding ethics in games journalism. However, despite presenting themselves as a reaction to the supposedly poor ethical practices of certain games journalists, a great number of gamergate supporters engaged 'in concentrated harassment of game developers, feminist critics, and their male allies on Twitter and other platforms' (Massanari, 2015: 6). Most of the individuals targeted by gamergate supporters were pejoratively labelled as 'Social Justice Warriors' (SJW). SJW is a label that far right and conservative individuals have used for some time to define those who publicly sustain progressive point of views. In this regard, many of those who can be identified as belonging to the cultural-intellectual group would be catalogued as SJW; a label that many have even re-appropriated as a proud achievement.

Hence, this means that, once again, we are faced with a category that is to a large extent, constructed in opposition to the most stereotyped version of the gamer, the hardcore-subcultural type. As, Robert, a 47-year-old, male, director of a video game museum and organizer of video game events with journalists, developers, researchers, and those interested in the gaming culture, states: 'We are not shutting anyone out, and they [hardcore gamers] are. I feel like there is a constituency that feels that they own video games. Both critically and culturally'.

Without wishing to diminish the importance of challenging abuse and misogyny in all its forms and wherever it occurs, what we particularly want to focus on here is what gamergate can tell us about gamer identity, and in particular the gamer as 'an iteration of geek masculinity' (Braithwaite, 2016: 2). Of course, gamergate was not the start of this aggression, nor the start of the abuse of women in the games industry (and beyond), nor is this isolated from wider social movements, such as the rise of the (far-)Right (what some call euphemistically the 'alt-right') in the mid to late 2010s, as characterized by the arrival of Donald Trump in the White House, Brexit in the UK, the growing popularity of Marine Le Pen in France, and other worldwide examples of retreatism and xenophobia (Lees, 2016). However, gamergate brought a certain antagonism and strand of misogyny clearly into the light and (literally) gave it a label under which it could be identified.

In particular, it is clear that in the weeks following the initial online post that sparked gamergate, some of the key discussions here revolved around this idea of the gamer identity; a debate ignited by the publication of a number of articles declaring 'the end of gamers'. The two texts that drew particular attention were those written by Dan Golding (2014) and Leigh Alexander (2014), who themselves clearly incarnate a cultural-intellectual approach to video games. Here, Golding argues that the gamer identity was born when playing games was an 'unusual activity' and primarily a 'masculine culture'; however, as the activity of playing video games moved beyond this niche, 'the gamer identity remained fairly uniformly stagnant and immobile' (Golding, 2014: online). The gamer identity, Golding argues, was not flexible enough to simultaneously include people as different as, for example, on the one hand, players of *Candy Crush*, and on the other, *Call of Duty* players. Therefore, video games changed but 'the gamer identity did not stretch, and so it has been broken'. Hence, Golding's conclusion is that we are witnessing the 'end of gamers', and the 'traditional gamer identity' has now become 'culturally irrelevant'. In a similar vein, Alexander addresses video game writers, media outlets, and the game industry to argue that the stereotypical young white male gamer, does not need to be their only target audience. According to Alexander, the gamer is not just 'a dated demographic label', it is directly 'over'. In particular, one of our interviewees, Edward, very much subscribes to this position:

> The word gamer is now discredited. If you look at Leigh Alexander's piece [...] she said, you know, 'gamer seems to mean a whole lot of people who are obsessed with a particular subset of experiences which fall into that category that we might call games'. There is a note of obsession and hence gamergate. Gamers are not good people. Players are, audiences are. In a sense [...] [if] gamers seem to be the type of people who make death threats to people on the Internet for pointing out that female representation in the medium of their choice is not as it should be, then I don't subscribe to that. It seems to me to be a subculture which is not one to be proud of.

It seems then, that the gamer label applied more readily in an era where this pastime was more niche and could be more clearly associated with a particular demographic of young white men. However, as the diversity of video games and the population of players has grown, the internal dissonance in terms of identity becomes so strong that the category implodes; provoking a reaction among some of those who still consider this label as applying to (solely people like) *them*. Hence, many gamers felt, and probably still do, that their very identity and community was under attack. Conan, a 23-year-old, male, video game (and sometimes also film) critic youtuber, who could be easily identified as belonging to the cultural-intellectual category, voices his concerns over an indiscriminate derogatory attack on the category of gamer:

> It's also ironic because when the idea of gamer is attacked, and considering that gamer is a term that encompasses so many things because we haven't defined what a gamer is or isn't [...] when you say every gamer is a misogynist, you may be attacking me as well. Because I don't know who you are referring to.

Not only does Conan point out that there could be some problems when the hardcore-subcultural type of gamer is exclusively equated with the gamer label, but he also indicates that the gamer is, identity-wise, an indefinite category or, at most, vaguely defined. This then leads us to start looking for more open definitions of gamers and, in doing so, face its constitutive vagueness.

Everyone is a gamer

The growth in different types of games and a more diverse population who are playing them (see Chapter 2) has helped contribute to the problematic nature, if not implosion, of the gamer label and identity. The industry no longer needs to exclusively target the young male niche that, in the 1980s and 1990s, 'was perceived as the key to dominance in the whole business' (Kline et al., 2003: 250).

This is illustrated by one of our research participants, Alfred, who has considered himself a gamer since childhood, and comes from a family where all its members play video games of one form or another. Although he does not live in the same city as his parents and brother, he speaks and plays online with them frequently. In particular, most of the interactions with his family and his closest friends happen through video games. Playing video games strongly mediates the way he socializes and interacts with his social and family network. In this case, it is interesting to see how though Alfred shares most of the characteristics of a hardcore-subcultural gamer (he identifies as such, though 'on the light end of the scale'), he opens up the definition of gamer to anyone who identifies as such; as he states: 'a gamer is whoever identifies himself as a gamer'.

This is then the fifth big type of 'gamer' definition that we found in our research. It is a definition completely open, almost to the point of diluting the category. A definition that is to a great extent tautological: a gamer is anyone who identifies as a gamer. It is purely based on self-identification. If you consider yourself a gamer, therefore, you are a gamer. According to Alfred, if someone plays games once a week or less, as long as they consider themselves gamers, they are gamers; by contrast, if they play thousands of hours per year and do not want to be considered gamers – because they just want to play games, then, they are not. Hence, for Alfred, gamer is a self-imposed label, it is a chosen identity, not a category with set parameters. As he adds, 'I think it's a mentality, that if you don't want to have it, you don't have to have it'. This a powerful image: gamer as mentality. However, as Kallio et al. (2011) showed in their three-year study on how to approach video game cultures and playing practices, there are various gamer mentalities (dependent on context), rather than just one monolithic mindset. In particular, they found that the majority of video gaming practices take place 'between "casual relaxing" and "committed entertaining"' (Kallio et al., 2011: 347), which overflows the stereotype of a gamer as someone who is completely immersed in the game and committed to its culture. This then highlights a reality and identity defined by fluid mentalities and situated practices that are located inside gamers' everyday lives. Video games are inexorably becoming normalized parts 'of the invisible everyday social realities for large groups of peoples' (Kallio et al., 2011: 348). Gaming is becoming an increasingly common and mundane activity (Crawford, 2012: 143–159), and everyone is starting to become a gamer.

Conan, the 23-year-old youtuber whose audience is mainly people who have a keen interest in video games, for instance, believes that 'there are a thousand ways of playing and understanding video games', and he considers himself 'a gamer but also a person who only plays *FIFA* and *Minecraft* is one'. And, the indie developer Noel (male, 24, self-identifying gamer) offers a very open definition of a gamer when he states that, for him, 'everyone's a gamer in some way'. He also adds:

> I play games, therefore I'm a gamer. If most people do play some games, technically, that makes everyone a gamer, because they're playing games.

According to Noel, there is a direct correlation between playing video games and being a gamer. In an almost, if not intentional, philosophical periphrasis, he states that 'I play games, therefore I am a gamer'. For Noel, as with some others we interviewed, there is no pre-condition to be a gamer, not even a process of self-identification; if someone plays a video game, whether they want to be it or not, they are a gamer. Thus, the universe of potential gamers increases exponentially and consequently the definition of gamer is immensely simplified: a gamer is anyone who plays video games, anyone who plays video games is a gamer. The principal consequence of this is obvious: if everyone is technically a gamer, then the category loses its defining power. Hence, this label becomes so generic that it does not create any real sense of belonging or differentiation.

Conan claims that, if someone told him he was speaking to gamers, he would not know to whom he was speaking; for Conan, a 'gamer is an indefinable amalgam' and also adds:

> Worst of all is we keep using 'gamer', and I use it a lot, and I don't know why. I'm that stupid because, in the end, it's trying to define what cannot be defined. People who stand up for the word 'gamer' are defending a ghost, because it's nothing, you can't touch it. I don't know what you are clinging to when you say 'gamer', I don't know. It's simply [...] when I use the word 'gamer' it's like: 'gamer, whoever that plays video games'.

At the end of *Casual Revolution*, Juul (2010: 152) concludes that his text 'documents that cultural moment when video games became normal; when it is no longer exceptional to play games'. In 2010, video games were already 'fast becoming games for everyone'. And if video games are for everyone, that means they are an essential part of our society and not just a subset of it:

> Certainly some gamers do seem to belong to a culture distinct from mainstream society. The term subculture, however, is too limited to adequately explain the broader world of games and game players that currently exists.
> *(Consalvo, 2007: 3)*

In particular, most of our interviewees seem to assume this normalization of video games is now part of our shared social landscape. Zelda, a regular attendant at video game-related events (such as conventions, conferences, and concerts) and a dedicated gamer, considers that playing video games 'has become part of our culture'. Also, Albert, a 25-year-old, male, indie game artist, and self-identifying gamer, suggests that the time when gamers were 'only nerds and geeks' is now truly over. For him, 'the geek is [now] cool' and 'everything is referencing video games to a degree'. Hence, Albert and many of our other interviewees, are pointing to how video games have become not only a common leisure activity for many, but that the popularity (if not dominance) of this cultural industry has seen it blurring with, and impacting on, many other areas of social and cultural life.

Ian Bogost (2011), in the conclusion of *How to Do Things with Videogames*, argues that as video games become more entangled in the general fabric of society, and those playing them become increasingly diverse, then the idea of gamers as an identity will lose its meaning. Bogost (2011: 154) suggests that as video games 'broaden in appeal, being a "gamer" will actually become less common', and playing video games will not be deemed 'as a primary part of one's identity'. Playing video games will become a mundane activity, with no particular capacity to shape a person's identity. Emmett, the director of a museum on video games, summarizes this projection as follows:

> I think more people have been in contact nowadays than the past with video games, and of course that helps them to understand it. But on the other hand, this development bears the tendency that you don't understand it as something special anymore, just common, just normal. For example, we wouldn't say there is a community of jeans people who wear jeans [laughter]. This might be an issue one hundred years ago, in the rock and roll era, in the 1950s […]. But today […] there are millions of people wearing jeans as trousers. I think the same thing happens with video games.

As playing video games becomes more like wearing jeans, mundane, then, it is no longer special. If it is not special, therefore it means that is not distinctive. And if it is not distinctive, the gamer category is hardly going to be something around which an individual or community can build an identity or a sense of belonging. There is thus a significant tension here between more restrictive notions of gamers, and those that open this label up to anyone and everyone – emptying it of meaning. The gamer identity is, at the same time, strong and weak, solid and liquid, bounded and limitless. 'Gamer' is a category that defines individuals and communities as much as it does not say anything (of relevance) about them.

Although for some 'gamer' is still seen as a strongly bounded identity, the indefiniteness of the gamer category creates this apparent impossibility of determining what a gamer is, or who can be considered as a gamer. Gamers seem not to know if they, or others, are gamers. 'Gamer' becomes, in this way, a changing label.

In this regard, Zelda is not sure how to answer when she is asked if she identifies as a gamer: 'Sometimes I do and sometimes I don't'. Even though Zelda is one of the most involved individuals among the interviewees in certain aspects of gaming culture, she is incapable of giving a clear response. Her fluctuating gamer label appears to vary depending on who she is with:

> My boyfriend definitely does not call me a gamer, because he plays so much more games than I have. Whereas my sister would consider me as a gamer, because she doesn't play any games. It depends who you talk to, really.

Or when it is:

> Is a gamer a gamer that plays every day? Is a gamer who spends a lot of time in a game in the past or now? Because if you asked me this question a few years ago when I was playing Final Fantasy, yes, I was a gamer. But now, maybe not so much.

People as close to Zelda as her partner and sibling have opposing opinions on Zelda's gamer status. The perception of an individual as a gamer depends on different factors that do not always align, particularly between the opposing forces that imply the processes of self-identification and external interpellation (Hall, 1996; Butler, 1999). The insecurity of anyone to call themselves a gamer is completely understandable given that people that surround them – and presumably know them well – sustain such different representations.

One way or another, the gamer identity figuratively dances around the different versions of identity imagined by social scientists, without settling on any particular type; it's obstinate, solid, and perennial, but also open, free, and ethereal. In any case, the disjunction of the act of playing and the identification as gamer evinces some of the contemporary debates around identity, where, for instance, work (traditionally, what you do), and nationality or citizenship (traditionally, what you are) do not necessarily define people's identity. Identity becomes part of the insecurities that populate contemporary society, and, among them, the gamer identity reflects and fosters those processes.

In relation to this, Darius, the 28-year-old, male, indie game designer, picks up his discourse on gamers and explains the processes that they, as a community, have experienced over the last decades. Darius suggests, that in the past, around the 1980s, gamers might have had the opportunity to form a community; there was a subcultural substratum that allowed that kind of collective assembly. But now, in Darius' opinion, only a residual body of individuals would locate their identities within that community, which has become almost obsolete by means of its fragmentation. There are so many and diverse kinds of games and people who play them – whether they call themselves gamers or not – that it is very difficult to build a strong bounded identity around them.

It is the realization of the gamers' social landscape described by Bogost (2011: 154) in his version of the *end of gamers* idea: 'there'll be many smaller groups, communities, and individuals with a wide variety of interests, some of them occasionally intersecting with particular videogame titles'. Normalization of video games brings the fragmentation and, eventually, dissolution of their identity. The gamer identity then anticipates, paradoxically, a post-identity scenario.

The post-identity hypothesis

All of what we have seen so far turns the gamer identity into a conundrum. The gamer identity is, in this way, an identity categorization that does not define the identity of those who are defined by it. As any conundrum, the gamer identity is a tricky one, and it is full of contradictions: A non-defining definition? An identity that does not give a sense of identity? As surprising and counterintuitive as it might seem, this is the corollary of the gamer identity. Although it is difficult to put into words, some of our interviewees express themselves in a way that resembles this conundrum:

> Gamer is a fair way to summarize that I love video games and be able to say: 'I'm a lifelong gamer'. But not as a way to define myself.
> *(Víctor Somoza, male, 26, director of a documentary on video games)*

In this case, the gamer category helps Víctor Somoza make public one of his passions and refer to what seems to be an important part of his life (that he has a history with video games). However, he refuses to use gamer as a defining category of his persona. He is, at the same time, a gamer and not a gamer. He does not have a problem identifying as gamer as long as that does not mean he has to be identified as gamer. The tension is palpable as the gamer conundrum emerges. Karla Zimonja, the 37-year-old artist, developer, and co-founder of Fullbright (developers of the video game *Gone Home*), who does not identify as a gamer, helps to see a different angle, equally paradoxical, of the conundrum:

> If somebody said to me 'you play games, you're a gamer', I'd say 'ok sure, fine'. I'm not gonna get real upset about it. I'm just not going to put it that way for myself, I think.

Unlike Somoza, Zimonja does not seem too concerned about the possibility of being identified as gamer; although she does not identify as a gamer herself. She would accept being called gamer, as a plausible label since she plays video games, but she will not use that kind of identification herself. Of course, it is not new for someone to be identified as something that they do not particularly identify with, but it is less common to consider that categorization as acceptable, while refusing to use it for themselves. In any case, the fundamental aspects of the conundrum, mainly sustained by a non-defining identity category, are still in place. These are, after all, two sides of the same coin. In a similar vein, Laura, a 26-year-old, female, indie developer, expounds her relationship with the notion of gamer:

168 Video gamers and (post-)identity

> I think 'gamer' defines me, but well, not necessarily […] I play video games, I'm a gamer. I don't know. I like exploring the worlds, the stories, all of those things that video games are. But I do it beyond the label 'gamer'.

Doubts surface all the time; the insecurities that surround the gamer identity are always there. And those uncertainties make the gamer identity a fringe identity. Although Laura clearly defines herself as a gamer, almost immediately she tries to transcend that categorization. It is about being a gamer without being a gamer. 'Gamer' is a category that is associated with these interviewees, to the point of stating 'I am a gamer', but, at the same time, it is not defining them. 'I am a gamer who is not a gamer,' they seem to say.

The gamer conundrum incarnates the conundrum of identity. Identity is still a necessary concept to make some aspects of social reality thinkable, but, simultaneously, it is a concept with which we cannot – properly – approach those aspects. We need to talk about identity in order to talk about things that identity cannot explain. Video games prefigure, then, the post-identity hypothesis; that we are entering a type of society in which identity will lose its defining characteristics. We identify three elements that define the post-identity era hypothesis: short facts, the creation of communities without anything in common, and the rupture of the defining axes of identity.

Short facts

It was the first week of June, in 2014. The launch party of Big Brother UK 2014 was on TV.[3] Every time someone entered the house, it was preceded by a description of the contestant using three short facts, which were also superimposed on the screen. The facts did not follow any particular pattern beyond some common opinions about choosing money over love (or vice versa), ambitions, or certain preferences. Due to their succinctness and randomness, these facts were paradoxically generic and specific, meaningless and defining, irrelevant and pertinent. Facts that could hardly help to define someone, but were somehow meaningful, at least in that place and time. Short facts such as 'Hates veggies, animal rights people, and the unemployed', 'Uses tarot cards to decide what to wear', 'Goes to church every Sunday', 'Rescued a dog from a burning building', 'Scared of failure', 'Turned down a marriage proposal', 'Never been in a relationship', 'Once drank champagne with Sir Sean Connery', 'Went clubbing with her mum', and 'Wants to open a Turkish kebab shop'. Television, now an *old* medium seems to be mediated by newer media, particularly Internet and its social networks, in which the presentation of the self is done in a – not necessarily interrelated – sequence of hashtags, short statements, pictures, gifs, memes, status messages, comments, 'likes', 'shares', and 'retweets'. We say and show several aspects about our lives and ourselves, but we do it in short, fragmented, and chaotic ways.

This poses a number of questions for us, such as: Can we be defined by a number of short statements – expressed either discursively or by other means? Is that how identity formation works today? Is identity a pastiche of (almost) unrelated statements, images, and tags about oneself or others? Has identity become a non-defining categorization? Far from letting these thoughts drift away, we lingered on them.

Only a few days before Big Brother's launch party, the video game *Watch Dogs* (Ubisoft, 2014) appeared in the stores, and, surprisingly, we found noticeable similarities with the television show (and, indirectly, with the gamer identity). In the universe of *Watch Dogs*, there exists an Orwellian surveillance system called ctOS (disguised as an operating system), which can be hacked in order to access and control any electronic device or element that is digitally governed (from smartphones and computers to steam pipes and explosives). The system is constantly recording and storing what the citizens of (the in-game fictionalized) Chicago say, do, write; anything that can be grasped through those devices that surround them in their everyday life.

However, what is particularly interesting about this game is, again, the appearance of defining short facts. Whenever the player uses the profiler (a hacking tool that allows us to access the guts of ctOS), a myriad of information about the people (Non-Playable Characters, NPCs) who are around the player pops up on the screen. Yet again, sentences such as 'Joined aerophobia group', 'Dyslexic', 'Cited for animal cruelty' or 'Explosives expert' frantically appear and disappear in front of the players' eyes. Everything is also accompanied by information on their age, occupation, and income. In this way, *Watch Dogs* enables us to perform a sociology of short facts,[4] letting us grab a glimpse of what could be deemed as a post-identity categorization system. We invite the reader to have a look at the following classification:

> In its distant pages it is written that animals are divided into (a) those that belong to the emperor; (b) embalmed ones; (c) those that are trained; (d) suckling pigs; (e) mermaids; (f) fabulous ones; (g) stray dogs; (h) those that are included in this classification; (i) those that tremble as if they were mad; (j) innumerable ones; (k) those drawn with a very fine camel's-hair brush; (l) etcetera; (m) those that have just broken the flower vase; (n) those that at a distance resemble flies.
>
> *(Borges, 1999: 231)*

We have to admit that every time we read this classification of animals (a fictional account extracted from the vivid imagination of Borges, who attributes it to a certain Chinese encyclopedia), it makes us laugh. The list is disconcerting, if not hilarious. Why does this classification have this effect on us? Foucault (1989: xvi), at the beginning of *The Order of Things*, and after bringing up this delirious classification, concludes that, when confronted with other systems of thought, we start to understand the limits of our own: 'the stark impossibility of thinking that'. That extravagant classification belongs to a different fundamental form of knowledge, what Foucault calls 'episteme', and that makes thinking within its limits impossible for us:

> In any given culture and at any given moment, there is always only one episteme that defines the conditions of possibility of all knowledge, whether expressed in a theory or silently invested in a practice.
>
> *(Foucault, 1989: 183)*

The episteme delimits the space of the thinkable inside a particular society at a specific time. The further we move from those temporal and spatial coordinates, the greater is the possibility of coming across a different ground of positivity – episteme. In a way, the bewilderment that probably most people feel when they read some of the short facts presented by ctOS, Big Brother, Twitter, or Instagram hashtags, for example, displayed on our screens, could be explained by this approach. It shows the seams of our old episteme in its transition to the new conditions of possibility, where the way we think about identities – or what comes next – is radically changing.

In terms of identity, why should very specific aspects of someone's life or bite-sized statements define them? Here, our hypothesis is that there are no longer core elements that define identity in contemporary societies; the old coordinates by which people were understood (such as nation, gender, and class) have been decentred, and now new elements, almost randomly, are becoming as important as them in order to define someone's identity. That would explain, for instance, why our most frequent searches on the Internet might be as important for our processes of identity formation as the illnesses we have (as seen in *Watch Dogs*). Or why tweeting with the hashtag '#parentslife' is as relevant as participating in the Parent–Teacher Association of your children's school. According to Maffesoli (2001: 68), *presentism* has been installed in our societies, and we do not consider that 'there are things that are more important than others'. In everyday life, if nothing is important, then, everything is important.

The key question is then whether it is possible to be defined by one or various short facts or statements, such as the 140 characters of a Twitter post, an Xbox Live gamertag, or a picture posted on Facebook or Instagram? Once our identities seem not to be attached to specific meta-narratives (Lyotard, 1984), other fragments of meaning, more and more specific and global at the same time, are occupying the stage of identity. Once again, experience is both unique and shared (Chapter 4). That is why we are defined by what pops up in that moment, by what is relevant at that point: it can change at any time, with new events, when individuals are in different contexts, with different people; it can shift in the same day several times, in a continuous overlapping process. What these short defining statements do is highlight what matters in that moment, what is relevant for that time and place. Precisely because individuals cannot be defined by something that encompasses everything they are, they can be defined by anything that describes them in a particular moment; as we saw above with regard to the notion of 'gamer'. Identity therefore is contextual and mutational (Zingsheim, 2011). The very notion of identity is being challenged, entering into a post-identity era.

Communities with nothing in common

We have insisted throughout this book on how video games are a fertile, theoretical terrain to observe issues of social relevance in contemporary society. In some cases, it even helps to envisage some aspects of the society that is to come. This is also the case of the idea of community as a collective expression of identity formation. For example, Emmett, the 48-year-old head of a museum on video games, considers that the digital has fundamentally changed our culture and the way people live together, and, furthermore, that video games offer valuable hints on what kind of community we are headed to:

> I think the digital changed our culture of living together and building and developing communities radically. These new technologies, if you want to have an idea what this will mean for the global human society, you could have a look at even old multiplayer online games, which gave us a good impression how the future communities will look and how they will work, what's relevant and what's not relevant, what you can do and what we lose compared to earlier kinds of living together.

Looking at video games could give us useful information about the current and future modes of living together, including a refurbished (or maybe totally re-imagined) community. In particular, the community of gamers appears as a community that does not generate a sense of community. We base our assertion in two interrelated characteristics that surfaced during the interviews: the lack of social interaction and commonality. The fragmentation of the universe of gamers and their micro-communities leads to a lack of interaction between them that makes it almost impossible to create a global community of gamers. Interactions only occur, when they happen at all, inside very specific (often mostly online) spaces, usually linked to particular games:

> Somebody who plays *Minecraft* and somebody who plays *Bloodborne* may never actually interact. So they're part of a larger gaming's community, but then they're part of the *Minecraft* community or the *Bloodborne* community.
>
> *(Alfred)*

According to Alfred, there are groups of people that belong to large communities, who, most probably, will never come in contact with each other. What it is noteworthy about Alfred's statement is the fact that he alludes to a general community of gamers, even though they are, apparently, not part of the same communities and do not share the same social interaction spaces. In this sense, Carl lays out a similar disjointed and contradictory scenario:

> I can say "I'm a gamer. I play Smash, I play puzzle games", you can say "well, you're a gamer, but I play Call of Duty. I enjoy first person shooters". There's probably not that much interaction.

Yet again, people who share an identity – that of gamer – probably have very little else in common, and have little to no interaction with each other. Carl shares the widespread assumption that there are different 'specific communities' rather than a big community of gamers, and yet he asserts that if someone belongs to one of those particular communities, they are 'suddenly part of that community' of gamers. The constitutive contradiction of the formula is that *to be part of a community but without being a community* reflects a trend in contemporary society that follows in the non-defining identities' wake. This precisely resembles Bauman's (2001: 68) representation of communities that are mediated by electronic technologies, a 'community of non-belonging, a togetherness of loners'. Similarly, in relation to those communities, Bauman (2001: 69) also explores the communities that are formed around idols or celebrities, which 'conjure up the "experience of community" without real community, the joy of belonging without the discomfort of being bound'. The important thing is the *experience of identity* and not *identity*. These are communities that create a sense of (temporal) belonging without generating social bonds.

These new communities, and particularly the community of gamers, only seem to exist as part of a continuous, collective, effervescent (Durkheim, 1995: 216–225) situation. Bauman (2004: 31) coined the notion of 'cloakroom communities' to allude to those social formations that 'are patched together for the duration of the spectacle and promptly dismantled again once the spectators collect their coats from the hooks in the cloakroom'. These are communities that 'tend to be volatile, transient and "single-aspect" or "single-purpose"' (Bauman, 2000: 199), and, like gaming communities, they bring individuals together 'for a stretch of time when other interests – those which divide them instead of uniting them – are temporarily laid aside' (Bauman, 2000: 200). In this sense, we find among our research participants the ultimate definition of the community that revolves around video games:

> This is a very common misunderstanding that people tend to approach gamers as a community. There is no community of gamers. There are communities around certain games, maybe around certain genres. But gamers are so different that they don't have anything in common.
>
> *(Emmett)*

Communities with nothing in common; 'gamers' as a notion that unites a group of people so different they cannot be united under any notion. The coming community, Giorgio Agamben (1993: 85) predicted in the early 1990s, would therefore be 'mediated not by any condition of belonging (being red, being Italian, being Communist) nor by the simple absence of conditions (a negative community [...]), but by belonging itself'. This is a community that, Agamben (1993: 86) adds, would form 'without affirming an identity', where individuals 'co-belong without any representable condition of belonging (even in the form of a simple presupposition)'. Almost 25 years later, in the late 2010s, video games and their culture seem to corroborate Agamben's prognosis. Video games anticipate the post-identity nature of the social settings that are starting to emerge in contemporary society.

Just a gamer: outside the defining axes of identity

The notion of identity, we would like to suggest, can be approached using two axes of analysis. The first axis makes reference to the form and shape of identity: is it solid, consolidated, stable, and permanent? Or is it fragmented, weak, unstable, temporary, multiple, and liquid? In social sciences, as we saw above, this narrative is constructed around the idea that traditional and (early) modern societies were dominated by a solid type of identity, and post- or late- modern societies are closer to a fluid one, which is, in the end, evidence of a category that it is starting to dissolve.

The second axis refers to how identity is assembled: is identity a position, a starting point, from where individuals are able to enunciate and act? Or is it rather a point of arrival, the non-preexisting outcome of different associations, mediations, and processes? According to Latour (1993: 1–3), already at the beginning of the 1990s, the proliferation of hybrids was more than visible: the emergence of those 'imbroglios of science, politics, economy, law, religion, technology, fiction' that populate the world and are easy to detect everywhere. For example, in relation to an article in a newspaper about AIDS, Latour (1993: 2) says:

> The smallest AIDS virus takes you from sex to the unconscious, then to Africa, tissue cultures, DNA and San Francisco, but the analysts, thinkers, journalists and decision-makers will slice the delicate network traced by the virus for you into tidy compartments where you will find only science, only economy, only social phenomena, only local news, only sentiment, only sex.

Modernity, then, was built on a discourse about sphere differentiation (social, cultural, natural, biological, human, animal, economic, technological, political, and so forth), be it a functional differentiation within a social system (Luhmann, 1996; Parsons, 2012; Durkheim, 2013), the dialectical polarization of social forces (Marx, 1976; Horkheimer and Adorno, 2002), or an inevitable individualization and expert specialization process (Bell, 1976; Giddens, 1991; Stehr, 1994). However, as Latour claims, modernity, and particularly late modernity, has fostered an incessant process of de-differentiation between entities that were previously isolated or inexistent. In this context of augmented hybridization between heterogeneous elements, identity appears as an effort to compartmentalize what it is expressed, by definition, in diverse, complex, and hybrid terms. This also hints that identity has become a category overflown by the tides of the times, incapable of containing a promiscuous and ever-changing social reality.

The real contradiction surfaces in contemporary society, when the two axes crumble as soon as they attempt to capture a sense of identity. As Bauman (2004: 16) argues, the 'frailty and the forever provisional status of identity can no longer be concealed'; 'the secret is out'. The gamer identity, as we have seen throughout this chapter, could be understood as a prototypical example of an emerging social reality dominated by post-identity positions.

The gamer identity, as with many other contemporary identity constructions, cannot find accommodation in the spectrum of solidity/liquidity of the first axis. As we saw above, it jumps from extremely solid and rounded definitions of the gamer to radically liquid and fragmented ones. The gamer identity restlessly circulates between these two poles and, eventually, escapes their coordinates to stay in an undetermined state. In relation to the second axis, video gamer identity is incapable of providing a definite and (at least moderately) stable outcome to become a point of enunciation or action for the individuals that identify (or are identified) with it. Gamer identity is a perennial struggle to become (or not become) a gamer. As other aspects of social reality (see Chapters 4 and 5), identity is becoming, at most, an experience of identity, not an identity itself. The gamer identity is, thus, an assemblage of an essence; the articulation of different discourses, practices, and experiences that allows individuals to occupy the category without any (pre-) condition of belonging.

Therefore, video games and their culture question the very notion of identity. After all, the video gamer identity is based on a series of gaming (or para-gaming) experiences, which are a disjointed accumulation of singular – but also shared – facts and situations (acknowledged even in their ephemeral status); this is what defines today's social reality. We are defined by what does not (essentially) define us, and that is the fundamental paradox that video gaming practices are making spectacularly visible. The gamer is what Agamben (1993: 65) calls 'a singularity without identity', which overcomes the idea of the search for an 'individual property' with 'a proper identity'. Building on Agamben (1993: 9–11), we consider that the gamer is like 'the example', neither 'particular, nor universal'; it is 'one singularity among others, which, however, stands for each of them and serves for all'. Gamers are then like these singularities that 'communicate only in the empty space of the example, without being tied by any common property, by any identity'. In this case, we argue that we are faced with a sequence of related experiences that never fully emerge as an identity, but rather as the experience of that identity; it is close to what Martínez de Albeniz (2017: 3) identifies as an *identity 3.0*, an 'identity that expresses by means of its unfolding'. Identity as a 'circulating reference' (Latour, 1999: 24–79), without beginning or end.

As we saw before, Bogost (2011: 154) thinks that 'gamer' will soon be an anomaly, or, even, a category that will probably disappear. But even though our research findings could be interpreted in a direction that corroborates Bogost's prognosis, we do not think this means that 'gamer' will just disappear or become an anomaly.

The gamer category might even become more relevant than ever, but emptied of identity content. It is the notion of identity that will become the anomaly.

The post-identity scenario we discuss here is like video games: an embodied postphenomenological experience that articulates a sense of belonging without belonging; it is the experience of identity, its shell so to speak, not identity itself. This approach does not refuse the notion of identity to construct identity (a negative identity, as Pulkikinen (2015) proposes), but it embraces particular identity constructions in order to refuse the notion of identity. Alfred summarizes all this with pristine clarity: 'Really, I'm just a gamer'. This is a simple and direct way to define himself, using a label that is presented as self-evident, but one that does not actually say that much about him.

Conclusions

In this chapter we have focused on what the video gamer category tells us about the notion of identity in contemporary society. In particular, we suggest that video game culture provides a useful vantage point to observe the process of identity formation in today's world. Thus, in accordance with social theorists that have approached the crisis of identity (along with other institutions of modernity) in late modernity, we present a theoretical framework that illustrates the transition from a model of identity construction based on solid and permanent identities to another that revolves around fluid and fragmented identities. In this sense, we argue that the gamer identity corroborates some aspects of this transition and, moreover, anticipates new modes of meaning construction.

After reviewing some of the theoretical discussions on identity that have taken place in recent years, we looked at the different conceptualizations of the video gamer and its communities that stem from our interviews. Thus, we have explored different categories of 'gamers', along with diverse approaches to video game culture. This includes the hardcore-subcultural gamer, the casual gamer, the gamer as foodie-connoisseur, the cultural-intellectual, and the idea of 'everyone is a gamer'. In this process, we reached the conclusion that video game culture and video gamers impeccably depict the conundrum that defines identity in contemporaneity, and, furthermore, offer partial answers to it. The gamer identity shows us the road towards the post-identity hypothesis, which explains how the processes of identity formation has changed radically in the present and how the very notion of identity becomes jeopardized.

Therefore, video game culture sets out the post-identity hypothesis, where the gamer identity and the communities built around video games appear as one of the first empirical examples that offer plausibility to it. We saw how the gamer identity breaks free of the axes of analysis that usually seize identity: on the one hand, its form (if identities are solid or liquid); on the other hand, the way in which identities are assembled (if identities are to be considered as a substance or as a process). The gamer identity cannot be defined according to these axes, because it endlessly moves between the two poles of the first axis (the gamer identity sometimes seems to be sturdily solid and other times seems to be completely fluid and unstable) and, in relation to the second axis, it is neither a point of enunciation of action for those that identify (or are identified) as gamers, nor a process that eventually reaches an end. Video game culture, as in many other elements that define contemporary society, describes our current social settings as much as it anticipates the coming society. The gamer identity can be deemed as the first example of relevance in an emerging post-identity era.

Notes

1 Interpellation is the process by which an individual is given an idea, identity, or social location, through how dominant social practices and ideologies are enacted in everyday life, and then accepts (or refuses) this as their own. Such as, when someone shouts 'hey you!', they are identifying you as 'you', giving you a label and a role in this interaction, which 'you' then accept and adopt as your subject position or, in contrast, decide to challenge. Interpellation, although a powerful and dominant identity-conditioning process, always implies the possibility to resist it.
2 https://www.youtube.com/watch?v=ILMiw9KGJd8&list=PLRfJP25LI5vTT6qHBm9h mYrT4WMXDROc0
3 The launch party can be seen on YouTube. Part 1: https://www.youtube.com/watch?v=e9rZRx7s0sU; Part 2: https://www.youtube.com/watch?v=MjwA9NtiFJY
4 An extended 'sociology of short facts' based on *Watch Dogs* can be accessed here: https://danielmuriel.com/2016/11/07/sociology-of-short-facts-watch-dogs-and-post-identity-social-settings/

References

Aarsand, Pal (2012). 'The Ordinary Player: Teenagers Talk about Digital Games', *Journal of Youth Studies*, 15 (8): 961–977.
Agamben, Giorgio (1993). *The Coming Community*. Minnesota: University of Minnesota Press.
Alexander, Leigh (2014). '"Gamers' Don't Have to be Your Audience. 'Gamers' are Over"', *Gamasutra*, [http://www.gamasutra.com/view/news/224400/Gamers_dont_have_to_be_your_audience_Gamers_are_over.php] [Last accessed: 22/02/2017].
Althusser, Louis (1971). *Lenin and Philosophy and Other Essays*. London: New Left Books
Bauman, Zygmunt (1989). *Legislators and Interpreters*. Cambridge: Polity Press.
Bauman, Zygmunt (1993). *Modernity and Ambivalence*. Cambridge: Polity Press.
Bauman, Zygmunt (2000). *Liquid Modernity*. Cambridge: Polity Press.
Bauman, Zygmunt (2001). *Community: Seeking Safety in an Insecure World*. Cambridge: Polity Press.
Bauman, Zygmunt (2004). *Identity*. Cambridge: Polity Press.
Bauman, Zygmunt (2005). *Work, Consumerism and the New Poor*. London: Open University Press.
Beck, Ulrich (1992). *Risk Society: Towards a New Modernity*. London: Sage.
Beck, Ulrich (2002). 'The Cosmopolitan Society and Its Enemies', *Theory, Culture & Society*, 19 (1-2): 17–44.
Beck, Ulrich and Beck-Gernsheim, Elisabeth (2001). *Individualization: Institutionalised Individualism and its Social and Political Consequences*. London: Sage.

Beck, Ulrich; Giddens, Anthony; Lash, Scott (1994). *Reflexive Modernization*. Cambridge: Polity Press.
Bell, Daniel (1976) [1973]. *The Coming of Post-Industrial Society*. New York: Basic Books.
Berger, Peter L. and Luckmann, Thomas (1995). *Modernity, Pluralism and the Crisis of Meaning*. Gütersloh: Bertelsman Foundation Publishers
Bergstrom, Kelly; Fisher, Stephanie; Jenson, Jennifer (2016). 'Disavowing "That Guy": Identity Construction and Massively Multiplayer Online Game Players', *Convergence*, 22 (3): 233–249.
Blackshaw, Tony (2013). *Leisure Life: Myth, Masculinity and Modernity*. London: Routledge.
Bogost, Ian (2011). *How to Do Things with Videogames*. Minneapolis: University of Minnesota Press.
Borges, Jorge Luis (1999). *Selected Non-Fictions*. London: Penguin.
Braithwaite, Andrea (2016). 'It's About Ethics in Games Journalism? Gamergaters and Geek Masculinity', *Social Media + Society*, 1–10.
Bryce, Jo. and Rutter, Jason, (2005). 'Gendered Gaming in Gendered Space', in Raessens, J. & Goldstein, J. (editors). *Handbook of Computer Game Studies*. Cambridge, MA: MIT Press, 301–310.
Burke, Peter J. and Stets, Jan E. (2009). *Identity Theory*. Oxford: Oxford University Press.
Butler, Judith (1993). *Bodies that Matter. On the Discursive Limits of "Sex"*. London: Routledge.
Butler, Judith (1999). *Gender Trouble. Feminism and the Subversion of Identity*. London: Routledge, 2nd edition.
Castells, Manuel (2010). *The Information Age: Economy, Society and Culture. The Rise of the Network Society Vol 1*. Oxford: Wiley-Blackwell.
Consalvo, Mia (2007). *Cheating. Gaining Advantage in Videogames*. Cambridge, MA: MIT Press.
Drucker, Peter (1994). *Post-capitalist Society*. New York: HarperCollins.
Dubet, François (2006). *El declive de la institución*. Barcelona: Gedisa.
Durkheim, Émile (1995) [1912]. *The Elementary Forms of Religious Life*. New York: The Free Press.
Durkheim, Émile (2013) [1893]. *The Division of Labour in Society*. New York: Free Press.
Foucault, Michel (1989) [1966]. *The Order of Things*. London: Routledge
Foucault, Michel (1991). 'Governmentality', in Burchell, Graham; Gordon, Colin; Miller, Peter. *The Foucault Effect. Studies in Governmentality*. Chicago: University of Chicago Press, 87–101.
Gee, James Paul (2003). *What Video Games Have to Teach Us about Learning and Literacy*. New York: Palgrave MacMillan.
Giddens, Anthony (1990). *The Consequences of Modernity*. Cambridge: Polity Press.
Giddens, Anthony (1991). *Modernity and Self-Identity*. Cambridge: Polity Press.
Giddens, Anthony (2002). *Runaway World: How Globalisation is Reshaping our Lives*. London: Profile Books, 2nd edition.
Golding, Dan (2014). 'The End of Gamers', *Tumblr*, [http://dangolding.tumblr.com/post/95985875943/the-end-of-gamers] [Last accessed: 22/02/2017].
Hall, Stuart (1996). 'Who Needs Identity?', in Hall, Stuart and Du Gay, Paul (editors). *Questions of Cultural Identity*. London: Sage, 1–17.
Hall, Stuart and Du Gay, Paul (editors) (1996). *Questions of Cultural Identity*. London: Sage.
Hayward, Keith (2012). 'Pantomime Justice: A Cultural Criminological Analysis of "Life-stage Dissolution"', *Crime, Media, Culture: An International Journal*, 8 (2): 197–212.
Horkheimer, Max and Adorno, Theodor W. (2002) [1944]. *Dialectic of Enlightenment*. Palo Alto, CA: Stanford University Press.
Jameson, Frederic (1991). *Postmodernism, or, The Cultural Logic of Late Capitalism*. Durham: Duke University Press.

Jayanth, Meg (2014). 52% of Gamers are Women – But the Industry Doesn't Know It', *The Guardian*, [https://www.theguardian.com/commentisfree/2014/sep/18/52-percent-people-playing-games-women-industry-doesnt-know] [Last accessed: 11/04/2017]

Jenkins, Richard (2008). *Social Identity*. London: Routledge, 3rd edition.

Jenkins, Richard (2014). *Social Identity*. London: Routledge, 4th edition.

Jones, Steven G. (1998). *Cybersociety 2.0: Revisiting Computer-Mediated Community and Technology*. Thousand Oaks, CA: Sage.

Juul, Jesper (2010). *A Casual Revolution: Reinventing Video Games and Their Players*. Cambridge, MA: MIT Press.

Kallio, Kirsi P.; Mäyrä, Frans; Kaipainen, Kirsikka (2011). 'At Least Nine Ways to Play: Approaching Gamer Mentalities', *Games and Culture*, 6 (4): 327–353.

Kapalo, Katelynn A.; Dewar, Alexis R.; Rupp, Michael A.; Szalma, James L. (2015). 'Individual Differences in Video Gaming: Defining Hardcore Video Gamers', *Proceedings of the Human Factors and Ergonomics Society 59th Annual Meeting*, 878–881.

King, Geoff and Krzywinska, Tanya (2006). *Tomb Raiders and Space Invaders. Videogame Forms and Contexts*. New York: I.B. Tauris.

Kirby, Alan (2006). 'The Death of Postmodernism and Beyond', *Philosophy Now*, 58 (Nov/Dec): 34–37.

Kirkpatrick, Graeme (2015). *The Formation of the Gaming Culture: UK Gaming Magazines, 1981-1995*. London: Palgrave.

Klimmt, Christoph; Hefner, Dorothée; Vorderer, Peter (2009). 'The Video Game Experience as "True" Identification: A Theory of Enjoyable Alterations of Players' Self-Perception', *Communication Theory*, (19): 351–357.

Kline, Stephen; Dyer-Whiteford, Nick; De Peuter, Greig (2003). *Digital Play. The Interaction of Technology, Culture, and Marketing*. Montreal: McGill Queen's University Press.

Kowert, Rachel; Griffiths, Mark D.; Oldmeadow, Julian A. (2012). 'Geek or Chic? Emerging Stereotypes of Online Gamers', *Bulletin of Science, Technology and Society*, 32 (6): 471–479.

Latour, Bruno (1993). *We Have Never Been Modern*. Cambridge, MA: Harvard University Press.

Latour, Bruno (1999). *Pandora's Hope. Essays on the Reality of Science Studies*. Cambridge, MA: Harvard University Press.

Lawler, Steph (2014). *Identity. Sociological Perspectives*. Cambridge: Polity Press, 2nd edition.

Lees, Matt (2016). 'What Gamergate Should Have Taught us About the "Alt-right"', *The Guardian*, [https://www.theguardian.com/technology/2016/dec/01/gamergate-alt-right-hate-trump] [Last accessed: 14/04/2017].

Lyon, David (1999). *Postmodernity*. Maidenhead: Open University Press.

Lyotard, Jean-François (1984). *The Postmodern Condition*. Manchester: Manchester University Press.

Luhmann, Niklas (1996). *Social Systems*. Palo Alto, CA: Stanford University Press.

Maffesoli, Michel (2001). *El Instante Eterno* [The Eternal Instant]. Paidós: Buenos Aires.

Martínez de Albeniz, Iñaki (2017). '¡Funtziona! La identidad como ensamblaje', [It Works! Identity as Assemblage], *unpublished paper*.

Marx, Karl (1976) [1867]. *Capital*. London: Penguin Books.

Massanari, Adrienne (2015). '#Gamergate and The Fappening: How Reddit's Algorithm, Governance, and Culture Support Toxic Technocultures', *New Media and Society*, 19 (3): 1–18.

Mäyrä, Frans (2008). *An Introduction to Game Studies. Games in Culture*. London: Sage.

Miller, Peter and Rose, Nikolas (2008). *Governing the Present. Administering Economic, Social and Personal Life*. Cambridge: Polity Press.

Mortensen, Torill Elvira (2016). 'Anger, Fear, and Games: The Long Event of #GamerGate', *Games and Culture*, 1–20. DOI: https://doi.org/10.1177/1555412016640408
Parsons, Talcott (2012) [1951]. *The Social System*. New Orleans: Quid Pro Books.
Perreault, Gregory P. and Vos, Tim P. (2016). 'The GamerGate Controversy and Journalistic Paradigm Maintenance', *Journalism*, 1–17. DOI: https://doi.org/10.1177/1464884916670932
Pulkikinen, Tuija (2015). 'Identity and Intervention: Disciplinarity as Transdisciplinarity in Gender Studies', *Theory, Culture and Society*, 32 (5–6): 183–205.
Pulos, Alexis (2013). 'Confronting Heteronormativity in Online Games: A Critical Discourse Analysis of LGBTQ Sexuality in World of Warcraft', *Games and Culture*, 8 (2): 77–97.
Richardson, Ingrid (2011). 'The Hybrid Ontology of Mobile Gaming', *Convergence*, 17 (4): 419–430.
Rose, Nikolas (1999a). *Governing the Soul. The Shaping of the Private Self*. London: Free Association Books, 2nd edition.
Rose, Nikolas (1999b). *Politics of Freedom. Reframing Political Thought*. Cambridge: Cambridge University Press.
Shaw. Adrienne (2014). *Gaming at the Edge. Sexuality and Gender at the Margins of Gamer Culture*. Minneapolis, MN: University of Minnesota Press.
Shepherd, Tamara; Harvey, Alison; Jordan, Tim; Srauy, Sam; Miltner, Kate (2015). 'Histories of Hating', *Social Media + Society*, 1 (2): 1–10.
Smith, Oliver (2014). *Contemporary Adulthood and the Night-Time Economy*. London: Palgrave.
Stehr, Nico (1994). *Knowledge Societies*. London: Sage.
Tönnies, Ferdinand (2001) [1887]. *Community and Civil Society*. Cambridge: Cambridge University Press.
Touraine, Alain (1971). *The Post-Industrial Society*. New York: Random House.
Weber, Max (1968) [1925]. *Economy and Society*. Berkley, CA: University of California Press.
Zingsheim, Jason (2011). 'Developing Mutational Identity Theory: Evolution, Multiplicity, Embodiment, and Agency', *Cultural Studies, Critical Methodologies*, 11 (1): 24–37.

Ludography

Activision, Infinity Ward (2003 to date). *Call of Duty* series.
Bungie, Microsoft (2001–to date). *Halo* series.
dotGEARS (2013). *Flappy Bird*.
EA Sports (1993–to date). *FIFA* series.
King (2012). *Candy Crush Saga*.
Mojang (2011). *Minecraft*.
Nintendo (1999–to date). *Super Smash Bros.* series.
Nintendo, Bandai Namco (1996–to date). *Pokémon* series.
PopCap Games (2001). *Bejeweled*.
Quinn, Zoe (2013). *Depression Quest*.
Riot Games (2009). *League of Legends*.
Rovio Entertainment (2009). *Angry Birds*.
Sony Online Entertainment (1999). *EverQuest*.
Square Enix (1987–to date). *Final Fantasy* series.
Ubisoft (2014). *Watch Dogs*.
Valve (2000). *Counter Strike*.
Valve (2013). *Dota 2*.
Zynga (2009). *Words with Friends*.

7

CONCLUSION

This is not a video game, or is it?

At the end of the first episode of the video game *Life is Strange* (Dontnod Entertainment, 2015), Max, the character controlled by the player, confesses to her best friend, Chloe, that she has the ability to reverse time (it is the central mechanic of the game). Chloe, disconcerted, tries to calm her friend down: 'Okay. I see you're a geek now with a great imagination, but this isn't anime or a video game'. *Life is Strange* generates its own crisis of representation *à la* Magritte. René Magritte, a Belgian surrealist painter, is the author of the popular painting *La Trahison des Images* ('*The Treachery of Images*'), which depicts a pipe. Below the pipe, Magritte wrote the following sentence: 'Ceci n'est pas une pipe' ('This is not a pipe'). What Magritte seems to be trying to convey is that this is not a *pipe*, but rather a *painting* of a pipe; the word 'pipe' is not a *pipe* either. The x on the map does not (usually) refer to a real x on the ground, and even if it does, the x on the map *is not* the x on the ground. It is a *re*-presentation. And this re-presentation is not what is re-presented, the signifier is not the signified, and the map is not the territory.

However, how is it possible that a video game contains the affirmation 'this is not a video game'? *Life is Strange* is not a representation of a video game; it is a video game. Moreover, this question is particularly relevant for a video game like *Life is Strange*, which integrates as its main mechanic – the possibility of reversing time to explore new courses of action or try to succeed after failure – something that is attributed to most video games: the lack of (important) consequences for the player, since they can most typically reload a savegame or checkpoint, or replay an area again from the beginning. Intentionally or not, *Life is Strange* is implicitly a meta-game. However, if it is possible to affirm within a video game that 'this is not a video game', it is because video games are also representations of reality (or experiences of reality as we saw in Chapter 4), and that affirmation allows the game to refer to 'real life' as the opposite to a game, a fantasy, or a fiction. In video games, you (typically) get as many chances as you like. In this sense, video games represent the quintessential activity without consequences. Conversely, in 'real life', as in the Eminem song *Love the Way You Lie* where he states, 'you don't get another chance, life is no Nintendo game', every action has consequences that cannot be reversed. If you are reading this, you can say it aloud: 'This is not a video game'. And yet, several dimensions of social reality are starting to be understood in video game, or videoludic, terms.

In the introduction we set out the main aim of this book; in that, it is our intention to explore key aspects of contemporary reality through the lens of video game culture. In this sense, video games reflect and steer the fundamental transformations that give shape to contemporary society and culture. In that introduction, we also delineated a map that guides us on the intellectual journey we had before us. We did it showing the contents of our bags for the trip ahead: a three-year research project, a solid and original qualitative dataset, and a theoretical framework built on a rich and diverse interdisciplinary pool (amongst others, sociology, media studies, game studies, cultural studies, anthropology, philosophy, governmentality studies, and social psychology). Hence, during this journey, we have traversed some of the fundamental social issues and transformations of contemporary society that video games can help us comprehend, such as the digital, education, work, agency, neoliberalism, participatory culture, experience, technology, the body, empathy, identification, identity, and community. Obviously, video game culture is not the only filter or lenses through which we can understand reality, but, in today's world, it is a powerful one.

Within the context of a rising digital culture, we define video game culture as the institutionalization of video game practices, experiences, and meanings in contemporary society. Thus, we see how video game culture is pervading every corner of reality, giving to numerous aspects of our society and culture properties usually associated with video games. Even if these are not directly seen, their influence is palpable. For example, the presence and influence of video game culture can be perceived in different situations such as a flourishing and growing video game industry, in how video games are increasingly played by more diverse people, in the fact that video games are becoming an important cultural, academic, and artistic product, in the way video games are turning into a focus of interest for old and new types of media, and in the mode that video games significantly contribute to the blurring of the fields of education, play, and work. But, above all, this widely extended video game culture that affects society as a whole can be summarized in the ongoing process of *videoludification* of society, through which several aspects of contemporary society are being (video)gamified. Video games and their culture are, accordingly, the beta test version of the society to come.

We also explored how video game culture fosters different ways of understanding the nature of agency and its political articulations. Therefore, at an ontological level, the nature and form of agency can be defined as the multiple, distributed, and dislocated transformation of reality. The complex interrelations between the different types of actors in video game culture, including gamers, networks, hardware, software, and many others, along with its prosthetic, hybrid, and distributed nature, challenge the received notions of agency. This led us to rethink agency in the context of heterogeneous and post-humanist assemblages.

At a sociopolitical level, video game culture shows us that agency is part of both emancipatory and alienating practices. The notion of agency is strongly influenced by the hegemonic political rationalities of neoliberalism, as we saw in the way that video game culture fosters the idea of free, active, and powerful individuals who are held responsible for their own actions and self-government (this is reflected in wider society in those individuals who are responsible for their own safety, well-being, and education). However, precisely using the same forces that power neoliberalism as a hegemonic set of rationalities, video game culture also shows us that agency can be articulated in more collaborative and participatory ways. This is the case of participatory culture, which finds in video game culture the perfect breeding ground to develop. Although agency is the generic force that transforms reality, agency is also altered and propelled through the social fabric when it is enacted within video game culture, reproducing the hegemonic forms of agency – linked to neoliberalism – but also facilitating new and more promising modes of agency. Video game culture therefore helps us to visualize the contemporary materializations of these two, interrelated, social and political dimensions of agency.

Additionally, we looked at how video game culture could help us understand society as a set of designed experiences that are realized in a postphenomenological framework. We identified the fundamental characteristic that is present in almost every definition of video games: experience. In particular, video games were often understood as designed experiences mediated by digital technology. Hence, video games are normally seen as experiences for different reasons: video games are technologically mediated experiences of other experiences (real or imagined); social actors often recount their game experiences as they would do with other experiences in their everyday lives; the interactive nature of video games makes them experiences that must be enacted; and video games are articulated, prosthetic, and cyborgian embodied experiences. This, then, drives us to analyze the role of experience in contemporary society and its particular nature. Experiences, video games teach us, are unique, personal, and contingent, and, at the same time, shared, collective, and structural. In this case, experiences are not just a collection of phenomena, but the network of heterogeneous elements that make those phenomena emerge. Experiences emerge, then, within a postphenomenological context and give way to a society that can be understood as a group of designed experiences. In this regard, society is progressively becoming an assemblage of technologically mediated experiences – as we saw, amongst others, in the fields of tourism, culture, leisure, gastronomy, social relationships, politics, and work – and the logic and practice of video games is, again, anticipating and informing this very process.

In relation to this, we explored how video games are windows that, to a certain extent, enable the player to access other experiences and realities. Thus, video games can be seen as mediation devices that allow players to experience (re-presentations, re-creations, or re-enactments of) situations that they have not had or would not have otherwise. That is why video games are able to facilitate empathy and identification processes among players, letting them connect with a varied range of situations. Not only do video games function as tools for escapism, they also make possible different ways to help players create links with the social reality – far or close – that surrounds them. These game experiences are, nonetheless, experiences on their own. Video games convey some aspects of the experiences they are recreating, but video game experiences are not, themselves, the experiences recreated. The relationship that is established between the player and those realities expressed in a video game is therefore not defined in terms of correspondence but of connection, emergence, or (re)enactment. It is in this complex connection between video games, players, and social reality that the game experience reflects and transforms 'real life' experiences. The videoludification of society progresses inexorably.

Finally, we focus on what video gamers' identities can tell us about the contemporary processes of identity formation. Drawing on social theorists that have approached the crisis of identity (along with other institutions of modernity) in contemporary society, we set out a theoretical framework that describes the shift in the identity construction models from those based on solid and permanent identities to those centred around fluid and fragmented identities. Exploring different categories of video gamers and approaches to video game culture, including the hardcore-subcultural gamer, the casual gamer, the gamer as foodie-connoisseur, the cultural-intellectual gamer, and the everyone-is-a-gamer idea, we come to the conclusion that video game culture perfectly portrays the question of identity in contemporaneity and, moreover, goes beyond it. Not only do video games express the fluid, contingent, and volatile nature of identity in today's world, but they also anticipate social settings in which the very notion of identity is under scrutiny. Video game culture lays out the post-identity hypothesis, where the gamer identity and the communities built around video games seem to be one of the first empirical examples to give plausibility to the hypothesis. The gamer identity escapes the axes of analysis that usually capture identity: its form (solid or liquid) and the way it is assembled (as a starting point, a substance; or as a point of arrival, a process). The identities that emerge within video game culture do not rest between either of these axes. The gamer identity restlessly circulates between the two poles of the first axis (solid/liquid) and is incapable of providing a definite and (at least moderately) stable outcome to become a point of enunciation or action for the individuals that identify (or are identified) as gamers in relation to the second axis. Video game culture infiltrates how we think about ourselves and others. The *identity game* acquires a new dimension.

In the brief text – disguised as a quote from a seventeenth century book – *Of Exactitude in Science*, Jorge Luis Borges (1975: 131) writes:

> In that Empire, the craft of Cartography attained such Perfection that the Map of a Single province covered the space of an entire City, and the Map of the Empire itself an entire Province. In the course of Time, these Extensive maps were found somehow wanting, and so the College of Cartographers evolved a Map of the Empire that was of the same Scale as the Empire and that

coincided with it point for point. Less attentive to the Study of Cartography, succeeding Generations came to judge a map of such Magnitude cumbersome, and, not without Irreverence, they abandoned it to the Rigours of sun and Rain. In the western Deserts, tattered Fragments of the Map are still to be found, Sheltering an occasional Beast or beggar; in the whole Nation, no other relic is left of the Discipline of Geography.

There have been many interpretations of this Borges' text, but most of them revolve around the question of the scientific representation of reality. As we see above, the map is not the territory, and, consequently, a map that coincides with the territory would be of no use. However, in the introduction, we wrote about the 'x' that marks the spot both in the map and the territory on the eponymous Monkey Island. And we asked ourselves: what 'x' was first, the one imprinted on the map or the one ingrained on the land? The map is intended to be an easy-to-handle representation of the territory; however, the map is not an 'innocent' representation, but rather the map also contributes to producing the territory.

Video game culture is, then, a magnificent map that helps us understand contemporary society. It reflects fundamental aspects of today's world and also anticipates the emerging or coming society. But video game culture is more than this; it also informs the shape of contemporary culture and society. Between the map and the territory there is not a simple correspondence; they influence each other in many ways. This is what happens with video game culture and the social context in which it has emerged. Reality is not a video game, but it is starting to be pervaded by video game culture in more areas than we could imagine. In a sense, this book is a map of that map of contemporary society. We will need more maps to actually grasp all what video game culture has to offer. We hope this book becomes a fine work of cartography for a better understanding of video game culture and contemporary society; the first map of this nature that opens the field to other works that study the links between video games, and wider society and culture.

Therefore, this is not a video game; *this book* is not a video game, but it only makes sense in a society that has been traversed and thoroughly affected by a growing and pervading video game culture. This is not a video game. Or is it?

Reference

Borges, Jorge Luis (1975). *A Universal History of Infamy*. London: Penguin Books.

Ludography

Dontnod (2015). *Life is Strange*.

GLOSSARY

AAA Pronounced 'triple A'. This is an informal term, the video game equivalent of the 'blockbuster movie'. That is to say, they are mainstream, well-funded, and heavily promoted, major releases from the big video game publishers. Also see *Indie games*.

Agency Agency is the capacity of acting on reality. It is what produces any sort of transformation, whether small or big. We should approach agency by focusing on its consequences rather than on other intangible and difficult to observe elements that might or not precede it, such as intentionality.

Assemblage The articulation of different actors and systems that behave, though temporarily, in an organic way.

Augmented Reality (AR) A system that supplements our existing sight with additional computer-generated images or information. Examples include the use of mobile smartphone cameras and AR technology, so that smartphones can be held up to the user's eyeline and additional information or images displayed in front of them. Also see *Virtual Reality*.

Beta tester Individuals who work, paid or unpaid, to test a game before official release.

Casual gamer A type of gamer who engages in discontinuous gaming practices, with loose commitments and a limited involvement with video game culture. Also see *Gamer*, *Hardcore gamer*, and *Video game culture*.

Community Traditionally, a group of people that lives together in the same locality, sharing a culture, customs, and ways of doing and living. More recently, community tends to be used more loosely to refer to a group of people who share common interests, without any other precondition of belonging, or the necessity of face-to-face interaction.

Cyberspace See *Virtual Reality*.

Cyborg A cybernetic organism, that is, a biological organism that integrates some kind of technology in order to increase its abilities and capacities. Also see *Prosthetic*.

Digimodernism According to Alan Kirby, digimodernism is the dominant cultural logic of the twenty-first century, one mediated and dominated by digital culture. Also see *Digital culture*.

Digital culture Digital technology has transformed reality at all levels. This means that almost every aspect of our social and personal lives has become digitally mediated, which makes digital culture the dominant cultural logic and transforming force in contemporary society.

Dispositif The network of relations between heterogeneous elements such as discourses, institutions, architectural forms, laws, administrative measures, scientific statements, philosophical, moral, and philanthropic propositions. Also see *Assemblage*.

Embodiment A theoretical tool that helps us analyze our relationship with society and the environment, which gives the body an important role in our everyday life experiences and calls into question the divide between the corporeal and the cognitive.

Empathy Someone's ability to put themselves in someone else's place.

Enaction Certain aspects of social reality that must be performed in order to be created or maintained.

Ergodic The requirement of explicit and non-trivial efforts to interact with a product.

Escapism The process through which individuals temporarily escape from some aspects of their current lives, such as boredom, work, routine, or stress.

Esports The playing of video games in organized, often professional, competitions.

Experience What we apprehend and understand through our senses. However, crucially, experience is not only determined by our perception, it is also conditioned by other factors (including other people's experiences) that structure it.

FPS First Person Shooter. A video game played from the first-person perspective (through the eyes) of the game's main protagonist, where the primary action undertaken is shooting other player or non-player characters (PC or NPCs).

Game mechanic The different kinds of actions that a video game player is able to perform within the game world.

Gamer A video game player who constructs an identity and a culture around video games.

Gamification The use of game elements or dynamics in non-game environments, such as in work, education, or marketing.

Hardcore gamer A type of gamer who invests a great deal of time playing video games and is highly involved in video game culture. They strongly identify as gamers and usually are seen as the prototypical gamer. Also see *Gamer*, *Casual gamer*, and *Video game culture*.

Identification The process by which individuals establish a connection with other individuals or situations without becoming part of them.

Identity Identity is the way we think about ourselves and others. It is how we see ourselves as individuals and as part of a group, and at the same time, how we understand others as different to us.

Indie games An informal and loose term used to describe games produced by small independent games companies, most typically without the direct support of a publisher. Also see *AAA*.

Interpellation The process by which an individual is given an idea, identity, or social location, through how dominant social practices and ideologies are enacted in everyday life, and then accepts (or refuses) this as their own.

Ludology The perspective and study of video games as primarily forms of play and games, which are shaped and bounded by rules and (at least partially) separated from everyday life. Also see *Narratology*.

Magic circle, the In Game Studies this is the argument that games take place in a (at least partially) demarcated play space, separate from ordinary everyday life.

Mediation Mediations are what intercede between the different agents, processes, and elements that configure our world and make it possible. For example, a game controller mediates the relationship between the player and the video game, transforming the way they interact with each other, but also enabling that interaction.

MMOG Massively Multiple Player Online Game. A video game played online with a large number of concurrent players. Sometimes shortened simply to MMO, or where the game is a role playing game, sometimes MMORPG (Massively Multiple Player Online Role Playing Game).

Narratology In Game Studies this is the argument that games can be studied using the same methodological and theoretical tools previously applied to other forms of media, such as films or literature. Also see *Ludology*.

Neoliberalism Neoliberalism is a twentieth century evolution of nineteenth ideas on individual freedom, which emphasizes individual responsibility and accountability, small government, and free-market capitalism.

Participatory culture The idea that there has been an evolution both in technology and the expectations and behaviour of audiences, which has led to a greater active involvement of audiences in the consumption and production of media.

Political rationality The regularities in the political discourse that justify an idealized way to represent, analyze, and act upon reality, particularly, populations.

Post-humanism Post-humanism is a paradigm that decentres the human being as the most important agent in the scientific, social, and cultural narratives.

Post-identity A social scenario in which the questions of the construction of meaning and a sense of belonging are held outside the theoretical coordinates of identity.

Postphenomenology Postphenomenology takes into consideration other aspects beyond what we experience through our bodies in order to understand what surround us. It addresses the notion of experience in a more complex way, including our perception of the world, along with the external elements that participate in the configuration of that perception. Also see *Experience*.

Prosthetic An artificial body part, sometimes leading to the articulation of cyborgs. Also see *Cyborgs*.

Quick time event Parts of a video game where the player has to act, with the controller, in a timely manner, typically following a sequence of prompts on the screen.

Serious games A term for video games, or similar digital tools, specifically designed for educational, business, or training purposes.

Video game culture The institutionalization of video game practices, experiences, and meanings in contemporary society.

Video games The most common term used to describe games (software) played on electronic devices (hardware), such as video games consoles, personal computers, mobile telephones, and tablet computers.

Videoludification The process by which everyday life is permeated by the logic of video games, including, among others, the fields of economy, work, leisure, education, health, and consumption.

Virtual Reality (VR) Virtual Reality describes operating in a space beyond the everyday and ordinary. The most common contemporary example of this is the use of VR headsets to play video games, which give the gamer a deeper sense of direct presence in the game. Also see *Augmented Reality*.

Walking simulator A sub-genre in video games that describes a strong narrative-driven experience of play. In them, the player is not rushed to act or fulfill specific aims, and there are no fail states that critically impede their progress (such as dying).

INDEX

AAA games 6, 9, 31–2, 154, 159; *see also* indie games
Aarsand, P. 155
Aarseth, E. 4, 8, 41, 100
Abt, C. 26
Adorno, T. 43, 44, 173
advanced liberalism *see* neoliberalism
Agamben, G. 4, 145, 172, 174
agency: distributed 27, 61, 64–5; as multiple 63–4, 95; and neoliberalism 68–74, 79; and participatory culture 74–9; players' agency 60–1, 66–7, 69; as transformation 62–3, 109
Alexander, L. 126, 161–2
Alien: Isolation 46, 63
Althusser, L. 149
Amnesia 63
Angry Birds 32, 156
Anthropy, A. 123, 136
Appelbaum, M. 123
Arsenault, D. 62
Assassin's Creed 9
Assassin's Creed series 31, 40, 70
assemblage 2, 8, 11–12, 27, 64–6, 93, 96, 131, 174
audience 21, 24, 30, 33–4, 44–6, 75–6, 135, 137, 151, 155, 162–3; video gaming 37–41
Augé, M. 100
augmented reality 26–7, 99

Bachen, C. 129–30
Bagnall, G. 100

Bastion 31
Batman: The Telltale series 61
Baudrillard, J. 16, 102
Bauman, Z. 4, 16, 145–8, 172–3
Beck, U. 16, 144–5
Bejeweled 156
Bell, D. 145, 173
Berger, P. L. 146
Bergstrom, K. 32, 36, 152
beta test 78, 101, 181
Beyond: Two Souls 39, 61
The Binding of Isaac 32
Black, D. 96
Blackshaw, T. 148
Bloodborne 10, 105–7, 171
Bogg, J. 33
Bogost, I. 23, 42, 84, 85, 129, 165–6, 174
Boltanski, L. 36–7
Booth, P. 74
Borges, J. L. 169, 183–4
Bourdieu, P. 1
Braithwaite, A. 160–1
Brookey, R. A. 74
Brothers: A Tale of two Sons 123
Bryce, J. 154
Bulut, E. 33
Burke, P. J. 145
Burn, A. 19
Burrows, R. 94
Butler, J. 130, 150, 166

Caillois, R. 22
Calleja, G. 60, 116–18, 120

Call of Cthulhu: Dark Corners of the Earth 107
Call of Duty 4: Modern Warfare 90
Call of Duty series 2, 31, 94, 154, 156–9, 161, 171
Candy Crush Saga 2, 32
Cart Life 123
Castells, M. 1, 4, 16, 47, 145
Castronova, E. 34, 120
CBeebies Playtime 9
Centola, D. 132
Chalmers, D. J. 90
Championship Manager series 89
Charles, A. 67
Charsky, D. 36
Chatfield, T. 4, 30
Chen, S. 26
Chiapello, E. 36–7
Clark, A. 90
Cline, E. 46
Cogburn, J. 90
community 25, 49, 77–9, 105–6, 144–8, 153–4, 156, 158, 162, 165–6, 170–2
Consalvo, M. 164
Conway, S. 40, 92
Cook, J. M. 132
Copier, M. 119
cosplay 4, 77–8
Costello, B. M. 91–2
Craps, S. 126
Crawford, G. 5, 18–20, 29, 38–9, 42, 44, 60, 77, 79, 89–90, 94, 100–3, 119, 163
Creeber, G. 47
Crick, T. 94, 96
Csikszentmihalyi, M. 40, 92
Cuttell, J. 101
cyberspace *see* virtual reality
cyborg 95–6, 110, 182; *see also* prosthetic

Dark Souls 63, 90, 105
Dark Souls series 105
Davis, M. H. 124
Dean, C. 123–4
Dear Esther 39
Debord, G. 60
Deleuze, G. 74, 118
De Marinis, P. 69, 74
De Peuter, G. 163
Depression Quest 123, 160
Destiny 31
Deterding, S. 5, 21–3, 25
Detroit: Become Human 61
De Waal, F. 124, 130
Dewar, A. R. 152, 155

Dibbell, J. 34
digimodernism 4, 18, 47–8; *see also* digital culture
digital culture 3–4, 17–20, 47, 137
dispositive 65–70, 74, 80; *see also* assemblage
Don't Starve 31, 91
Donzelot, J. 69
Dota 2 33
Dourish, P. 95, 97–8
Dovey, J. 30, 77
Dreamfall Chapters 61
Dredge, S. 32
Drucker, P. 145
Dubet, F. 103–5, 145
Durkheim, E. 109, 145, 172–3
Dyer-Whiteford, N. 163
Dys4ia 123, 136

Egenfeldt-Nielsen, S. 28, 30, 36, 42, 71
Eguíluz, V. M. 132
The Elder Scrolls V: Skyrim 70
The Elder Scrolls series 40, 70
embodiment 93–8, 108–10
empathy 121–33, 135–8; empathy games 123, 135–6; *see also* identification
enaction *see* enactment
enactment 80, 92–3, 108–10, 134–5, 138–9
ERA 31
ESA 4, 28, 30–1, 33
Escape from Woomera 93
escapism 115–18, 120, 135
Eskelinen, M 39
esports 33–5, 38–41
Evans, A. 116
Eve Online 44, 70
Everybody's Gone to the Rapture 39
experience: embodied 85, 93–8, 108–10; gaming 47, 65, 87–9, 91–3, 96–7, 102, 108–9, 131, 174; player's experience 106, 120, 134; postphenomenological 107–10; shared experiences 20, 103–7; translation of 22, 85–7, 110; video games as 84–5, 109–10
everyday life 17, 21, 37, 49, 103, 110, 120, 135, 169–70

Fallout series 70
Featherstone, M. 94
Feifer, M. 102
Fez 31
FIFA series 154, 156, 163
Final Fantasy series 48, 166
Fine, G. A. 89–90
Firewatch 123

Fisher, S. 32, 152
Fizek, S. 23
Flappy Bird 156
Flow 44
Football Manager series 78, 89
Foucault, M. 11, 24, 61–2, 65–7, 70–1, 146, 169
freedom 4, 23, 61–3, 67–74, 80, 147
Frelik, P. 36
Fuchs, M. 23

Game of Thrones 61
gamer: casual 155–7, 159; cultural–intellectual 159–62; everyone is a 30, 48, 157, 162–4; as a foodie–connoisseur 155, 157–60; hardcore–subcultural 28, 38, 150–5, 157, 160–1; as the main figure of contemporary society 18; pro– 33–4, 36; as spectator–tourist 39–41; *see also* identity
gamergate 79, 160–2
gamification 21–5, 100
García-Catalán, S. 67
García Selgas, F. 48, 63–4, 94–5
Gee, J. P. 149
Geertz, C. 19–20
Gere, C. 4, 16–18, 47, 76
Gibson, W. 95, 117
Giddens, A. 4, 16, 145–6, 173
Giddings, S. 27, 65, 67, 109
Gilmore, J. H. 98–9, 101–3, 116
Gittleson, K. 39
Gods Will Be Watching 10
Goffman, E. 90, 103, 107
Goldberg, D. 42
Golding, D. 161
Goldstein, J. 42
Gone Home 6, 10, 35, 39, 87, 102, 123, 125, 127, 132–4, 167
González-Avella, J. C. 132
Google 37, 38, 100; Books 42; Consumer Survey 41; Trends 38
Gordon, C. 65–6, 68, 74, 116
Gorry, A. 137
Gosling, V. K. 38
Grand Theft Auto V 31
Grand Theft Auto series 31, 40, 70, 154, 158
Griffiths, M. 32, 152
Grodal, T. 85

Hakim, J. 37
Hall, S. 131, 143–5, 149, 166
Halo series 153–4
Hansen, M.V. 96
Haraway, D. 16, 80, 95, 109, 138

Harris, B. 127
Harrison, A. 48
Harvey, A. 160
Hayles, K. 95
Hayward, K. 147
Heavy Rain 39, 46, 61, 97
Hefner, D. 131, 149
Heineman, D. S. 100
Hepworth, M. 94
Hernández-Ramos, P. F. 129–30
Hill, C. 85
Hine, C. 5
Hjorth, L. 36, 42
Horkheimer, M. 43–4, 173
Hotline Miami 32
Huizinga, J. 117, 119
Humphreys, L. 127

identification 116, 130–5, 138, 144, 148–50, 158, 163–6
identity: formation 12, 130, 143–5, 147–9, 168–70, 173–5; gamer 19, 148–51, 158, 161, 165–70, 173–5; post-identity 144, 166–75
Ihde, D. 85, 109
Immune Attack 25
indie games 7, 9; *see also* AAA games
Ingress 26
Inside 123
interactivity 21, 39, 60, 67, 74, 80, 84, 91
interpellation 150, 166, 176n1
Invizimals 26
ISFE (The Interactive Software Federation of Europe) 28–9

Jakobsson, P. 120
Jameson, F. 47, 62, 145
Jenkins, H. 4, 16, 60, 75–7
Jenkins, R. 144, 145
Jenson, J. 32, 36, 152
Jones, S. G. 145
Jordan, T. 160
Journey 104
Julier, G. 102
Juul, J. 3, 29, 30, 42, 73, 120, 150, 152, 155–7, 164

Kaipainen, K. 163
Kallio, K. 163
Kapalo, K. 152, 155
Katsaliaki, K. 36
Kennedy, H. 30, 77
Keogh, B. 27, 85, 96, 109
Kerr, A. 3–4, 33, 36, 43–4, 79

King, G. 149–51
Kirby, A. 4, 18, 20, 47, 60, 72, 77, 145
Kirkpatrick, G. 3, 32, 38, 150–1
Klimmt, C. 131, 149
Kline, S. 163
Knorr Cetina, K. 16
Kossinets, G. 132
Kowert, R. 32, 42, 152
Krzywinska, T. 67, 149–51
Kücklich, J. R. 36

L.A. Noire 126
Lahti, M. 94–6, 98
Larsson, L. 42
The Last of Us 101
Latour, B. 5, 62–6, 92, 173–4
Law, J. 5, 72, 92–3, 138–9
Law, Y.-Y. 4, 47–8
Lawler, S. 145
League of Legends 35
Lees, M. 161
Leonard, D. 101, 117, 136
Life is Strange 10, 61, 88, 102, 135, 180
Light, B. 38
Limbo 31
Lin, H. 34, 40
Linder, J. 24
Linehan, C. 24–5
Luckmann, T. 146
Luhmann, N. 173
Lyon, D. 145
Lyotard, J.-F. 72, 145, 170

MacCannell, D. 16, 101, 116
McGuigan, J. 68
McPherson, M. 132
Madden NFL series 136
Madigan, J. 126
Mad Max 46
Maffesoli, M. 37, 170
magic circle, the 27, 116–17, 119–20
Martin, R. 47
Martínez de Albeniz, I. 174
Marx, K. 173
Mass Effect 70
Mäyrä, F. 5, 8, 19–22, 27, 42, 151
mediation 65, 92–3, 97, 108, 115, 127–9, 134–5, 173
Metal Gear series 46
Metal Gear Solid 46
Michael, D. 26
Miége, B. 44
Miller, P. 68–9, 148
Millington, B. 63

Miltner, K. 160
Minecraft 31, 35, 91, 158, 163, 171
MMOG 21, 45, 70, 118
Mortensen, T. E. 79, 160
Muñoz, J. E. 133
Muriel, D. 9, 62, 92, 99, 110
Mustafee, N. 36
Myst 44

Nakamura, L. 136
Navarro-Remesal, V. 67
NBA Live series 136
neoliberalism 23–4, 62, 68–74, 79–80, 148
Newman, J. 4, 19, 39, 42, 77–8
No Man's Sky 31

Oestreicher, J. 123, 130
Oldmeadow, J. A. 32, 152
Oliva, M. 72
The Order: 1886 46
Outlast 63

Pac-Man 44
Pajares Tosca, S. 42
Papers, Please 10, 115, 121–3, 126
Pargman, D. 120
Parsons, T. 173
participatory culture 21, 23, 61–2, 74–9, 105
PeaceMaker 25
Pearce, C. 20, 42
Pérez-Latorre, O. 72
Perreault, G. P. 160
Perron, B. 4, 41–2, 62
Petrie, M. 100
Pine, J. 98–9, 101–3, 116
Pitts, R. 35
Planells, A. 76
Pokémon GO 9, 21, 26–7, 32
Pokémon series 158
political rationalities 23, 37, 61–2, 68, 71, 73–4, 80, 146, 148
Poltronieri, F. 80
Poremba, C. 93, 134–5
Postigo, H. 34
postphenomenology 85–6, 93, 103, 107–10
Preciado, P. B. 95
Prescott, J. 33
Pro Evolution Soccer series 40
prosthetic 95–7, 110, 181–2
Proteus 39
Pulkikinen, T. 174
Pulos, A. 154

Quandt, T. 42

Raessens, J. 5, 21–2, 42
Raphael, C. 129–30
Real Lives 129
Reinald, B. 72
Re-Mission 25
Re-Mission 2 25
representation 38, 64, 69, 72, 74, 84, 95, 100–1, 108, 118, 124–5, 131–2, 149–50, 152–5, 158, 162, 166, 180, 184
Resident Evil 46, 104
Richardson, I. 156
Rifkin, J. 123–4, 126–7
Robertson, R. 48
Rose, N. 4, 16, 23, 68–71, 73, 146, 148
Roussos, G. 136
Ruffino, P. 23
Rupp, M. A. 152, 155
Rusch, D. C. 127
Rutter, J. 44, 154
Ryan, M.-L. 96

Salen, K. 84, 87, 91, 93, 98, 103, 119–20
San Miguel, M. 132
Schiesel, S. 28
Schrape, N. 23–4
Schutt, B. 100
Scutti, S. 123
Second Life 118
The Secret of Monkey Island 10, 133
serious games 22–3, 25–6, 35
Shattell, M. 127
Shaw, A. 74, 86, 131–3, 136, 157
Shepherd, T. 160
Shilling, C. 94
Sicart, M. 25, 27, 42
Silcox, M. 90
Simkins, D. W. 127
Simmel, G. 1–2
The Sims 44
The Sims series 31
Skrebels, J. 135
Smethurst, T. 126
Smith, J. 42
Smith, L. 99–100
Smith, O. 148
Smith-Lovin, L. 132
Spec Ops: The Line 123
Spent 136
Srauy, S. 160
Staiger, J. 133
Stallabrass, J. 102
The Stanley Parable 31

Starcraft II 41
Star Wars: Knights of the Old Republic 46
Stehr, N. 145, 173
Steinkuehler, C. 127
Stets, J. E. 145
Street Fighter II 44
Stuart, H. 131, 143
Stuart, K. 31, 37, 43
Super Meat Boy 32
Super Smash Bros. series 157
Szalma, J. L. 152, 155

Tales from the Borderlands 61
Taylor, T. L. 4, 34, 36, 42, 46, 64, 71, 120
To the Moon 123
The Tearoom 127
Tetris 44
That Dragon, Cancer 115
This War of Mine 6, 10, 63, 86, 88, 101–2, 115, 120, 123, 125, 128, 129
Thornham, H. 5, 63
Titan Souls 10
Titchener, E. 124
Toffler, A. 98
Tönnies, F. 146
Touraine, A. 145
Tredinnick, L. 18
Tronstad, R. 39
Tuan, Y.-F. 116
Tulloch, R. 67
Turner, B. 94

Ukie 4, 28, 31, 33
Uncharted series 46
Until Dawn 61

Valiant Hearts 123
video game culture 2–7, 21–4, 27, 29–30, 32, 34, 37, 41, 43, 46, 48–9, 62, 64, 72–4, 78–9, 100–1, 148–9, 160, 163; definition of 16, 18–20
videoludification 16, 21–2, 26, 49, 181–3
virtual reality 21, 94–6, 101, 116–18
Vorderer, P. 131, 149
Vos, T. P. 160

Walkerdine, V. 96
The Walking Dead series 61, 115, 126
walking simulator 39–40
Walz, S. 5, 21–2
Warr, P. 35
Watch Dogs 10, 168–70
Watts, D. J. 132
Webb, J. 101

Webber, J. E. 122, 128
Weber, M. 20, 36, 145
Westecott, E. 94
Weststar, J. 33
What Remains of Edith Finch 39
Williams, P. 25
Wilson, T. 33
Winch, A. 37
The Witcher 3: Wild Hunt 9
Wolf, M. 4, 41–2, 45
The Wolf Among Us 61

Words with Friends 156
World of Warcraft 2, 31, 70, 118

Yang, R. 127–8

Zackariasson, P. 33
Zefeldt, M. J. 127
Zichermann, G. 24
Zimmerman, E. 5, 21–2, 84, 87, 91, 93, 98, 103, 119–20
Zingsheim, J. 170